South
South
South
Soth South

SRA Reading Mastery

Signature Edition

Textbook A

Siegfried Engelmann
Susan Hanner

McGraw Hill SRA

A Division of The McGraw-Hill Companies
Columbus, OH

Illustration Credits

Rick Cooley, Leslie Dunlap, John Edwards and Associates, Simon Galkin, Heidi King, Susan Jerde, Paul Montgomery, Den Schofield, James Shough, Karen Tafoya, Jessica Stanley

Photo Credits

11 ©Corbis; **56** ©Jonathan Blair/Corbis; **287–346** ©Corbis.

SRAonline.com

 SRA

A Division of The McGraw-Hill Companies

Send all inquiries to this address:
SRA/McGraw-Hill
4400 Easton Commons
Columbus, OH 43219

ISBN: 978-0-07-612581-4
MHID: 0-07-612581-5

6 7 8 9 10 QPD 13 12 11 10 09

Table of Contents

A

1	**2**	**3**	**4**
1. female	1. months	1. Henry	1. male
2. select	2. yearly	2. chest	2. migrate
3. migration	3. ponds	3. goose	3. shorter
4. Florida	4. lonely	4. geese	4. hatch
	5. markings	5. flapping	

B # Facts About Geese

You're going to read a story about geese. Both geese and ducks are water birds, but geese are a lot bigger than ducks.

There are many different kinds of geese. Snow geese are white. The geese in the story you'll read are Canada geese. They are gray, black and white.

The picture shows a person standing near ducks, snow geese and Canada geese.

Male geese and female geese have the same color and markings. But male geese are bigger than female geese.

Baby geese hatch from eggs that are a lot bigger than chicken eggs. The babies are born in June. They are yellow, but as they grow older they change color. Geese are not full-grown by the time they are a year old.

When geese are three years old, they mate for the first time. Each female goose selects a mate, and the two geese stay together until one of them dies. As you will find out in the story, it may be a long time before one of them dies.

C

Old Henry

The other geese called him Old Henry. His name tells you one thing about him. He was old. Most geese live about 30 years. That's a long time for a bird. But Old Henry was 35 years old.

You couldn't tell he was that old by looking at him. He was sort of a gray color with a white chest, just like the other Canada geese. If you saw Old Henry swimming on Big Trout Lake with the other geese on a warm summer day, you would not be able to tell that he was the oldest goose in the flock.

If you saw Old Henry three months later that year, you might get the idea that he was an old goose. ✦ He was the only goose that was still on Big Trout Lake. All the other geese in the flock had gone south for the winter. They wanted Old Henry to go with them. But he told them, "No, I'm getting too old to fly two thousand miles. I've done it too many times, and I'm just too tired."

The other geese told him, "But if you stay here, you may never make it through the winter. The lakes will freeze and you'll die."

Henry replied, "Maybe I won't die," but he didn't really believe that at all. So, he waved goodbye to the other geese as they took off from the lake, and he watched them form a great V that moved slowly south.

A

1	2
1. flocks	1. Florida
2. migration	2. yearly
3. answers	3. sudden
4. flapping	4. breeze
5. fliers	5. migrate
6. shorter	6. lonely

B

More Facts About Geese

Most wild geese are born in Canada and spend every summer in Canada. Geese live in flocks that may have more than 50 geese in them. In the fall, flocks fly south to their winter home. Then in the spring, they return to their summer home in Canada. This yearly flying to the south and to the north is called a migration. When geese migrate in the fall, they fly south. In which direction do they migrate in the spring?

The geese that you're reading about migrate to a place in Florida. The map shows the path of the migration from Big Trout Lake in Canada to Crooked Lake in Florida.

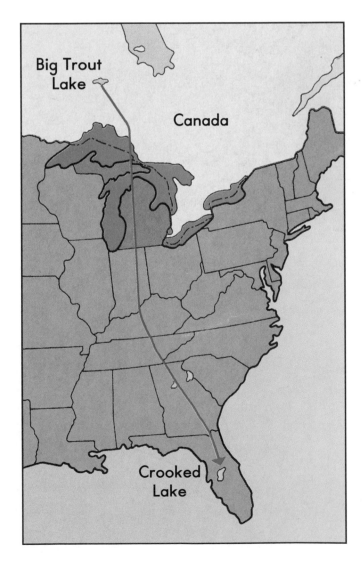

Geese migrate south in the fall because the lakes and rivers freeze in Canada. Farther south, lakes and rivers do not freeze.

Not all flocks migrate to the same place in the south. Some flocks migrate over three thousand miles to their winter home. Some migrate only a thousand miles.

C ## Henry Meets Tim

Henry stayed in Canada while the other geese in the flock went south for the winter. It was lonely being all alone on Big Trout Lake, but Henry had felt lonely for the last five years. That was when his wife had died. Henry still missed her. She had been his mate since they were both three years old.

So Henry waited for winter. He spent time walking, swimming and looking at the sky. Every now and then a flock of geese would fly by. Henry would listen to the leader as he honked directions to the other geese.

The days were getting shorter and colder. Henry knew that very soon Big Trout Lake would freeze. Nine days after the others had left, Old Henry saw another Canada goose walking along the shore. Old Henry could tell that it was a very young goose. It wasn't very big, and it didn't seem to know where it was going.

"Hey, there," Henry called. "What are you doing here? You're

supposed to be on your way to Florida."

The young goose said, "Oh, I couldn't learn to fly because my leg was hurt."

Old Henry knew about that problem. When young geese learn to fly, they start out by running faster and faster. They hold their wings out to the side as they run. Then they flap their wings and fly. But if they can't run fast, they can't fly. Later, geese learn to take off from the water, but that's not the first thing they learn about flying.

"Well," Henry said. "If you don't have anything better to do, swim out here and join me. I would be glad to have your company."

 Number your paper from 1 through 11.

Review Items

1. What's the name of geese that are gray and black and white?

2. What's the name of geese that are all white?

3. What color are all geese when they are born?

4. You can tell male geese from female geese because ░░░░░ .
   - male geese have brighter colors
   - male geese have longer feathers
   - male geese are larger

5. How old are geese when they mate for the first time?

6. After male and female geese mate, they stay together ░░░░░ .
   - for the summer
   - for a full year
   - until one goose dies

7. Most geese live for about ░░░░░ years.

8. What was the name of the lake where Henry's flock stayed during the summer?

9. In which season did the flock leave the lake?

10. In which direction did the flock fly?

11. How far was the flock going?

A

1
1. equator
2. flocks
3. breeze
4. answers
5. above
6. fliers

2
1. glided
2. sudden
3. training
4. anymore
5. dived

B

Directions on Maps

The geese in the story you're reading go from Canada to Florida in the fall. In which direction do they go?

In which direction do they go when they go from Florida to Canada?

- Maps always show four directions—north, south, east and west.
- North is always at the top of the map.
- South is always at the bottom of the map.
- East is always on this side of the map. ⟶
- West is always on this side of the map. ⟵

Map 1 shows the directions on all maps.

Touch the circle in the middle of the map and move your finger to the top of the map. In which direction did you go?

Touch the circle and move to the bottom of the map. In which direction did you go?

Touch the circle and move to the number **2**. In which direction did you go?

Touch the circle and move to the **4**. In which direction did you go?

Map 1

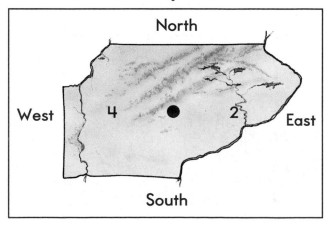

Map 2 shows Canada, the United States and some other countries. Is the red dot in the United States, or in Canada?

In which country is the blue dot?

Touch the red dot and go to the **4** on the map. In which direction did you go?

Touch the red dot and go to the **3**. In which direction did you go? The red dot is in the United States. What's the name of the **state** the red dot is in?

Map 2

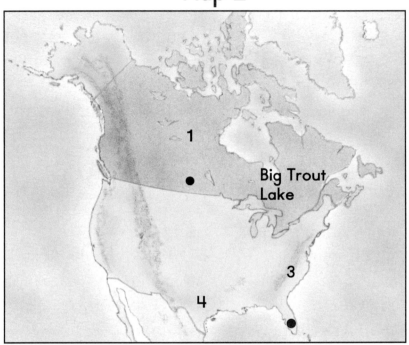

Big Trout Lake

Tim's Questions

Old Henry and a young goose were the only ones left on a pond in Canada. The young goose swam up to Old Henry and said, "My name is Tim. What's your name?"

Henry answered Tim's question, and then Tim said, "I have a lot of questions about geese. I was never able to ask my mom these questions because she was so busy getting my brothers and sisters ready for the flight down south."

Henry said, "So you have never made the trip to the south."

"That's right," Tim said. "I was born last June. So I'm less than half a year old."

"Well, ask me the questions," Old Henry said, "and I'll tell you the answers."

Tim said, "Well, Mom always told us that geese are the best high fliers there are. I don't know what she meant by that."

Old Henry laughed and said, "On the other side of the world are some mountains that are over five miles high. There's only one kind of bird that can fly over those mountains, and that's a goose."

Tim shook his head. "Wow," he said. "Do the flocks fly that high when they go south for the winter?"

"No, no," Henry said. "You only go that high if you have to get over something. We fly pretty high, sometimes two or three miles high, but that's about as high as we go."

"I can see that geese fly pretty fast," Tim said, "but do you know how fast they go?"

"Of course I know," Old Henry said. "Geese can fly one mile a minute. That's sixty miles per hour,

and geese can fly at that speed all day long."

The geese stopped talking as a sudden breeze blew across the lake. It was very cold. Henry shook his head and said, "There will be some ice on Big Trout Lake tomorrow morning."

Tim said, "I wish I could fly south. My leg feels better now, but I don't know how to fly."

Henry said, "Well, if your leg is better, I could teach you how to fly." Henry shook his head. "And I suppose I could even tell you how to get to Florida."

"That would be great," Tim said. "It would be even better if you would come with me and show me the way."

"No, no," Henry said. "I have flown to Florida for the last time. But I'll tell you how to get there."

"Thank you," Tim said. "I would really love to go there."

D Number your paper from 1 through 13.

Review Items

1. What's the name of geese that are all white?
2. What's the name of geese that are gray and black and white?
3. What color are all geese when they are born?
4. How old are geese when they mate for the first time?
5. After male and female geese mate, how long do they stay together?
6. Most geese live for about ▭ years.
7. Geese live in large groups called ▭ .
8. Where are most wild geese born?

9. In which direction do geese fly in the fall?
10. What is this trip called?
    - migration
    - mating
    - hibernation

11. How had Henry felt ever since his wife had died?

12. When geese learn to fly, do they start in the water or on the land?

13. They run with their ▭ out to the side.

A

1	2
1. route	1. circles
2. receive	2. glided
3. unfrozen	3. barns
4. above	4. training
5. equator	5. dived
6. anymore	

B

Facts About the Earth

Some places on the earth are colder and some places are hotter. Here are some facts you need to know about the earth.

- The earth is shaped like a ball. It doesn't look like it's that shape because the earth is very large. Pictures of the earth that are taken from a spaceship show that the earth is shaped like a ball.

Picture 1

- The hottest part of the earth is called the equator. You can see the equator in picture 2.
- The equator is a pretend line that goes around the fattest part of the earth.
- The coldest parts of the earth are called the poles. You can see two poles in picture 2. The pole on top is called the North Pole. The pole on the bottom is called the South Pole.
- The farther you go from the equator, the colder it gets.
- The poles are the parts of the earth that are farthest from the equator.

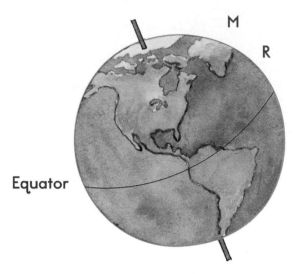

Picture 2

C Tim Has a Flying Lesson

The morning was cold and still. Ice had formed all around the shore of the lake. Tim said, "Wow, it's really cold this morning."

"Yes," Old Henry said, "and if you're going to get on your way to Florida before it gets even colder, we'd better start on your training today."

So Henry explained what Tim had to do. He had to run with his wings held straight out to the sides. Then Henry would honk. That honk told Tim to start flapping his wings. "I'll bet you can do it the first time we try," Henry said.

Henry and Tim went to a hill near the lake. Henry said, "Just run down this hill as fast as you can. Remember to keep those wings out to the side."

Then Henry took off and circled above Tim. "Go," Henry said, and Tim went—running as fast as he could.

Henry honked and Tim started flapping his wings. "That's it," Henry honked. "Keep flapping."

Tim took off, but as soon as he did, he became frightened and stopped flapping. Plop. He fell back

down to the ground and tumbled over and over.

Henry landed next to him and laughed. "Well," Henry said, "at least you got into the air. Now all you have to do is learn how to stay up there. ⭐ You have to keep flapping after you take off."

Tim said, "But I got scared."

Henry said, "Well, just remember: Geese are made for flying. It's nothing to be scared about. I'll fly in front of you. Just keep looking at me and do what I do."

So they tried again. This time, Henry made sure that he was right in front of Tim when he took off. Henry honked and honked. "Keep flapping and look at me."

The two geese flew all the way across the lake and over the hill on the other side. Henry turned around to look at Tim. He didn't look scared anymore. He had a big smile on his face. He honked, "This is great. I love it."

"Well, just keep doing what I do," Henry said.

Henry led Tim up higher and higher, more than a mile high. Then Henry held his wings out to the side and glided. Tim followed. The birds turned and swooped and dived and climbed. At last Henry said, "Now we're going to land. We'll go in the water. Remember to do what I do."

Henry came down and made a perfect landing in the water. Tim also made a landing, but it was not perfect. He was going too fast, and he landed with a great splash. Both geese laughed. Tim shouted, "I can fly."

"You sure can," Henry said.

D Number your paper from 1 through 11.

Review Items

1. You can tell male geese from female geese because ▮▮▮▮ .
   - male geese are larger
   - male geese have brighter colors
   - male geese have longer feathers

2. What was the name of the lake where Henry's flock stayed during the summer?

3. In which season did the flock leave the lake?

4. In which direction did the flock fly?

5. How far was the flock going?

6. Geese live in large groups called ▮▮▮▮ .

7. Where are most wild geese born?

Look at the map.

8. What country is the red dot in?

9. What country is the blue dot in?

10. What **state** is the blue dot in?

11. If you started at the red dot and went to the blue dot, in which direction would you go?

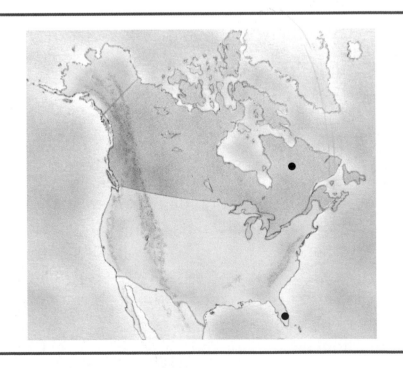

A

1
1. dangers
2. receives
3. barns
4. circles
5. lakes

2
1. foolish
2. below
3. daytime
4. unfrozen

3
1. trout
2. sprang
3. route
4. neck
5. confused

B

Facts About the Equator

You've learned about the poles and the equator. Let's see how much you remember.

- How many poles are there?
- What are they called?
- What do we call the line that goes around the fattest part of the earth?
- Where is the hottest part of the earth?

- Which parts of the earth are the coldest?

The heat that the earth receives comes from the sun. The equator is the hottest part of the earth because it receives more heat from the sun than any other place on the earth. The poles are the coldest places on the earth because they receive less heat from the sun than any other place on the earth.

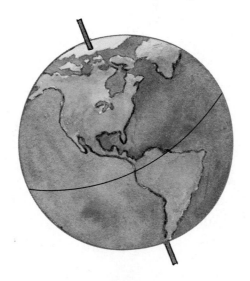

Tim Practices Flying

The two geese spent most of the next three days flying. Tim needed the practice, and Old Henry felt warmer when he was flying rather than swimming on that lake. There wasn't much room to swim anymore because most of the lake was frozen. Only some small circles near the middle were unfrozen. So Tim practiced and Old Henry gave him directions. By the third day, Tim could land on land and in the water. He still had trouble taking off from the water, but he could do it.

As the sun was setting on the third day, Old Henry said, "Well, my boy, the lake will be completely frozen tomorrow, so tomorrow is the time for you to go south."

Old Henry started to tell Tim how to get to Florida. The route was not simple. There were landing places about every 300 miles. Tim would have to land at each place and spend one or two nights. Then he would take off and go to the next landing place. Old Henry started to tell Tim about each landing place. But Tim had trouble understanding the directions.

Old Henry started out by saying, "You take off from this lake and fly south and east. By about the middle of the afternoon, you'll come to a field that is next to a pond. The field has two barns. One is red and . . ."

Tim said, "I don't know which way south is."

"Of course you do," Henry said. "All geese know north from south."

"But I . . ." Tim said.

Henry said, "Do this for me. Take off, go high and go in the direction that feels really good. Fly in that direction for a little while and then come back here."

Tim went up and circled around and then he started flying directly south. Soon he came back and landed next to Henry.

Henry said, "You were flying south. All geese like that direction in the fall. In the spring, they like the opposite direction, north."

Then Henry said, "Let's talk some more about the flight to Florida. The first stop is that field with the two barns. The next morning, you'll take off from that field, but you won't fly exactly south. You'll go a little to the east."

Tim looked confused. He said, "I'm not sure I can remember all this. I don't know how you can remember it."

Old Henry said, "Oh, once you go to a landing spot, you'll remember it for the rest of your life. You'll know exactly how to get there and exactly what it looks like."

Then Old Henry tried again to tell Tim about the landing places.

But by the time Henry had explained how to reach the third one, he could see that Tim was just about ready to start crying. "I'm sorry," Tim said, "but I just can't keep all this straight. How many landing places are there between here and Florida?"

Old Henry said, "Five," and Tim got a big tear in his eye.

"I can't do it," he said. "I'll never remember how to get there."

Old Henry said, "Well, we'll figure out some way to get you there."

D Number your paper from 1 through 16.

Review Items

Look at the map below.

1. What country is the green dot in?

2. What country is the purple dot in?

3. What state is the purple dot in?

4. If you started at the purple dot and went to the green dot, in which direction would you go?

5. The earth is shaped like a ▮▮▮▮ .

6. The hottest part of the earth is called the ▮▮▮▮ .
   - pole
   - desert
   - equator

7. What's the name of the line that goes around the fattest part of the earth?

8. What's the name of the spot that's at the top of the earth?

9. What's the name of the spot that's at the bottom of the earth?

10. The ▮▮▮▮s are the coldest places on the earth and the ▮▮▮▮ is the hottest place on earth.

11. How many poles are there?

12. The farther you go from the equator, the ▨ it gets.

- hotter
- fatter
- colder

Look at the map below.

13. What's the name of the place shown by the letter **C?**

14. Which letter shows the coldest place?

15. Which letter shows the hottest place?

16. Which letter is farthest from the equator?

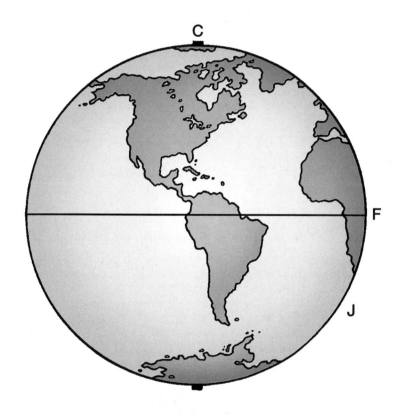

6

1

1. Michigan
2. Kentucky
3. crooked
4. triangle

2

1. foolish
2. dangers
3. rivers
4. sharper
5. lakes

3

1. trout
2. daytime
3. below
4. sprang
5. neck

B

The Sun Lights the Earth

The sun shines all the time. But you can't see the sun all the time. Only half of the earth is in sunlight. You can see the sun if you're on the side of the earth that is closer to the sun. It is daytime on the side of the earth where you can see the sun. It is nighttime on the side of the earth where you can't see the sun.

The earth turns around once every 24 hours. If you lived on the equator, you would have one day and one night during that 24 hours.

Picture 1

Picture 2

Picture 3

Picture 4

C The Geese Leave Big Trout Lake

Tim and Old Henry spent the night in a small woods near the lake. In the morning, the lake was completely frozen and the air was even colder than it had been.

Tim said, "I'm supposed to leave today. But I still don't know about all the landing spots. How long do you think it's going to take for me to learn about them?"

Henry said, "Oh, I thought of a different plan. I'll fly along with you part of the way. After we reach the third landing place, I'll head back here."

Tim smiled. "Thank you," he said. "I like this plan a lot better."

"Well, let's get going then," Henry said. "And remember to follow all the directions I honk out."

"I will," Tim said. And the two geese took off, circled above Big Trout Lake one time, and then headed south.

Old Henry led the way and Tim followed. But Tim got tired after the geese had flown about sixty miles. As they flew over a large lake, Tim said, "Let's land down there for a while. I see a few geese near the shore."

Old Henry laughed and said, "Never land where you see only a few geese. You'll find out they are not real geese at all. They are fake geese that hunters use to make other geese think it is safe to land there. But most of the geese that try to land there will get shot."

"Well, where can we land?"

"Two kinds of places are safe," Henry said. "One kind of safe place has hundreds of geese on the water. Another kind of safe place has no geese on the water." Then Henry said, "Pick a safe place for us to land."

Tim said, "That's easy. There are lots of lakes down there, and I don't see ducks or geese on most of them."

"Well, lead the way to a safe place then." And that's what Tim did. The two geese rested there for a while. ⭐ They ate some water plants and took a nap in a field. Then they took off and flew south again.

A few hours later the two geese flew over the landing place where they would spend the night. Old Henry didn't say anything about where they were. He wanted to see if Tim would recognize the place. He didn't. Henry asked him, "Do you see anything interesting down below us?"

Tim looked at the trees, the pond and the two barns in the field. Then he said, "No, what's interesting down there?"

At that moment, Old Henry knew that he would have to do something more than just tell Tim about how to get to Florida on his own.

The geese landed near the barns. They were empty except for some mice that lived in them. Something didn't smell right to Henry, however. Something told him to get out of this place. Just then, a red fox sprang from the grass and charged toward Tim. Before Tim could take off, the fox had grabbed his tail feathers. "Help," Tim yelled.

Old Henry put his head down and charged at the fox. He bit the fox on the neck and ears. The fox tried to attack Old Henry, but Old Henry kept biting the fox until it ran away.

Henry looked at where the fox had grabbed Tim to make sure that Tim was not hurt. Tim was all right.

Then Old Henry said, "That was a foolish fox. I guess she doesn't know that a full-grown goose is a much better fighter than a fox."

What Henry didn't tell Tim was that an old goose that tries to fight a fox might hurt itself. Old Henry had a very sore wing. He was glad that he wouldn't have to fly until the morning.

Tim and Henry walked all around to make sure that no other dangers were near the barn. Henry told Tim, "I think it will be safe here if we spend the night in one of these barns." And that's what the geese did.

D Number your paper from 1 through 20.

Story Items

1. Where did Henry and Tim spend their last night at Big Trout Lake?
   - on the water
   - in a barn
   - in the woods
2. In the morning, Henry told Tim that he would ______.
   - tell Tim more about the trip
   - fly part of the way with him
3. Henry told Tim, "Don't land where you see ______ geese."
   - many
   - a few
   - no
4. Write the letters of the **2** kinds of places that are safe for geese.
   a. places with many geese
   b. places with no geese or ducks
   c. places with a few geese
   d. places with a few ducks
5. When the two geese flew over the landing place, did Tim recognize it?
6. After they landed, which goose was attacked?
7. What attacked that goose?
8. What did Henry do?

9. Which is a better fighter, a full-grown goose or a fox?

10. After the fight, Henry had a sore ▓▓▓.

Review Items

11. How old are geese when they mate for the first time?

12. After male and female geese mate, how long do they stay together?

13. Most geese live for about ▓▓▓ years.

Choose from these words to answer each item:

- moon
- Florida
- sun
- Canada
- equator
- geese
- poles
- migration

14. The heat that the earth receives comes from the ▓▓▓.

15. The part of the earth that receives more heat than any other part is the ▓▓▓.

16. The parts of the earth that receive less heat than any other part are called the ▓▓▓.

---

17. Which letter shows the part of the earth that receives more heat from the sun than any other letter?

18. Which letter shows a part of the earth that receives less heat from the sun than any other letter?

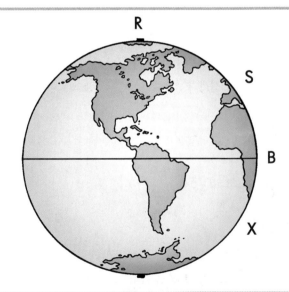

19. How many landing places are there on Henry's migration trip to Florida?

20. Was Tim able to understand what Henry explained about the landing places?

A

1
1. older
2. river
3. sharper
4. fewer

2
1. Reedy Lake
2. Kentucky
3. crooked
4. Michigan
5. triangle

B # Michigan and Kentucky

The map shows the migration path the geese are following. The map also shows the first three landing places.

Follow the path from Big Trout Lake to the first landing place.

What country is that landing place in?

Follow the path to the next landing place.

That landing place is in the United States. It is in a state named Michigan.

Follow the path from the landing place in Michigan to the next landing place.

That landing place is not in the state of Michigan. It is in the state of Kentucky.

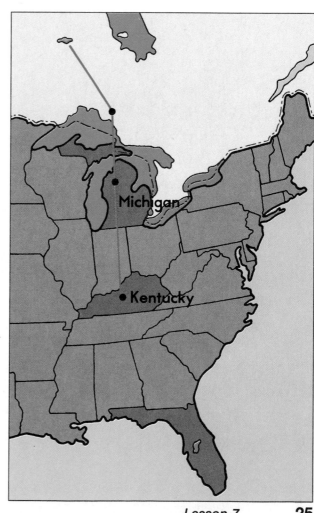

Old Henry Tests Tim

Old Henry's wing was very sore the next morning, but he didn't tell Tim about it. Before the geese took off, Old Henry tried to explain the next landing place to Tim. It was a field that had a stream running through it. The field was shaped like a triangle. It had a large grove of trees on the east side of the triangle. Old Henry even scratched a map in the dirt. It showed the landing place, the stream and the trees. "Remember, that's the place we're looking for this afternoon. I won't tell you when we're there. You'll have to tell me when we're there."

Henry didn't know how well Tim would do, but Henry had to find out. Henry knew that Tim didn't learn if Henry just described the place. But Henry hoped that Tim would do better if he saw a map.

So the geese took off and flew south. About an hour before they came to the landing place, Old Henry tested Tim. Old Henry said, "Look down there and tell me if you see anything that is interesting."

Tim looked down and then looked at Old Henry. Tim said, "I think that's where we are supposed to land. Am I right?"

"No," Old Henry said. "That is not the place."

Tim said, "I'm sorry. I guess I am not very smart."

"You're doing fine," Henry said. But Tim was not doing fine. An hour later the geese flew over the stream and the field shaped like a triangle. After they had flown past it, Old Henry said, "Our landing place is back there. Follow me." He knew that Tim would not be able to make the trip on his own.

After the geese had landed, Henry said, "What if we wanted to go back to our first landing place? Could you find the way back?"

"Oh, sure," Tim said. "That's easy. You just fly back that way until you come to some blue hills, then you turn a little and go more north until you come to the place where the two rivers cross . . ." Tim went on to tell all the important facts about how to get there.

Old Henry spent a lot of time thinking that night. And he thought a lot the next day. The geese did not fly on that day or on the day after that. On the first day, they rested and talked. It was warmer here than it had been farther north. The geese were not in Canada anymore. They were in Michigan. The trees were yellow and orange and the sun was warm.

Old Henry knew that Tim could not remember a place unless he

went to that place. So somebody would have to lead him all the way to Florida. Henry's problem was that his wing felt worse than ever. Henry didn't know how much more of the trip he would be able to make.

Tim and Henry rested a second day. That day was the first time they saw another flock of geese. The flock formed a great V in the sky. Both Henry and Tim had eyes far sharper than human eyes. So they were able to see all the geese in that flock. Henry said, "There must be more than 60 geese in that flock."

"Are they going to the same place we're going?" Tim asked.

"No," Henry said. "They are heading a little bit to the west, so they are probably going to Mexico."

Tim asked, "Have you ever been to Mexico?"

Henry said, "No. The only place I've ever gone in the winter is to Crooked Lake in Florida. And that's what you'll do. Every year, you'll fly to Crooked Lake. Then in the spring you'll go back to Canada."

 Number your paper from 1 through 13.

Review Items

1. The sun shines ▢ .
   - all of the time   - some of the time
2. Can you see the sun all day long and all night long?
3. If you cannot see the sun, it is ▢ on your side of the earth.
4. What is it on the other side of the earth?
5. The earth turns around one time every ▢ hours.

Look at the picture.
6. Which side of the earth is closer to the sun, A or B?
7. Which side of the earth is in nighttime?
8. Which side of the earth is in daytime?

9. Which letter shows the place that has the warmest winters?
10. Which letter shows the place that is closest to the equator?
11. Which letter shows the place that is closest to a pole?
12. Is the **North Pole** or the **South Pole** closer to that letter?

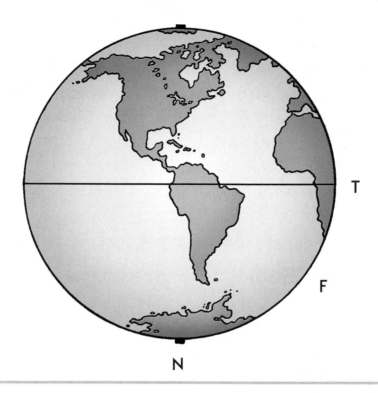

13. Write the letters of the **2** kinds of places that are safe for geese.

       a. places with many geese
       b. places with a few geese
       c. places with no geese or ducks
       d. places with a few ducks

A

1

1. <u>fewer</u>
2. <u>season</u>
3. <u>hurting</u>
4. <u>cloudy</u>
5. <u>older</u>

2

1. Reedy Lake
2. Clarks Hill Lake
3. Jackson Lake
4. shown

B

The Sun Heats the Earth

You can figure out which parts of the earth are hot and which are cold if you look at how the light from the sun gets to the earth.

The picture shows lines of heat that are going from the sun to the earth. Those lines are the same distance apart. Here's a rule about the lines of heat: **Places on the earth that have more lines of heat are hotter than places that have fewer lines of heat.**

Places A, B and C on the earth are the same size, but one of them is a very hot place and one is a very cold place. The hot place receives more lines of heat from the sun. So if you want to find out which place has more heat, you count the number of lines from the sun that hit that place.

Count the lines that hit place C.
Count the lines of heat at place B.
Count the lines of heat at place A.
Remember, the sun heats the earth, and the equator receives more heat than any other part of the earth.

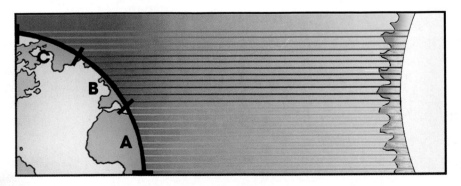

A New Plan

The next day's flight was very hard on Old Henry. His wing was sore, and the next landing place was a little more than 300 miles south of the landing place in Michigan. It would have made sense for the geese to travel only 200 miles and then spend the night at a new landing place. But geese don't always make sense. They always go to the same landing places. If those places are a little more than 300 miles apart, the geese fly a little more than 300 miles.

Tim and Old Henry reached the landing place by late afternoon. This landing place was between two lakes in Kentucky. One was large and one was small. Something about the large lake didn't seem right to Old Henry. There were some geese on the large lake, but they were too close to the shore.

Henry's wing was so sore that he really wanted to land and rest. So he told himself, "There's no problem down there," and he started to lead the way down to where the other geese were swimming. Tim flew up next to Old Henry and said, "I don't think we should land there."

"Why not?"

"You told me never to land in a place that had only a few geese on the water." Just then the geese heard a sound that was something like another goose calling, but Old Henry knew that it was not the sound of a real goose. He said, "You're right, Tim. There are hunters down there. Let's get out of here."

The geese made a great turn and started to climb higher and higher into the sky. Just then, there were loud banging sounds. Hunters were shooting at Tim and Old Henry, but they were too far away. "You may have saved our lives," Henry said to Tim. "You're a very smart young goose."

The two geese found another landing place about five miles away. It was a field that had a small pond in the middle of it. The geese landed, took a nap and then ate some seeds. Old Henry wanted to go the rest of the way to Florida, but he knew that he could not travel as fast as flocks usually go. If Henry was to make it, he would have to fly one day and rest the next. He couldn't fly two days in a row.

When the sun was growing red in the west sky, the two geese were sitting near the pond. Tim said, "So where do we go tomorrow?"

Henry told him the plan. "We're going to rest tomorrow. Then we'll fly the next day."

Tim said, "But I'm not tired. I'll be ready to fly tomorrow."

"I won't be ready," Henry said.

Tim looked at Henry for a long time. Then he said, "Well, you're in charge. Anything you want to do is fine with me."

So the birds rested the next day. Late that afternoon, a large flock of more than eighty geese landed near the pond. The leader of the flock and three of the older geese came over and talked to Henry and Tim.

The leader asked, "Where's the rest of your flock?"

Old Henry explained where the rest of the flock was and why Tim hadn't gone with them.

The leader of the other flock said, "We're from one of the big lakes between Canada and the United States."

Tim said, "I know those big lakes. We flew over one of them, didn't we, Henry?"

"Yes, we did," Henry said. Then he asked the leader, "Are you on your way to Florida?"

"We are," the leader said. "We go to Reedy Lake."

"That's wonderful," Old Henry said. "Tim is trying to go to Crooked Lake."

"Oh," the leader said. "That's only a few miles from Reedy Lake."

Old Henry said, "How would it be if Tim went with your flock? You could drop him off at Crooked Lake."

"We could do that," the leader said.

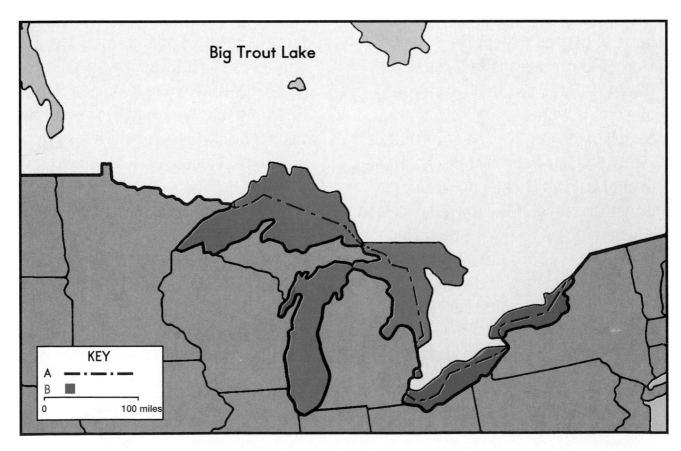

Big Trout Lake

KEY
A — · — · —
B ■
0   100 miles

D Number your paper from 1 through 28.

1. How many heat lines are hitting place A on the map?
2. How many heat lines are hitting place B?
3. How many heat lines are hitting place C?
4. Write the letter of the place that's the hottest.
5. Write the letter of the place that's the coldest.
6. Write the letter of the place that has the warmest winters.
7. Write the letter of the place that's the farthest from the equator.
8. You know that place A is hotter than place C because place A ▓▓▓▓ .
   - is closer to the poles
   - has more lines of heat
   - is in sunlight

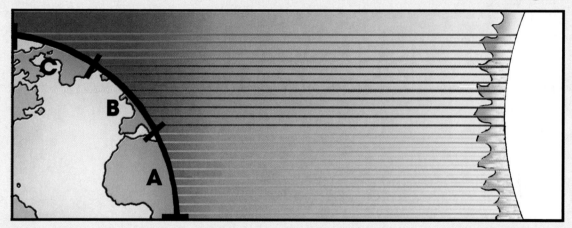

Story Items

9. About how far was it from the landing place in Michigan to the one in Kentucky?
10. How did Henry feel by the end of that trip?
11. Which goose wanted to land at the regular landing place in Kentucky?
12. What kept them from landing there?
    - The lake was frozen.
    - Hunters were at that landing place.
    - Too many geese were at that landing place.
13. Henry and Tim landed at a place that was about ▓▓▓▓ miles away.

14. Did Henry plan to stay at this landing place **one day** or **two days**?

15. Another ▬▬ landed at the landing place the next day.

16. How many geese were in that flock?

17. Where was that flock going?

18. That flock spent summers on one of the ▬▬ ▬▬.

19. Henry asked if ▬▬ could fly with that flock.

20. Did the leader of that flock think this plan was okay?

Review Items

21. In which direction do geese fly in the fall?

22. What is this trip called?

23. At which letter would the winters be very, very cold?

24. At which letter would the winters be very, very hot?

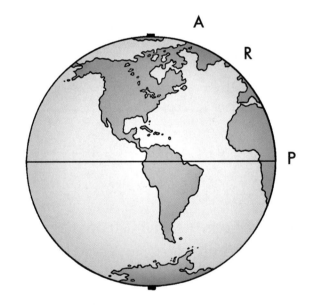

25. Write the letter of the earth that shows the person in daytime.

26. Write the letter of the earth that shows the person 6 hours later.

27. Write the letter that shows the person another 6 hours later.

28. Write the letter that shows the person another 6 hours later.

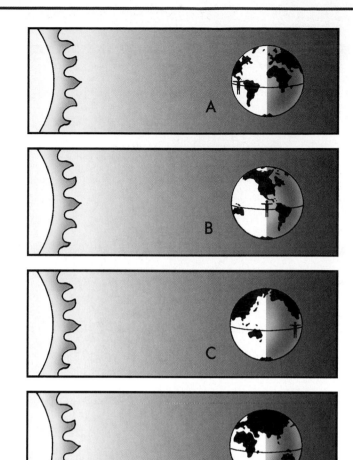

A

1
1. constant
2. sir
3. season
4. seventy
5. daylight
6. hurting
7. wintertime

2
1. tilted
2. cloudy
3. friends
4. splashing
5. reaches
6. honking

3
1. South Carolina
2. Georgia
3. Newmans Lake
4. Jackson Lake
5. Clarks Hill Lake

B

The Sun and the Earth

Here's a rule about the earth and the sun. The earth is moving around the sun all the time. The earth makes a complete circle around the sun one time every year. A year is 365 days, so it takes the earth 365 days to make a complete circle around the sun.

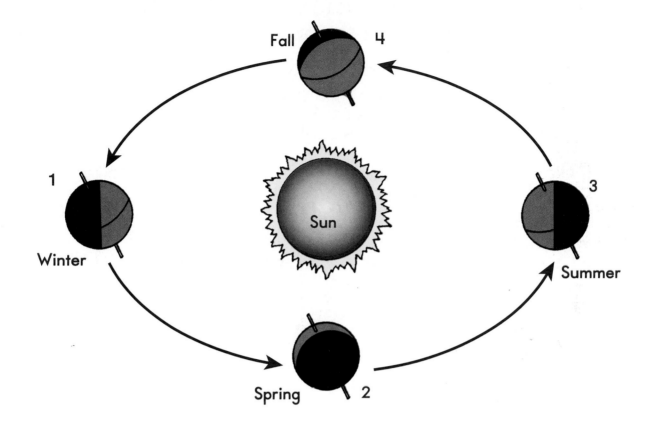

The picture shows the earth at four different times of the year as it circles the sun. Touch the picture of the earth during winter.

Notice how much of the earth is in shadow and how much is in sunlight.

Follow the arrow around the sun and name the season that is shown by each earth. Start with the earth at wintertime.

Remember, the earth is in different places at different seasons of the year.

Flying With the Flock

After the geese from the large flock finished talking with Old Henry, they went over to their flock. As soon as they had left, Tim said, "When is that other flock going to fly?"

"Tomorrow," Henry said.

"We planned to fly tomorrow, didn't we?"

"Yes," Henry said.

"Well, why did you say I would fly with them? I thought I was flying with you."

Old Henry said, "Tim, I'm not sure I can make it all the way to Florida. If you go with them, they'll drop you off at Crooked Lake."

"But what will you do?" Tim asked. "Aren't you going to fly with them, too?"

"Well . . ." Old Henry said. He wanted to tell Tim that he didn't plan to go any further south, but Tim looked very sad. So Old Henry said, "Well, I'll go with them as far as I can. I'll fly with them tomorrow and then I'll see how I feel at the end of the day."

"Well, I'm going where you go," Tim said. "If you fly with them after tomorrow, I'll fly with them. But if you don't fly with them after tomorrow, I won't fly with them."

"We'll see how it goes tomorrow," Henry said.

So the next morning, more than eighty geese took off from that pond in Kentucky and formed a great V in the sky. The leader was near the front of the V, but he was not at the very point of the V. He was back a few places so he could see the front of the V and honk out orders to the other geese. Old Henry and Tim were far behind the leader. Tim was right behind a young goose. Old Henry was in front of one of the older geese.

After the flock stopped climbing, it was nearly two miles high. ⭐ Tim called out to Henry, "I notice that it is a lot easier to fly than it was when you and I were alone."

"Right," Henry said. "It's easier flying in a large flock."

"Why?"

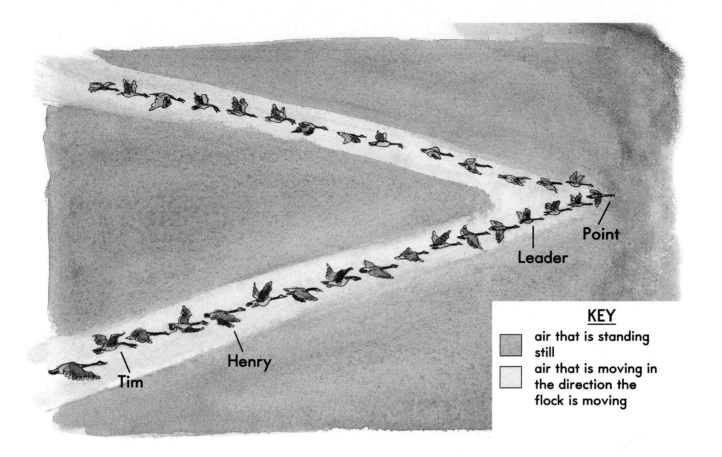

KEY

air that is standing still

air that is moving in the direction the flock is moving

🌼 Old Henry explained. "We are behind a lot of other geese. Those geese fly through the air and leave a trail of wind that moves in the same direction the geese are moving. We're flying through that air, so we don't have to work as hard as the geese up front."

Tim said, "That's good for us, but I sure wouldn't want to be one of those geese up front."

Henry said, "All the geese that are up front take turns at being the first goose in the V. They fly at the point for an hour or more and then change places with another goose."

Then Henry noticed that his wing wasn't as sore 🌼 as it had been. He hadn't been thinking about that wing because it hadn't been hurting. Henry realized that it hadn't been hurting because it didn't have to work as hard as it did when he and Tim flew alone. Henry said to himself, "If it doesn't get any harder than this, maybe . . ." He still wasn't sure how he would feel the next morning when the rest of the flock was ready to fly again.

Later that afternoon, when the sky was starting to get very cloudy, the great V of geese went lower and lower through the clouds and came out of them above a beautiful green lake. Tim asked Henry, "What's that lake?"

Henry said, "I don't know. This is not on the route I've taken. We always land at Clarks Hill Lake. It's much bigger than this lake and it's farther east."

Then Henry asked the old goose behind him, "What's the name of that lake?"

"Jackson Lake."

About ten minutes later the flock landed on Jackson Lake.

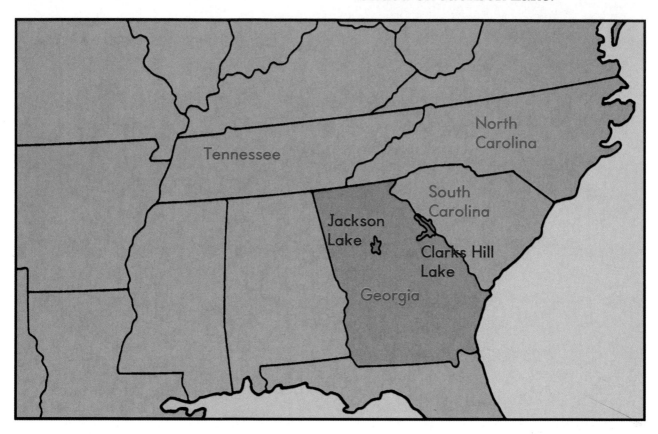

D Number your paper from 1 through 19.

Story Items

1. Henry noticed that his wing felt ▇▇ because it didn't have to work very ▇▇ .

2. What's the name of the lake where the flock landed?

3. In what state is that lake?

4. Had Henry landed there before?

5. At what lake did Henry's flock usually land?

6. Which lake is farther east?

7. Do you think Henry will be able to continue flying south with the flock?

Review Items

8. What's the name of the line that goes around the fattest part of the earth?

9. What's the name of the spot that's at the top of the earth?

10. What's the name of the spot that's at the bottom of the earth?

11. Write the letters of the 2 kinds of places that are safe for geese.

    a. places with many geese

    b. places with a few geese

    c. places with no geese or ducks

    d. places with a few ducks

---

12. How many heat lines are hitting place A on the map?

13 How many heat lines are hitting place B?

14. How many heat lines are hitting place C?

15. Write the letter of the place that's the hottest.

16. Write the letter of the place that's the coldest.

17. Write the letter of the place that has the warmest winters.

18. Write the letter of the place that's farthest from the equator.

19. Why is place A hotter than place C?

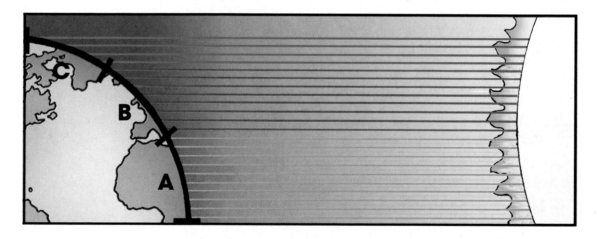

Number your paper from 1 through 35.

1. How old are geese when they mate for the first time?
2. After male and female geese mate, how long do they stay together?
3. Most geese live for about ▮▮▮ years.

4. In which direction do geese migrate in the fall?
5. In which direction do geese migrate in the spring?

6. Write the letter of the line that starts at the circle on the map and goes south.
7. If you start at the circle and move to the number 2, in which direction do you go?

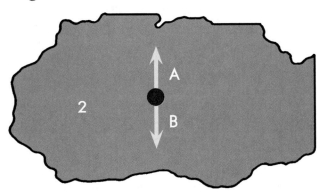

8. Which side of Earth 1 is closer to the sun, A or B?
9. Which side of Earth 1 is in nighttime?
10. Which side of Earth 2 is in nighttime?

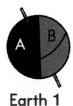
Earth 1

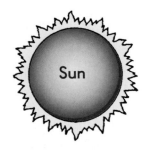
Sun

Earth 2

11. Write the letter of the earth that shows the person in daytime.

12. Write the letter of the earth that shows the person 6 hours later.

13. Write the letter that shows the person another 6 hours later.

14. Write the letter that shows the person another 6 hours later.

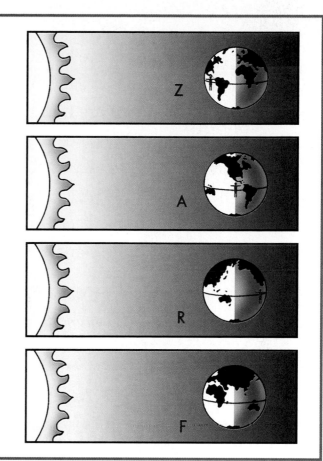

15. Which letter on the map shows Big Trout Lake?

16. Which letter shows the landing place in Kentucky?

17. Which letter shows the landing place in Michigan?

18. Which letter shows the landing place in Florida?

19. Which letter shows the landing place in Canada?

20. Which letter shows Crooked Lake?

21. Which letter shows the first landing place?

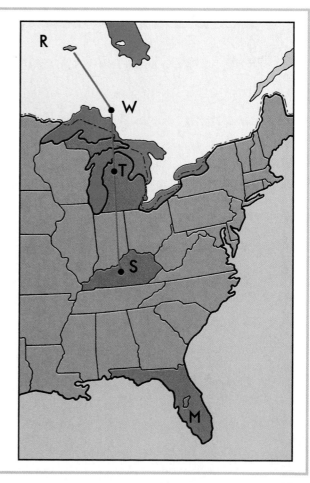

22. How many heat lines are hitting place X on the map?

23. How many heat lines are hitting place K?

24. How many heat lines are hitting place T?

25. Write the letter of the place that's the hottest.

26. Write the letter of the place that's the coldest.

27. Write the letter of the place that has the warmest winters.

28. Write the letter of the place that's farthest from the equator.

29. Why is place T hotter than place K?

30. How many Great Lakes are there?

31. The earth makes a circle around the sun one time every ▮▮▮ .

32. How many days does it take the earth to make one full circle around the sun?

33. Write **A, B, C** and **D** on your paper. Write the season each letter shows.

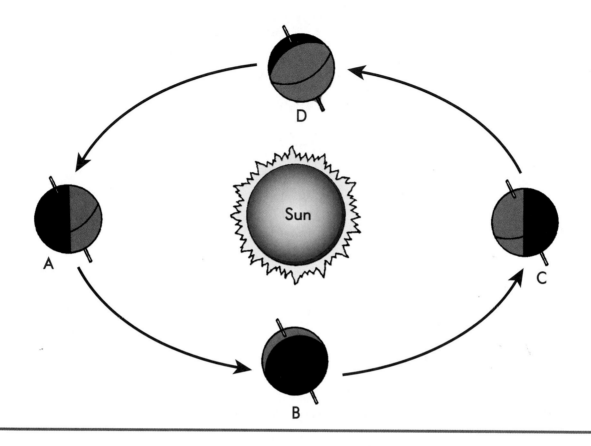

Skill Items

For each item, write the underlined word from the sentence in the box.

The horses became <u>restless</u> on the dangerous <u>route</u>.

34. What word tells how you feel when you want to do something different?

35. What word tells about how you get to a place?

Some maps have a key that lets you figure out how far apart things are on the map. The map on page 47 is like maps you've seen before. It shows the path that the geese took from Canada to Florida. The key down at the bottom of the map shows how long 100 miles is on the map. Follow the steps below to learn how to use the key to figure out distances on the map.

1. Place a piece of paper on the map so that one corner is on Big Trout Lake. Then hold the paper so that the edge is right next to the path that the geese took.

2. You're going to use your marking pencil to make three marks on the edge of your paper. Hold your paper very still and make the first mark at the first landing place.

3. Make the second mark at the landing place in Michigan.

4. Make the third mark at the landing place in Kentucky.

5. Find the corner of your paper that shows where the path from Big Trout Lake started.

6. Hold that corner of your paper at the beginning of the line in the key. Use your regular pencil and mark the other end of the line.

7. Now move your paper so the mark you just made is at the beginning of the line in the key.

8. Mark the other end of the line.

9. Keep repeating steps 7 and 8 until you get just past the last mark you made with your marking pencil.

Figure out how many hundred miles it is from Big Trout Lake to the first landing place.

Figure out how many hundred miles it is from the first landing place to the landing place in Michigan.

Figure out how many hundred miles it is from the landing place in Michigan to the landing place in Kentucky.

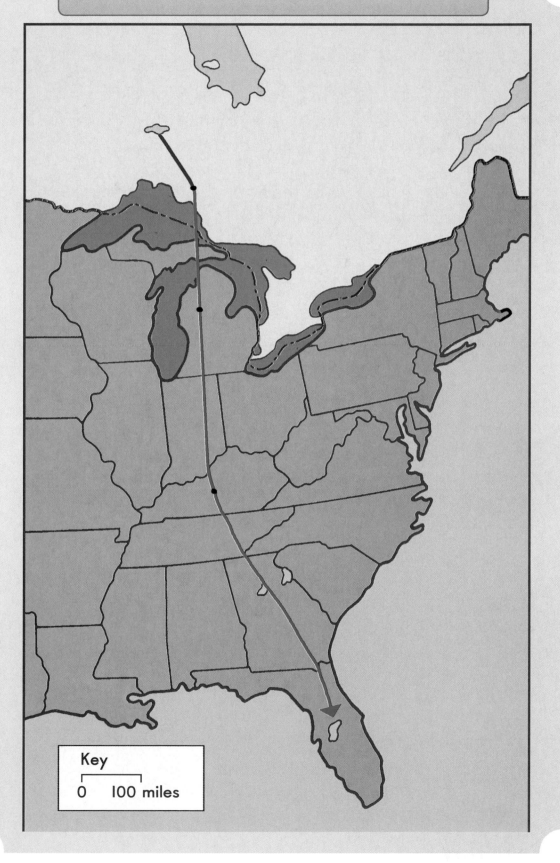

Key

0   100 miles

A

1
1. Eskimo
2. son
3. kayak
4. ordinary
5. scientist

2
1. <u>any</u>more
2. <u>day</u>light
3. <u>day</u>time
4. <u>winter</u>time
5. <u>rest</u>less

3
1. January
2. March
3. December
4. February

4
1. reaches
2. honking
3. friends
4. splashing
5. tilted

5
1. Newmans Lake
2. seventy
3. sir
4. constant
5. ignore
6. spear

B

The Tilt of the Earth

The earth is tilted. The poles are not straight up and down. Instead, they tilt. And the poles tilt the same way as the earth circles the sun.

Picture 1

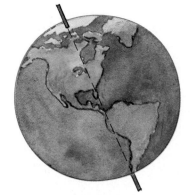

Picture 2

Picture 3 shows the tilt of the earth during the different seasons.

Touch the earth at wintertime. The North Pole tilts away from the sun during winter. You can see that half of the earth is in shadow and half is in sunlight. But the North Pole is completely in shadow. That means that as the earth spins around and around during wintertime, there is no daylight at the North Pole. There is constant darkness.

Touch the earth at summertime. The North Pole tilts toward the sun during summer. Half the earth is in shadow and half is in sunlight. But the North Pole tilts toward the sun, so it is completely in sunlight. That means that at the North Pole during summer, there is no night. There is daylight all the time during summer. The sun never sets.

Remember, if the pole tilts away from the sun, it's wintertime at the pole and there is no daylight. If the pole tilts toward the sun, it is summertime and there is no night.

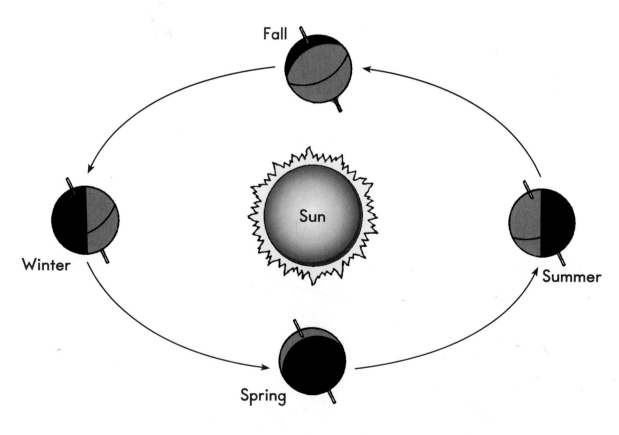

Picture 3

The Flock Reaches Florida

The next morning before the flock took off, Henry tried out his wing. He took off from the field and flew around the lake. When he landed, Tim came up to him and said, "I know what you were doing. You were trying to see if your wing is all right. Is it?"

"It feels pretty good," Henry said with a smile. "I can fly today."

And he did. The leader of the flock honked out directions to the goose that would be at the point of the V. Then, there were loud splashing and flapping sounds as more than eighty geese took off from Jackson Lake. Tim and Old Henry took their place near the back of the V and the flock went higher and higher.

"Why are we going so high?" Tim asked.

"When we're up high, we'll be able to ride some winds that are blowing toward Florida. We should be able to go far today without doing much work."

The winds blew and the flock flew. Around noon, Henry told Tim, "We're in Florida now."

"Wow," Tim said. "That means we're almost at Crooked Lake."

Henry laughed. "No, we still have a long way to go, and we won't get there today. It's more than two hundred miles to Crooked Lake."

Tim said, "So where will we spend tonight?"

"I don't know. Our flock always stops at Newmans Lake, which is about seventy miles from here. But I don't know where this flock lands."

Less than two hours later, Henry found out where the flock would land—at Newmans Lake.

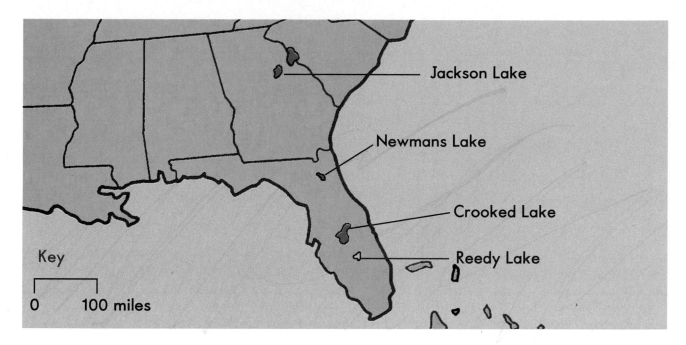

Key

0   100 miles

There were lots and lots of geese around Newmans Lake. Tim said, "It looks like ✦ all the geese in the world are right here."

"There are a lot of geese here," Henry said. "But wait until you see how many geese there are near Crooked Lake."

The flock circled Newmans Lake and landed near a shore that was covered with geese. Some of them were honking and showing off by flapping their wings. Others were napping. The leader of the flock swam over to Old Henry and said, "We're going to spend tomorrow resting here. Then we'll go to Reedy Lake the next day. Do you plan to fly with us?"

Henry flapped his wings and said, "I do. I feel fine."

Tim smiled and said, "Me, too."

So two days later, Tim and Henry were flying high above Crooked Lake. Henry told Tim, "This is where we leave the flock. Our lake is right down there."

Old Henry flew up near the front of the great V and called to the leader. "Thank you, sir," Henry said. "You're a fine leader and you have a wonderful flock. We were glad to have the chance to fly with you."

"Good luck to both of you," the leader said. Then Henry and Tim swooped down from the flock. "I can't wait to see my mom and dad," Tim said.

Henry was also looking forward to seeing his old friends and his children and grandchildren. But he also felt a little sad. As the two geese swooped closer and closer to the beautiful blue lake below, Henry knew that he would miss flying with Tim. This trip was the first time in years that Henry felt that somebody really needed his help. That was a good feeling for Henry.

D Number your paper from 1 through 16.

Review Items

1. What's the name of geese that are gray and white and black?
2. What's the name of geese that are all white?
3. What color are all geese when they are born?
4. Geese live in large groups called ▮▮▮.
5. Where are most wild geese born?

6. If you cannot see the sun, it is ▮▮▮ on your side of the earth.
7. What is it on the other side of the earth?
8. The earth turns around one time every ▮▮▮ hours.

9. Which letter shows the place that has the warmest winter?
10. Which letter shows the place that is closest to the equator?
11. Which letter shows the place that is closest to a pole?
12. Is the **North Pole** or the **South Pole** closer to that letter?

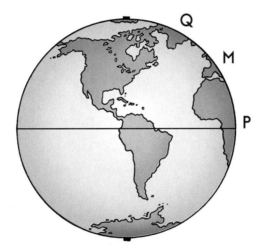

13. The earth makes a circle around the sun one time every ▮▮▮.
14. How many days does it take the earth to make one full circle around the sun?
15. Is it easier to fly alone or with a large flock?
16. Flying near the back of a large flock is like riding your bike ▮▮▮.

    • with the wind   • against the wind

1	2	3	4
1. polar bear	1. pebbled	1. killer whale	1. walrus
2. ice floe	2. splatter	2. Eskimo	2. kayak
3. Oomoo	3. Alaskan	3. spear	3. son
4. Oolak	4. scattered	4. January	4. restless
5. shoulder			

B

Facts About Eskimos

In the next lesson, you will read about Eskimos. The winters are very cold where Eskimos live. Eskimos live near the North Pole in Canada and Alaska.

Alaska is a state of the United States, but it is far north of the main part of the United States. Touch Alaska on the map.

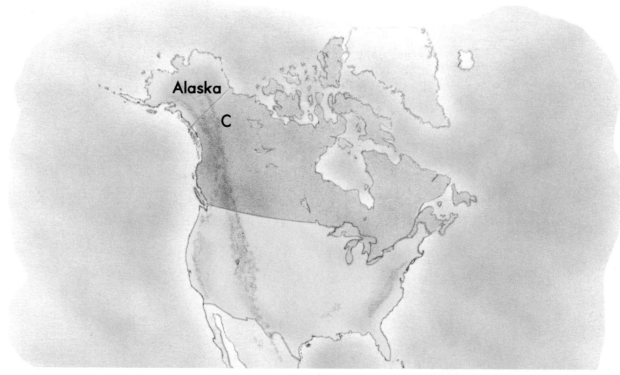

Picture 1

Picture 2 shows an Eskimo with some of the things that Eskimos use.

The Eskimo is holding a fishing pole in one hand.

The Eskimo is holding a fishing spear in the other hand.

The Eskimo is wearing warm clothes that are made from animal skins.

Near the Eskimo is a sled. The dogs that pull the sleds are called sled dogs.

The boat that Eskimos use in the summer is called a kayak.

Make sure you can read these words:

Eskimo	Alaska
kayak	spear

fishing pole

spear

sled

kayak

sled dogs

Picture 2

C Back to Canada

There were hundreds of geese on Crooked Lake and in the fields around it. Henry and Tim circled the lake twice before Henry spotted their flock. Then he pointed his wing toward the south shore and said, "There's our flock right there."

The two geese flew very low over the flock and honked loudly. As they made a sharp turn and headed back, Henry could hear some of the geese in the flock saying things like, "Who are those geese?" and "Doesn't that one goose look a lot like Henry?"

Tim and Henry landed right in the middle of the flock. Oh, how the geese honked and flapped their wings. Tim's mom flapped her wings so hard she sent little feathers flying all over the place. His dad rushed over and gave Tim a big old goose kiss. "My son," he said, "I didn't think we'd ever see you again."

Tim had tears in his eyes. As Tim ran off with his mom and dad, Henry's friends formed a big circle around him and honked so loudly that you could hear them for miles. A few minutes later, some of his children, grandchildren and great grandchildren came from their flocks to give Henry big old goose kisses. One of Henry's grandchildren said, "We didn't think you were coming, but we knew we would see you next summer when we went north again."

"Yes," a great grandchild said, "but now you'll be able to fly back to Canada with us next spring."

Henry started to say, "Oh, I don't know," but then he smiled and said, "Sure. We'll all go back to Canada in the spring."

And that's what happened. Henry spent the winter in the warm Florida sun, napping, eating, swimming and visiting with his friends and family. About two times every week, he would go flying with some of the geese who were less than a year old. He would always make sure that Tim went ★ with them. Henry would give the young geese practice at flying in a V. Henry would honk out orders as the V would swoop over Crooked Lake very low and very fast. Once in a while, Henry would have a sore wing after flying with the young geese, but his wing wasn't too bad.

Henry wasn't really worried about his wing because the trip back north was a lot easier than the trip down to Florida. The trip north started in January but the geese wouldn't reach Big Trout Lake in Canada until the middle of April.

At the beginning of January, Tim, Henry and all the geese began feeling restless. They wanted to fly north. Two days later, the first flocks took off. Over the next few days, Henry watched hundreds and hundreds of flocks take off. Finally, Henry's flock was ready. It flew into the sky and joined other flocks that were leaving Crooked Lake, Reedy Lake and the other nearby lakes. The geese flew in four great Vs. The sky was filled with geese.

Henry's flock followed the warm weather as it moved north. The flock would stay at a landing place long enough to make sure that the next landing place would not be frozen.

Finally, in the middle of April, the flock arrived at Big Trout Lake.

There was honking and flapping as the geese met other flocks that stayed at Big Trout Lake during the summer.

Two days after the flock landed at Big Trout Lake, Tim and Henry said goodbye. It was time for Tim and the other geese that were almost a year old to form their own flock and fly off to Sandy Lake. The young geese would spend the summer at that lake. Before Tim left, he gave Henry a big old goose kiss and said, "Thank you for everything you've done. And I hope that I'll see you next winter at Crooked Lake."

Henry said, "I'll be there."

D Number your paper from 1 through 11.

Review Items

1. When geese learn to fly, do they start in the water or on the land?

2. They run with their ▆▆▆ out to the side.

3. Which letter shows the part of the earth that receives more heat from the sun than any other letter?

4. Which letter shows a part of the earth that receives less heat from the sun than any other letter?

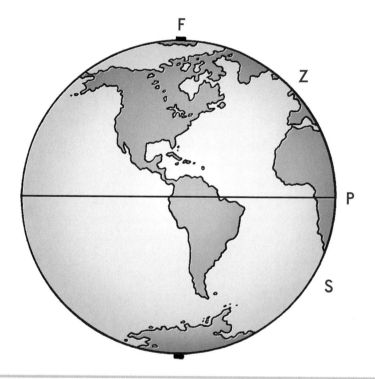

5. The sun shines ▆▆▆.
   - some of the time
   - all of the time

6. Can you see the sun all day long and all night long?

7. Write the letters of the 2 kinds of places that are safe for geese.
   a. places with many geese
   b. places with a few ducks
   c. places with no geese or ducks
   d. places with a few geese

8. During winter at the North Pole, how much does the sun shine?

    • never   • all the time

9. During summer at the North Pole, how much does the sun shine?

    • never   • all the time

10. What season is it at the North Pole when the North Pole tilts toward the sun?

11. What season is it at the North Pole when the North Pole tilts away from the sun?

SPECIAL PROJECT

Use a road map of your state to figure out how far it is between some of the cities in your state. Use the key to measure the distances.

Compare the distance you get using the key with the distance number that is shown on the map.

The distance numbers that are given on the map are often more than the distance you get by using the key. Why is that true?

Who would travel farther between two cities, a goose or a person driving on the road?

Why?

A

1
1. hind
2. Alaskan
3. December
4. shoulder
5. jacket
6. icy

2
1. snowball
2. playmate
3. snowdrift
4. slowpoke

3
1. repeated
2. playful
3. dangerous
4. walruses

4
1. killer whale
2. polar bear
3. ice floe
4. Oolak
5. March
6. splat

5
1. Usk
2. Oomoo
3. pebbled
4. February
5. scattered
6. fur

B

Animals in Alaska

The picture below shows some of the animals that live in Alaska. Here are the names of the animals in the picture: polar bear, elephant seal, killer whale, walrus and wolf.

Tell which animal in the picture is the biggest and which animal is the smallest.

walrus

male elephant seal

female elephant seal

polar bear

polar bear

killer whale

wolf

C Where Oomoo and Oolak Lived

In the next story, you will read about Oomoo and Oolak. They were Eskimos who lived in Alaska.

Pictures 1, 2 and 3 show the place where Oomoo and Oolak lived.

Picture 1

Pictures 1 and 2 show what their place looked like in the spring. Picture 1 shows how that place looks if you are standing on the beach. Picture 2 shows how that place looks if you are above that place looking down. Picture 2 is like a map of the place. You can see the ice floe in Picture 2.

The pebbled beach shows where the sand ends and the ocean begins. Seals are on the pebbled beach, far from the tent. Two walruses are closer on the pebbled beach. Near the end of the ice floe are killer whales.

The tent on top of the hill was Oomoo's summer home.

Picture 3 shows how the same place looked at the end of summer. Compare the place in spring and at the end of the summer. Tell three things that have changed.

In summer, the seals and the walruses moved away before the water froze. The killer whales also moved away. These animals came back in the spring.

Make sure you can read these words:

seal	walrus	killer whale
	ice floe	slope

Picture 2

Picture 3

Oomoo

Oomoo was an Eskimo girl who was twelve years old. Oomoo had a brother named Oolak. He was ten. Oomoo and Oolak lived in Alaska, near the ocean. When our story starts, Oomoo and Oolak are very happy. They are happy because it is April. April is a very good time of the year for the Eskimos along the Alaskan coast because April is in spring. And in the spring, the days start getting longer and warmer.

In the spring, you can notice the days getting longer. The days get longer because the North Pole of the earth is tilting toward the sun. As the North Pole tilts more and more toward the sun, the days get longer and longer.

If you live in Alaska, the days get very short in the winter and very long in the summer. The picture of the globes shows why. Globe W shows how the earth looks on the first day of winter. The X marks the place where Oomoo and Oolak live. Half of the earth is dark all the time. The place where Oomoo and Oolak live is so close to the North Pole that it is in darkness all winter long.

During Oomoo's winter, there is no daytime. There is only nighttime. That nighttime lasts for weeks and weeks. Imagine not seeing the sun for weeks. Then imagine what it is like to see the sun start coming out for a longer time each day.

Look at globe S. It shows the earth on the first day of summer.

You can tell that globe S shows summer because the North Pole is tilting toward the sun. On the first day of summer, it doesn't get dark where Oomoo and Oolak live. They are so close to the North Pole that they can see the sun all the time. For weeks, there is no night—just daytime. Then the sun starts disappearing for a longer time each day.

W

Sun

S

Remember, in summer the sun shines all the time where Oomoo and Oolak live. In winter, the sun does not shine at all. If you understand these facts, you can see why Oomoo and Oolak were happy when it was April. During the months of December and January, they had not seen the sun. During the months of February and March, the days got longer and warmer. In April, the days were getting much longer. Now the sun was shining more than 12 hours each day. The little flowers were starting to pop out on hills near the ocean. Thousands of seals were beginning to appear along the shore. Now the days were beautiful. "The sun," Oomoo said to herself and held her hands up. "The beautiful sun." She took a deep breath and smiled at Oolak. He smiled. They were standing on a hill next to the ocean. Tiny white clouds were scattered in the blue sky. The ocean was blue and gray, and it looked very cold. There was still a lot of snow on the ground, but it was wet snow, the kind of snow that made good snowballs.

Oolak made a good snowball. Oomoo figured out what Oolak was going to do, so she started to run away. She ran down the slippery hill and onto the ice chunks. She heard a snowball splat next to her, but she didn't stop. She ran and hollered over her shoulder, "Missed again!" She was smiling as she jumped to the next chunk of ice. She heard another splat next to her.

Then she stopped. In front of her, a huge polar bear was climbing from the water onto the ice. The polar bear was no more than three meters from Oomoo.

E Number your paper from 1 through 22.

Story Items

1. When days get longer, is the North Pole tilting **toward the sun** or **away from the sun**?
2. When days get shorter, is the North Pole tilting **toward the sun** or **away from the sun**?
3. Oomoo and Oolak might have a hard time going to sleep at night in the summertime. Tell why.
4. In April, the sun shines for more than ____ hours each day in Alaska.
5. What kind of animal did Oomoo see at the end of the story?
6. How far was Oomoo from that animal?
7. During Oomoo's winter, there is no ____.
   - daytime
   - nighttime

8. Write the letter of the globe that shows how the earth looks on the first day of winter.
9. Write the letter of the globe that shows how the earth looks on the first day of summer.

Review Items

10. Write the number of the earth that has the North Pole tilting away from the sun.

11. Write the number of the earth that has the North Pole tilting toward the sun.

12. Write the number of the earth that has darkness all around the North Pole.

13. Write the number of the earth that has daylight all around the North Pole.

Write which season each earth in the picture shows.

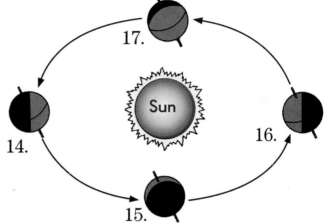

17.

Sun

14.

16.

15.

18. How warm is it during winter in Alaska?

19. Which letter on the map shows Alaska?

20. Which letter shows Canada?

21. Which letter shows the main part of the United States?

22. Which **2** letters show where Eskimos live?

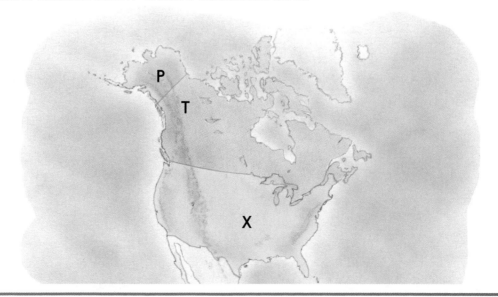

P

T

X

A

1	2	3
1. <u>nudged</u>	1. tumbling	1. snowdrifts
2. <u>scrambled</u>	2. hitch	2. dangerous
3. <u>growling</u>	3. ridge	3. slowpoke
4. <u>tossing</u>	4. hind	4. repeated
5. <u>jacket</u>	5. fur	5. playful
6. <u>playmate</u>	6. icy	

B

The Dangerous Season

The animals in Alaska are most dangerous in the spring. The male animals are ready to fight anything. The females have babies in the spring. After they have had babies, they will fight any animal that bothers their babies.

Polar bears are dangerous. So are wolves and walruses. The picture shows two animals fighting on the beach. The winner of the fight will keep his place on the beach. The loser will have to find another spot on the beach. The loser will probably have to fight another seal.

Remember, these animals are most dangerous in the spring.

Usk, the Polar Bear

"Usk," Oomoo shouted. "Usk, you big hill of white. Where have you been?"

The huge polar bear stood up and wagged his head from side to side. He was nearly three meters tall when he stood up on his hind legs. Oomoo started to run toward Usk, but then she stopped. She remembered what her father had told her last fall, when the days were starting to get short. Her father had told her that Usk was no longer a bear cub. He was a full-grown bear and full-grown bears arc not pets.

Now Oolak was standing on the ice chunk next to Oomoo. "Wow," he said, "Usk has grown a lot since last fall."

"Yes," Oomoo said. "Usk is beautiful." She was right.

Usk's coat was white-white, so bright in the sun that the color hurt Oomoo's eyes. As she looked at Usk, she remembered the first time she had ever seen him. Hunters had shot Usk's mother three years ago. Usk was just a baby, no bigger than a puppy. When Oomoo found Usk, he was very skinny and he could hardly move. For months she fed him milk from a bottle that she had made out of animal skins. Usk grew bigger and bigger. He became the best playmate that anybody ever had. He loved to run and wrestle in the snow. He slid down steep snowdrifts headfirst. He slid down them tail

first. In fact, he would sometimes slide down them as he turned around and around, with his legs sticking out in all directions as he swept a wide path down the snowdrift.

❀ As Oomoo stood near the great bear, she found it hard to believe that this same bear used to fit inside her jacket or that this bear used to sleep on the floor of her winter home.

Usk had been Oomoo's friend for over two years, but last fall something about him changed. He still liked to play sometimes, but ⭐ at other times he didn't seem to be interested in Oomoo or in being with her. Usk would go off by himself and walk along the high slopes, sometimes howling into the air like a dog. Sometimes he wouldn't come down to see Oomoo for three or four days at a ❀ time. And each time he came back, he didn't seem as playful as he had been the time before.

One day late in the fall, another polar bear came over the hills. It was a young male, about the same size as Usk. Usk attacked that bear and drove it away. That was the day that Oomoo's father told her and Oolak not to go near the bear anymore. "Usk is a bear," her father had told them. "And bears do what

bears do. They are not pets. Do not go near Usk anymore. He could hurt you."

Oomoo stood there on the ice chunk, looking up at Usk. She remembered what her father had told her.

Oomoo wanted to run over and give that great big bear a great big hug. She wanted to bury her face in his heavy white fur. She wanted to slide down the slopes with him. But she just stood there, smiling. "Hi, Usk," she said. Her brother repeated the greeting.

Usk dropped to all four legs and lowered his rear end, the way he always did when he wanted to play.

"Usk wants to play," Oolak hollered. Oolak was holding a wet snowball. He threw it at Usk and hit the bear in the shoulder. "Come on, Usk," he yelled, and ran back toward the shore.

Oomoo was going to remind her brother that they should not play with Usk. But before she could say anything, the bear bumped into her, almost knocking her into the icy water. Usk ran past her after Oolak, who was running toward the beach and hollering, "Here I am, you big white slowpoke."

Oomoo started running after the bear. She began to laugh.

D Number your paper from 1 through 16.

Review Items

Choose from these words to answer each item:
- Canada
- equator
- moon
- Florida
- migration
- geese
- sun
- poles

1. The heat that the earth receives comes from the ▮▮▮.
2. The part of the earth that receives more heat than any other part is the ▮▮▮.
3. The parts of the earth that receive less heat than any other part are called the ▮▮▮.

Write the name of each numbered object in the picture. Choose from these names:
- fishing pole
- sled dogs
- spear
- sled
- Eskimo
- kayak

10. When days get longer, is the North Pole tilting **toward the sun** or **away from the sun**?

11. When days get shorter, is the North Pole tilting **toward the sun** or **away from the sun**?

12. In April, the sun shines for more than ▇▇▇ hours each day in Alaska.

13. Which globe shows how the earth looks on the first day of winter?

14. Which globe shows how the earth looks on the first day of summer?

Q

Sun

F

15. What kind of boat do Eskimos use in the summer?

16. Why don't they use those boats in the winter?

A

1
1. mosquito
2. actually
3. punish
4. no-see-ums
5. scientists
6. ordinary

2
1. speckled
2. nudged
3. scrambled
4. sliced

3
1. forth
2. cliff
3. ignore
4. hitch
5. enter
6. careless

4
1. swarming
2. sloshing
3. growling
4. tumbling

B

Florida, Canada and Alaska

You've read about places in Florida, Canada and Alaska. See what you remember about those places.

- Which place in Canada did you read about?
- Who lived there?
- Who lived in Alaska?
- Which place is farthest south, Florida, Big Trout Lake or Alaska?
- Which place is farthest north?
- Which place has the warmest winters?
- Which place has the coldest winters?

Here's a map that shows Canada and Alaska.

You can see the route that goes from Big Trout Lake to where Oomoo and Oolak live.

Use the key to figure out about how far it is between these two places.

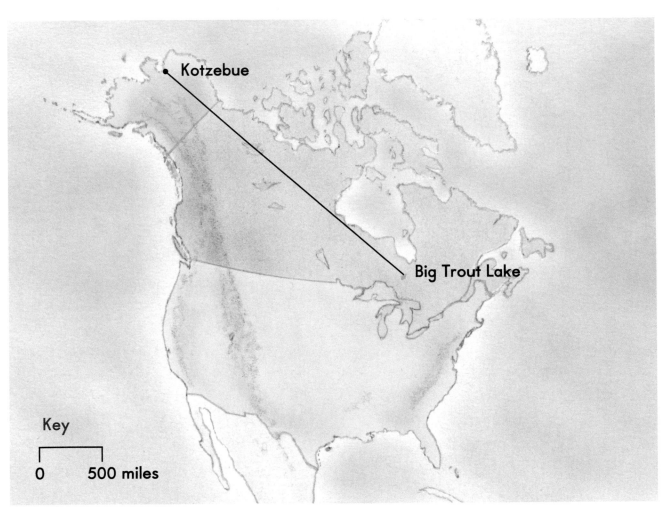

Kotzebue

Big Trout Lake

Key

0   500 miles

C Playing with Usk

Oolak ran very fast, but Usk ran even faster. Usk caught up to Oolak just as Oolak reached the beach. Usk nudged Oolak with his nose, and Oolak went tumbling in the pebbles. Usk made a growling sound and shook his head, but Oomoo knew that he was just playing the way dogs sometimes do. Oolak got to his feet and started to stumble through the pebbles. Before he got two meters down the beach, however, Usk caught up to him again, gave him a nudge in the back, and down went Oolak.

Oomoo ran to the edge of the beach where there was a snowdrift that was about a meter deep. She made a snowball and threw it at Usk. Splat! It hit him on the rear end. He turned around and stood up.

Usk made a growling sound and chased Oomoo. He caught up to her, grabbed her by the collar and pushed her over. She went face first into the snowdrift next to the pebbled beach.

She rolled over and laughed. Usk was sitting in the snow next to her, panting. With his big pink tongue hanging out, he looked like a great big white dog. She tossed some snow at his tongue. He licked his chops, and then started to pant again.

"Hey," Oolak said. "Let's hitch him up to the sled."

Oomoo remembered the fun that she and Oolak ⭐ used to have sledding down the hills with Usk. She used to hitch him to a dog sled and let him run down the hills. Sometimes he would stop halfway down and the sled would run into him. Then everybody would tumble down the hill. Sometimes he would run very fast and then make a turn at the bottom of the hill. The sled would slide in a great circle and then turn over, tossing Oomoo and Oolak into the snow. Sometimes Usk would . . .

"Oomoo," her father shouted.

Oomoo stopped thinking of sledding with Usk and looked up on the top of the hill, where her father was standing. "Oomoo," he shouted again. "Oolak, come here now." Oomoo and Oolak scrambled up the slope through the wet snow.

The top of the hill was free of snow. Oomoo stamped the snow from her feet and looked down. She did not want to look at her father. She could feel that he was looking at her.

"Oomoo, I am ashamed of you," he said. "What season of the year is it?" Oomoo answered quietly.

Her father said, "And in what season are bears the most dangerous?"

"Spring," she said.

"And what did I tell you about playing with Usk?"

Oomoo replied, "We should not go near him."

Her father said, "If you cannot stay away from that bear, you will have to stay where he will not go."

 Number your paper from 1 through 20.

Skill Items

Here are three events that happened in the story:

  a. Her father said, "And in what season are bears the most dangerous?"
  b. Oolak got to his feet and started to stumble through the pebbles.
  c. With his big pink tongue hanging out, he looked like a great big white dog.

1. Write the letter of the event that happened near the beginning of the story.

2. Write the letter of the event that happened near the middle of the story.

3. Write the letter of the event that happened near the end of the story.

Use the words in the box to write complete sentences.

ignore	splat	route	Eskimos	ordinary
playful	scientists	restless	constant	

4. The horses became ▢ on the dangerous ▢.
5. ▢ do not ▢ ▢ things.

Review Items

6. In which direction do geese fly in the fall?

7. What is this trip called?

8. The earth is shaped like a ▢.
9. The hottest part of the earth is called the ▢.
  * pole   * desert   * equator
10. The ▢s are the coldest places on the earth and the ▢ is the hottest place on the earth.
11. How many poles are there?
12. The farther you go from the equator, the ▢ it gets.
  * colder   * fatter   * hotter

13. At which letter would the winters be very, very cold?

14. At which letter would the winters be very, very hot?

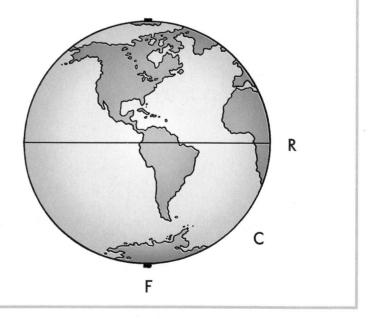

15. Is it easier to fly alone or with a large flock?

16. Flying near the back of a large flock is like riding your
bike ▨▨▨.

- with the wind
- against the wind

17. What season is it at the North Pole when the North Pole tilts
toward the sun?

18. What season is it at the North Pole when the North Pole tilts
away from the sun?

19. In what season are animals most dangerous in Alaska?

20. During what season do female animals in Alaska have babies?

A

1
1. numb
2. shrank
3. ridge
4. sliced
5. cliff
6. itch

2
1. <u>grind</u>ing
2. <u>glanced</u>
3. <u>punish</u>ment
4. <u>swarm</u>ing
5. <u>nicer</u>
6. <u>speckled</u>

3
1. groans
2. creaks
3. mosquitoes
4. no-see-ums

4
1. ignore
2. enter
3. sloshing
4. forth
5. schoolyard

B

Facts About Killer Whales

You'll be reading more about killer whales. Here are facts about killer whales:

- Killer whales are about 12 meters long. Most other whales are much longer than killer whales.
- Killer whales are not fish. Fish are cold-blooded. Whales are warm-blooded, like bears, humans and dogs.
- Killer whales are very smart. Some scientists think that killer whales are smarter than dogs.
- Killer whales hunt in packs. They kill larger whales, polar bears, seals or any other animal that is in the water.

C

The Beach

Oomoo's father said, "You must stay away from Usk."

Then he ordered Oomoo and Oolak to stay near their summer house for two full days. Oomoo and Oolak were not to go down to the beach or on the ice floe or into the hills. Oomoo's family had just moved into their summer home, which was a tent on a ridge near the ocean.

Their winter home was at the bottom of a cliff, right next to the beach. The winter home was a cave dug into the side of the cliff. The screaming winter wind could not get inside the cave. The summer home was much nicer, and it was much larger than the cave. It was made from animal skins. The only problem with the summer home was the bugs.

As soon as the snow starts to melt in Alaska, insects come out. Mosquitoes come out in clouds—millions and millions of them. The mosquitoes don't seem to bother the bears or the dogs, but they sure bother humans. There are also biting flies in Alaska. Biting flies look like ordinary flies, but they bite like mosquitoes. They leave red bumps that itch.

There are other biting flies—very small ones. And there are also little insects so small that you have to look very carefully to see them. They come out when the sun goes down, and they bite. Their bites feel like mosquito bites, but they do not leave a red mark. These tiny bugs are called no-see-ums.

Oomoo didn't like the bugs, but she managed to ignore them most of the time. And Oomoo's summer home was in a place where the wind blew hard. When the wind blew, the bugs stayed away.

Oomoo was being punished, but she really didn't mind sitting there on the hill near her summer home, looking down at the beach. The beach was like a ★ circus that had a million different acts. There were acts from the elephant seals. They were swarming on the beach about half a mile from Oomoo's summer home. Male seals were fighting for the best places on the beach.

Closer to Oomoo was another act. Two walruses were lying on a part of the beach that was speckled with thousands of birds. In the ocean were the killer whales, swimming back and forth just beyond the end of the ice floe. The killer whales were waiting for the seals to enter the water.

As Oomoo watched the killer whales she remembered a time when she had been very close to them. She had been out in a kayak with her father. It was late spring and the ocean was very calm. Oomoo's father paddled the kayak past the end of the ice floe. Suddenly, three huge killer whales appeared in the water. The fins of the killer whales sliced through the water as they circled the boat. Then one of the whales lifted its head out of the water and seemed to look right at Oomoo. The whale opened its mouth and Oomoo could see the shiny white row of knives. The whale was only a few meters from the kayak. It looked at Oomoo for a few seconds, then slipped back into the water, making a sloshing sound. Oomoo and her father sat silently in the kayak. Oomoo was so frightened that her hands were shaking. Then slowly, the three killer whales moved away from the kayak.

As Oomoo sat on the ridge looking out at the killer whales and thinking about what had happened, she could feel goose bumps on her arms. "I never want to be that close to killer whales again," she said to herself. Then the sounds on the beach caught her attention. Some of the birds near the walruses were fighting.

Review Items

Write the name of each animal in the picture.

1.

2.

3.

4.

5.

6.

7. Which animal in the picture is the biggest?
8. Which animal is the smallest?

9. Female animals fight in the spring to protect ▬ .
10. Name 2 kinds of Alaskan animals that are dangerous in the spring.

11. The map shows a route. What state is at the north end of the route?
12. What country is at the south end of the route?
13. About how many miles is the route?

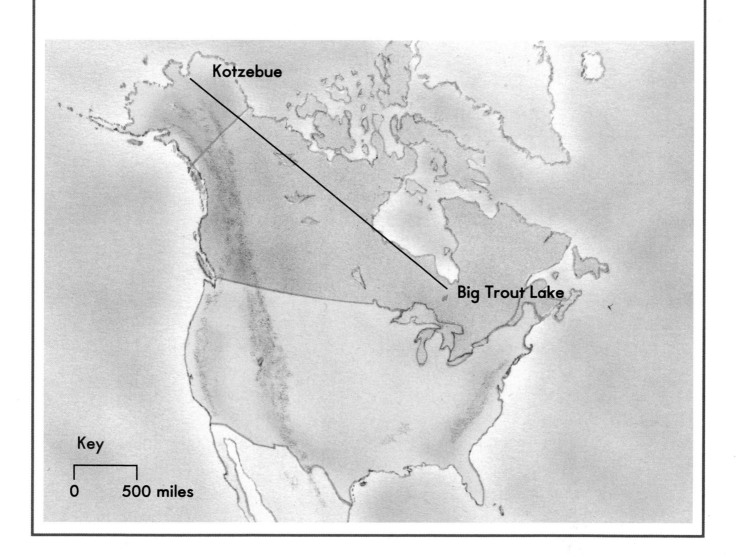

Kotzebue

Big Trout Lake

Key

0   500 miles

A

1
1. surface
2. current
3 careless
4. schoolyard
5. punishment

2
1. creaks
2. glanced
3. shrank
4. numb
5. groans
6. grinding

B

The Ice Floe

Ice floes melt in the spring. During the winter, parts of the ocean are covered with very thick ice. In some places, the ice is three meters thick. During the winter, you can walk far out on the frozen ocean. Then the spring comes and ice starts to melt. When it melts, chunks of ice break off and float into the ocean. Some of these chunks are as big as a schoolyard. Some are no bigger than a table.

When an ice floe begins to break up in the spring, you can hear it. At night, as you lay in your summer home, you can hear many sounds. You can hear the sound of wolves and sometimes bears growling. You can hear a million buzzes from a million bugs that circle above you. You can hear the occasional bark of the seals. And you can hear the ice floe. It moans and groans. It creaks and it cracks. Sometimes, it squeaks and squeals. It's a sound that you'll never forget and that you learn to love.

Ice floes also make noise in the winter. The ice floes creak and groan when the air is so cold that sweat freezes to your face. The air is so cold that a deep breath hurts and makes you cough.

In the winter, the ice floes creak and groan because great sheets of ice are crowding together and there is not enough room for them. So the ice floes buckle. Sometimes great chunks of ice break off and are pushed over other chunks. The chunks make noise when they move around.

But the sound that the ice chunks make in the spring is different. Now the chunks are melting and sliding back into the water. To Oomoo, the chunks sounded happy in the spring. They seemed to say, "I'm free to float into the ocean."

Oomoo loved to play on the ice chunks in the spring, but she knew that she had to be careful and follow the rule. The rule was that she could never go out to the chunks near the end of the ice floe. That was where the killer whales were.

During the spring there was always a small pack of whales waiting in the water just beyond the end of the ice floe. ✦ Here's why it was very dangerous to be on the ice chunks near the end of the ice floe. If the ice chunk that you were standing on drifted out into the ocean, you could not get back. Someone would have to save you. But you would be very far from shore—maybe more than a mile. Maybe the people from your village would not hear your calls for help. If they didn't, the chunk of ice would float farther and farther into the ocean. Then it would melt. It would

get smaller and smaller. As it shrank, the killer whales would move closer and closer to the ice chunk. But even if the killer whales didn't attack you, you would die within minutes after you went into the water. The water is so cold that it would take only a few minutes for your arms and legs to become so numb that you could not move.

•　　•　　•

Oomoo's punishment was over. She had just finished lunch. She could see her breath as she ran along the pebbled beach. She listened to the grinding sound of the pebbles under her feet. "Here's a good one," Oolak shouted. He was on the ice floe, pointing to a chunk of ice that was right in front of him. The chunk was a perfect size. It was about five meters across. Oomoo ran over to her brother. Then they jumped onto the ice chunk. The ice chunk rocked a little bit when they landed on it.

The ice floe was shaped like a giant letter C. The ice chunk that Oomoo and Oolak were on was near the bottom end of the C. Oolak pointed across the water to a place near the top of the C. He said, "The ice chunk will drift over there. Then we can walk back."

For a moment, Oomoo was going to say, "That's a pretty long way to drift." Then she turned around and faced the wind. It was blowing from the east. If it kept on blowing, it would move the ice chunk to the place Oolak pointed to. She glanced at the killer whales just beyond the end of the ice floe. Then she said, "Okay, let's go." The ice chunk had already drifted a few meters.

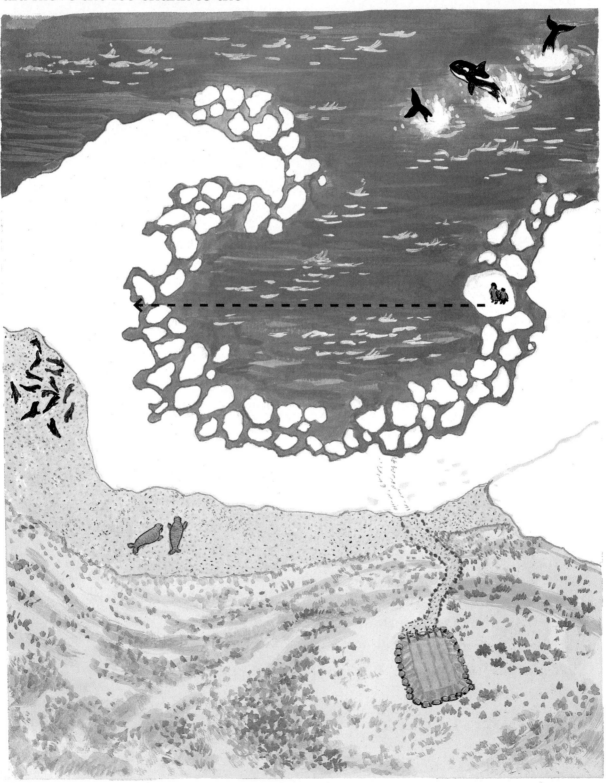

Review Items

1. Write the letter of the earth that shows the person in daytime.
2. Write the letter of the earth that shows the person 6 hours later.
3. Write the letter that shows the person another 6 hours later.
4. Write the letter that shows the person another 6 hours later.

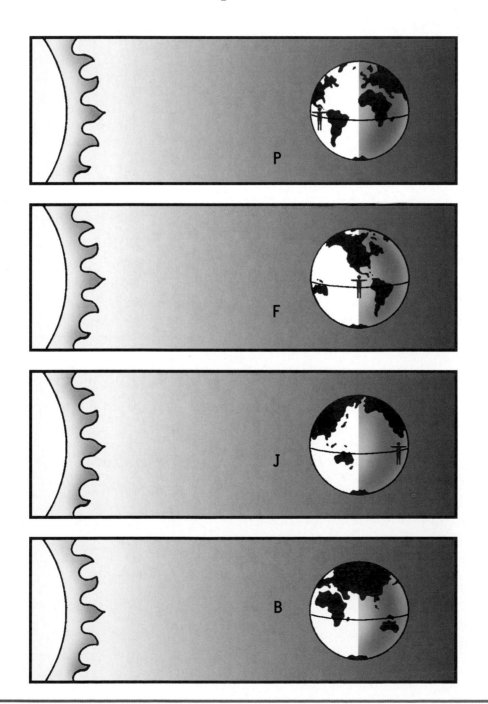

5. Which letter on the map shows Alaska?

6. Which letter shows Canada?

7. Which letter shows the main part of the United States?

8. Which 2 letters show where Eskimos live?

9. How warm is it during winter in Alaska?

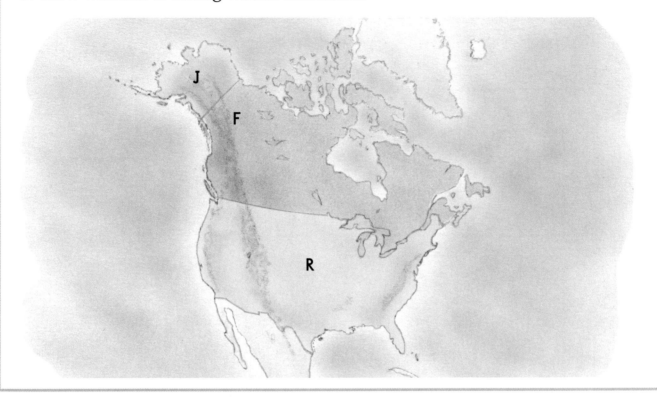

10. About how long are killer whales?

11. Compare the size of killer whales with the size of other whales.

12. Are killer whales fish?

13. Tell if killer whales are **warm-blooded** or **cold-blooded**.

14. Name 3 animals that are warm-blooded.

15. Name 3 animals that are cold-blooded.

16. Which globe shows how the earth looks on the first day of winter?

17. Which globe shows how the earth looks on the first day of summer?

Z

Sun

B

A

| 1 |
| 1. careless |
| 2. gripping |
| 3. stung |
| 4. surface |
| 5. current |
| 6. drowned |

B

Facts About Drifting

You're reading about an ice chunk that is drifting. Here are facts about how things drift in the ocean:

- Winds make things drift.

If the wind blows hard, the wind will push things and make them move. The wind will make things move in the same direction the wind blows. The picture shows wind blowing a cloud. Which direction is that wind coming from?

- Ocean currents also make things drift.

Ocean currents are like great rivers of water within the ocean. An ocean current moves. If you are in an ocean current, you will move in the same direction the current moves.

The picture shows two ocean currents, A and B. In which direction is ocean current A moving?

In which direction is ocean current B moving?

Remember the facts about how things drift. Winds make things drift. Currents make things drift. Something in a wind moves in the direction the wind is moving. Something in a current moves in the direction the current is moving.

C Drifting on an Ice Chunk

The sun felt very warm as Oomoo and Oolak stood on the drifting chunk of ice. The flies and mosquitoes were thick near the shore, but when the ice drifted into the open water, the insects were not as thick. Soon there were very few insects bothering Oomoo and her brother. Slowly, the ice drifted west, toward the other side of the C-shaped ice floe.

"Let's rock the ice," Oolak said, and began to jump up and down on one end of the ice chunk. Oomoo moved next to him and began to jump at the same time that Oolak jumped.

The ice began to rock more and more, making waves and a great sloshing sound. The cold ocean water swirled and jumped, sometimes coming over the surface of the ice.

Oomoo was looking at the water, careful not to get too close to the edge of the ice chunk. She did not want to fall into the ocean. Suddenly, she noticed that the water turned dark—from a sparkling blue to a purple, and her shoulders were no longer warm. Everything looked darker.

She looked south to see the sun, but it was behind a cloud. The cloud was not the kind of cloud you see when the weather is nice. It was a low storm cloud, a fat cloud that had a bottom layer that looked almost green. Oomoo knew about these clouds. Her father and the other men of the village had told many stories of the green clouds and how they brought winds that could sweep a boat out into the ocean. The men

of the village told that anybody going into the ocean should look at the sky—always look at the sky. Oomoo knew that as soon as you spotted a green cloud, you should get to shore immediately. Even if that cloud seemed to be many miles away, ⭐ you should not wait. The cloud would move in very fast, and when it did, it would bring terrible winds and rain. Oomoo had seen green clouds before. Once they came and almost destroyed Oomoo's tent. The winds blew so hard that they knocked down the strong posts that held up the tent. Oomoo remembered that she and Oolak stretched out on the tent and held onto the tent posts as hard as they could. If they had tried to stand up, the wind would have blown the tent into the ocean.

Oomoo remembered those things. But as she looked up at the great cloud that had covered the sun, she realized that she and Oolak had been careless. They hadn't followed the rule about watching the sky.

Suddenly, the wind tore across the ocean like a great rake. The wind made a dark path as it raced across the surface of the water. The water was smooth in front of the place where the wind touched down. Where the wind hit the water, the surface was rough with sprays of water blowing into the air.

"That wind will blow us north into the open water," Oomoo shouted. "Get down, Oolak, and find something to hang on to."

Oomoo and Oolak got down and watched the wind moving from the shore. The wait seemed very long, but it was only a few seconds. The wind was moving about 40 miles per hour.

Suddenly, the wind hit them. With a whistling sound, it hit. Oomoo held on with one hand over the edge of the ice chunk. She stuck the other one in a hole on the surface of the chunk. The spray of the water hit them. More wind. More spray. Now bigger waves, blowing and washing over the top of the ice chunk. The water was icy, and the wind was blowing. The ice chunk was drifting straight north, out into the ocean.

D Number your paper from 1 through 19.

Skill Items

She actually repeated that careless mistake.
1. What word means **to do something again**?
2. What word means the opposite of **careful**?
3. What word means **really**?

Here are three events that happened in the story:
   a. The wind tore across the ocean like a great rake.
   b. And the cloud was not the kind of cloud you see when the weather is nice.
   c. Soon there were very few insects bothering Oomoo and her brother.
4. Write the letter of the event that happened near the beginning of the story.
5. Write the letter of the event that happened near the middle of the story.
6. Write the letter of the event that happened near the end of the story.

Review Items

7. Which letter shows the place that has the warmest winters?
8. Which letter shows the place that is closest to the equator?
9. Which letter shows the place that is closest to a pole?
10. Is the North Pole or the South Pole closer to that letter?

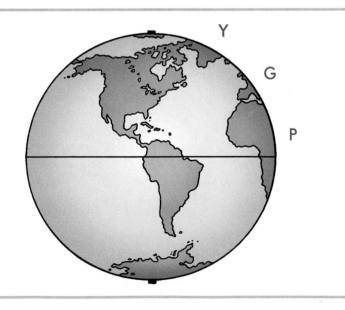

11. The earth makes a circle around the sun one time every ▨.

12. How many days does it take the earth to make one full circle around the sun?

13. When days get longer, is the North Pole tilting toward the sun or away from the sun?

14. When days get shorter, is the North Pole tilting toward the sun or away from the sun?

15. In April, the sun shines for more than ▨ hours each day in Alaska.

16. During which season do ice floes start?

17. During winter in Alaska, you can walk far out on the ocean. Tell why.

18. Do ice floes make noise in the winter?

19. Why do ice floes make noise in the spring?

19

A

1	2
1. kneeled	1. actually
2. hailstone	2. stung
3. gripping	3. marble
4. drowned	4. dents
5. playfully	

B

The Storm

If the wind hadn't started to blow, Oomoo and Oolak would have drifted west to the other side of the C-shaped ice floe. But the wind blew them off course. The wind was blowing from the shore, directly from the south. The wind blew everything north. The last place in the world that Oomoo and Oolak wanted to go was north. Oomoo noticed that the ice chunk was already very close to the end of the ice floe. Once the ice chunk went past the ice floe, there were currents that would take it farther and farther into the ocean, where it would melt.

"Help! Help!" Oomoo shouted, but her voice was small against the sounds of the wind.

The wind howled. It whistled. It made great blowing sounds, and it threw water so hard that the drops stung when they hit. "Help!" Oomoo shouted.

The waves were crashing over the side of the chunk now, almost washing Oomoo into the ocean. She tried to keep her face turned toward shore. "Help!" she hollered.

Suddenly, she heard Oolak's voice behind her. It was almost drowned out by the sound of the wind. "Oomoo," he called. She turned around and looked at the ice chunk. But she couldn't see Oolak. He had been washed into the water. Then she saw his hands. They were gripping the top edge of the ice chunk. She slid over and looked down into the water. "I can't get up," he shouted.

She rolled on to her back and let her legs hang over the side of the ice chunk. "Grab my legs," she shouted.

Picture 1

He grabbed her legs. He started to climb up, but when he did, he almost pulled Oomoo into the water with him. She started to slide, and she probably would have slid into the water if that big wave hadn't hit the ice chunk.

Oolak was on the side of the ice chunk that faced the ocean. The waves were coming from the shore side of the ⭐ ice chunk. Just as Oomoo was sliding off, a huge wave hit the shore side of the ice chunk. It lifted up the shore side and then pushed it very hard. The wave actually slid the ice chunk right under Oomoo and Oolak. In fact, it moved the chunk so fast that Oomoo and Oolak ended up right in the middle of the chunk.

Picture 2

Picture 3

🌸 Oolak looked very frightened and cold. His eyes were wide. Oomoo tried to hold on to him and keep him from slipping off. "Are we going to die?" he shouted.

"No, we're okay," Oomoo said. She was lying. She didn't see any way that she and Oolak could survive.

Then suddenly the wind died. The waves still rolled and continued to push the ice chunk beyond the floe. But the big wind had stopped. Rain and hail started to fall. The rain and hail made more noise than the wind had made. "Help!" Oomoo shouted. But she was starting to lose her voice.

"Let's shout together," she said to Oolak. "One, two, three: help!" 🌸 They repeated the shout again and again, until they could not yell anymore. Still the rain and the hail pounded down. Even though the rain was cold, it was much warmer than the ocean water.

After half an hour, the rain began to die down. When the rain had been coming down very hard, Oomoo had not been able to see more than a few meters. Now she could see where they were. The ice chunk was near the top of the C-shaped ice floe and it was still moving north. Oomoo looked to the ocean, past the ice floe, and she could see them—five or six of them. Sometimes they would roll out of the water so that she could see the black-and-white marking around their heads. Sometimes they would move along with only their fins above the water. Oomoo saw the killer whales but she didn't say anything to Oolak.

C Number your paper from 1 through 20.

Skill Items

Use the words in the box to write complete sentences.

ordinary	repeated	enter	scientists	ignore
careless	rootless	actually	hitch	

1. ____ do not ____ ____ things.
2. She ____ ____ that ____ mistake.

Here are three events that happened in the story:

a. Oomoo noticed that the ice chunk was very close to the end of the ice floe.

b. Sometimes they would roll out of the water so that she could see the black-and-white markings around their heads.

c. Just as Oomoo was sliding off, a huge wave hit the shore side of the ice chunk.

3. Write the letter of the event that happened near the beginning of the story.
4. Write the letter of the event that happened near the middle of the story.
5. Write the letter of the event that happened near the end of the story.

Review Items

6. Name 2 things that can make an ice chunk drift.
7. In which direction will you drift when you're in an ocean current?
8. In which direction will you drift when you're in a strong wind?
9. What kind of boat do Eskimos use in the summer?
10. Why don't they use those boats in the winter?

11. Write the number of the earth that has the North Pole tilting away from the sun.

12. Write the number of the earth that has the North Pole tilting toward the sun.

13. Write the number of the earth that has darkness all around the North Pole.

14. Write the number of the earth that has daylight all around the North Pole.

Write which season each earth in the picture shows.

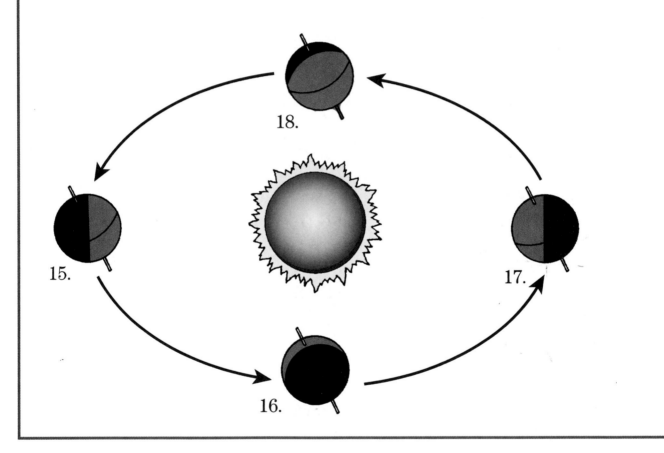

19. During winter at the North Pole, how much does the sun shine?

• never   • all the time

20. During summer at the North Pole, how much does the sun shine?

• never   • all the time

Number your paper from 1 through 29.

1. What season is it at the North Pole when the North Pole tilts toward the sun?

2. What season is it at the North Pole when the North Pole tilts away from the sun?

3. Which letter on the map shows Alaska?

4. Which letter shows Canada?

5. Which letter shows the main part of the United States?

6. Which 2 letters show where Eskimos live?

7. How warm is it during winter in Alaska?

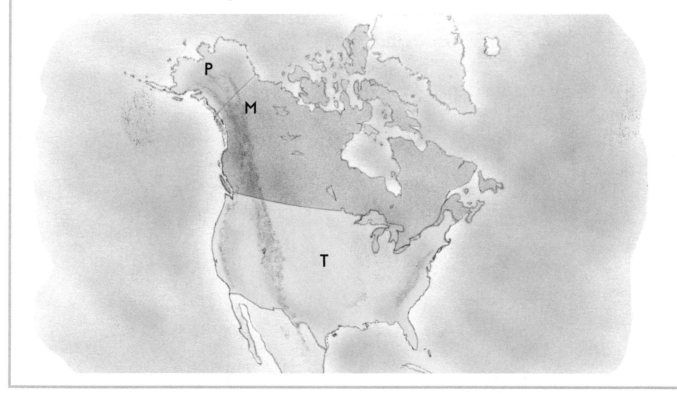

8. When days get longer, is the North Pole tilting **toward the sun** or **away from the sun**?

9. When days get shorter, is the North Pole tilting **toward the sun** or **away from the sun**?

10. In April, the sun shines for more than ▮▮▮▮ hours each day in Alaska.

11. Which globe shows how the earth looks on the first day of winter?

12. Which globe shows how the earth looks on the first day of summer?

 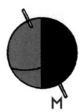 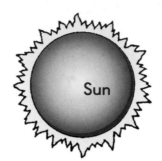

13. In what season are animals most dangerous in Alaska?

14. During what season do female animals in Alaska have babies?

15. In which direction is ocean current **P** moving?

16. In which direction is ocean current **L** moving?

17. Which direction is the wind coming from?

18. In which direction will ice chunk **F** move?

19. In which direction will ice chunk **M** move?

20. Are killer whales fish?

21. Tell if killer whales are warm-blooded or cold-blooded.

22. Name 3 animals that are warm-blooded.

23. Name 3 animals that are cold-blooded.

Skill Items

For each item, write the underlined word from the sentences in the box.

> Scientists do not ignore ordinary things.
> She actually repeated that careless mistake.

24. What word means **really?**

25. What word means that you don't pay attention to something?

26. What word means **did something again?**

27. What do we call highly trained people who study different things about the world?

28. What word means **the opposite of careful?**

29. What word tells about things that you see all the time?

END OF TEST 2

21

A

1
1. mukluks
2. wrist
3. hailstone
4. playfully

2
1. gulped
2. gently
3. owed
4. wavy
5. kneeled
6. dents

3
1. rose
2. sight
3. marble
4. dove

B **Facts About Clouds**

You have read about a big storm cloud. Here are facts about clouds:

- Clouds are made up of tiny drops of water.
- In clouds that are very high, the water drops are frozen. Here is how those clouds look.

Picture 2

- Some clouds are storm clouds. They are flat on the bottom, but they go up very high. Sometimes they are five miles high.

Picture 1

- Some kinds of clouds may bring days of bad weather. These are low, flat clouds that look like bumpy blankets.

Picture 3

The arrows in picture 3 show how the winds move inside a storm cloud. The winds move water drops to the top of the cloud. The drops freeze. When a drop freezes, it becomes a tiny hailstone. The tiny hailstone falls to the bottom of the cloud. At the bottom of the cloud, the tiny hailstone gets covered with more water. Then it goes up again and freezes again. Now the hailstone is a little bigger. It keeps going around and around in the cloud until it gets so heavy that it falls from the cloud. Sometimes it is as big as a baseball. Sometimes it is smaller than a marble.

If you want to see how many times a hailstone has gone to the top of the cloud, break the hailstone in half. You'll see rings. Each ring shows one trip to the top of the cloud. Count the rings and you'll know how many times the hailstone went through the cloud. Hailstone A went through the cloud three times.

How many times did Hailstone B go through the cloud?

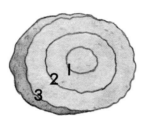

Hailstorm A

Hailstorm B

C The Killer Whales Wait

Oomoo took off one of her boots. She kneeled down and slammed the boot against the surface of the ice. The boot made a loud spanking sound. Oolak watched for a moment, then took off one of his boots and slapped it against the surface of the ice. "Maybe they'll hear this," Oomoo said. "I hope they do," she added. But she knew that it was still raining a little bit and that the rain made noise. She also knew that she and Oolak were far from shore—too far. They were more than a mile from the tent. She guessed that the sounds they made with their boots were lost in the rain and the slight breeze that was still blowing from the south.

From time to time, Oomoo glanced to the ocean. She hoped that she would see the killer whales moving far away. She hoped that the sound of the boots would scare them away. But each time she looked in their direction, she saw them moving back and forth, just past the top of the C-shaped ice floe.

Suddenly, Oolak tugged on Oomoo's shoulder and pointed toward the whales. His eyes were wide. He looked as if he was ready to cry. "I know," Oomoo said. Her voice was almost a whisper. "Just keep trying to signal," she said. "Maybe the people on the shore will hear us."

As she pounded her boot against the surface of the ice, she stared toward the shore. She wanted to see a kayak moving silently through the rain. She wanted to hear the signal of a bell ringing. She wanted to . . . .

Suddenly, she saw something white moving through the water. At first, she thought that it was a chunk of ice. But no, it couldn't be. It was not moving the way ice moves. It was very hard to tell what it was through the light rain. It wasn't a kayak. It wasn't a long boat. It was . . . Usk.

Usk ⭐ was swimming directly toward the ice chunk. And he was moving very fast.

"Usk!" Oomoo yelled as loudly as she could. "Usk!" She stood up and waved her arms.

The huge polar bear caught up to the ice chunk when it was not more than a hundred meters away from the killer whales. "Will they go after Usk?" Oolak asked.

"They'll go after Usk if they're hungry," Oomoo replied. "We've got to get out of here fast."

The huge bear swam up to the ice chunk, put his huge paws on the surface, and started to climb onto it. When he tried that, he almost tipped it over.

"No," Oomoo said. "Stay down." She tried to push him back. He rolled into the water and made a playful circle. "Give me your laces," Oomoo said to Oolak. Oomoo and Oolak untied the laces from their boots. These laces were long, thick straps of animal skin. Oomoo tied all the laces together. Quickly, she glanced back. The ice chunk was less than a hundred meters from the killer whales.

She called Usk. He playfully swam around the ice chunk, rolling over on his back and slapping the water with his front paws. Oomoo waited until Usk got close to the shore side of the ice chunk. Then she slipped the laces around his neck. "Hang on tight," she told Oolak, and handed him one end of the laces. She and Oolak sat down on the ice chunk and tried to dig their heels into dents in the surface of the ice.

"Play sled," she told Usk. "Play sled. Go home."

At first, Usk just rolled over and almost got the laces tangled in his front paws. "Home," Oomoo repeated. "Play sled and go home."

Usk stayed next to the ice chunk, making a playful sound. "Home," Oomoo shouted again.

Then Usk seemed to figure out what he was supposed to do. Perhaps he saw the fins of the killer whales. He got low in the water and started to swim toward shore.

D Number your paper from 1 through 12.

Story Items

1. What were Oomoo's boot laces made of?
2. What did Oomoo do with the laces after she tied them together?
3. What did she want Usk to do?
4. Did Usk immediately understand what he was supposed to do?
5. What did Usk start doing at the end of the story?

Review Items

6. The map shows a route. What state is at the north end of the route?

7. What country is at the south end of the route?

8. About how many miles is the route?

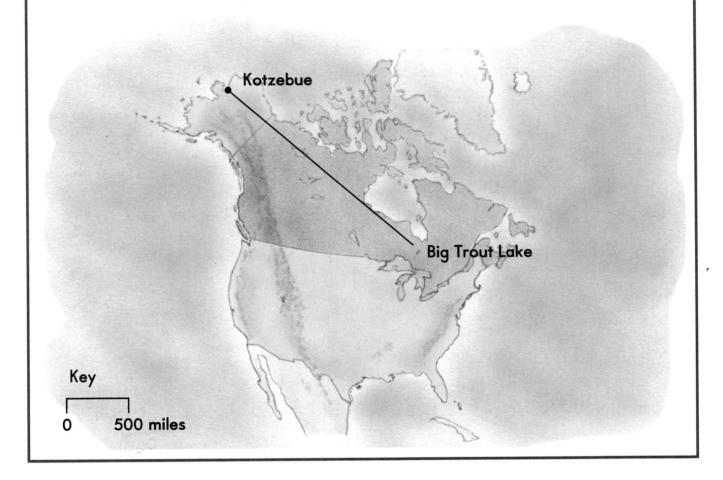

Kotzebue

Big Trout Lake

Key

0   500 miles

9. Female animals fight in the spring to protect ▮▮▮▮.
10. Name 2 kinds of Alaskan animals that are dangerous in the spring.
11. Is it easier to fly alone or with a large flock?
12. Flying near the back of a large flock is like riding your bike ▮▮▮▮.
    • with the wind   • against the wind

A

1	2	3
1. Mesozoic	1. earlier	1. figure
2. dinosaur	2. mukluks	2. sight
3. skeleton	3. wavy	3. rose
4. Triceratops	4. gulped	4. dove
5. Tyrannosaurus	5. gently	5. wrist
	6. owed	

B

Piles

Here's a rule about piles:
Things closer to the bottom of the pile went into the pile earlier.

Here's a pile:

Which thing is closest to the bottom of the pile?

So the shoe went into the pile first. The shoe went into the pile before the bone went into the pile. The shoe went into the pile before the cup went into the pile.

Look at the cup and the bone. Which object is closer to the bottom of the pile? So which object went into the pile earlier?

Look at the pencil and the rock. Which object is closer to the bottom of the pile? So which object went into the pile earlier?

The rule tells us that things closer to the bottom of the pile went into the pile earlier. Use this rule to figure out which object was the **last** one to go into the pile.

Use the rule to figure out which object went into the pile just after the shoe went into the pile.

Use the rule to figure out which object went into the pile just after the pencil went into the pile.

Usk and the Killer Whale

When Usk began to swim toward shore, he moved with so much power that he almost pulled Oomoo and Oolak off the ice. They leaned back and dug their heels in. They hung on to the laces as hard as they could hang on.

Oomoo looked over her shoulder. She saw a terrible sight. One of the fins was moving toward them. The fin rose out of the water, and she could see that the whale was looking at them. Its mouth was open and she could see the row of knives in its mouth. She clearly saw the wavy black-and-white markings on its body. Then it dove into the water. Its fin disappeared. But the whale was moving very fast.

Quickly, Oomoo tied the laces around her wrist so that she had a free hand. With that hand, she slapped the ice. "Maybe this sound will scare it off," she said to herself. "Oh, please go away," she said out loud. "Please."

She looked into the water and suddenly she saw the huge form of the whale pass under them. Her heart was pounding so hard that she seemed to shake all over. She kept looking down, but she didn't see

anything for about a minute. Then she saw the whale roll out of the water about five meters in front of them. The bear made a growling sound and pricked up his ears. For a moment, Usk stopped swimming. Then he continued.

"Oh, please go away," Oomoo repeated to herself. Again, the form of the great whale moved under them, making a slight turn to the right. Oomoo continued to slap the ice with her hand. Oolak was saying something, but Oomoo couldn't think about that. She thought about one thing—that whale.

Suddenly, the whale rolled out of the water behind them. It seemed to be turning away, toward the other whales. "Please go away," Oomoo said. Usk swam, Oomoo and Oolak held on to the laces. And Oomoo kept looking behind to see what the whale would do next. Suddenly, she saw it  roll out of the water again. It was more than sixty meters from them. That whale was moving toward the other whales.

• • •

The mosquitoes were terrible. So were the biting flies. There was no breeze at all, and the bugs were thick. But Oomoo didn't mind. She and Oolak had to stay near the tent. Oomoo and Oolak couldn't go on the slopes or down the path to the beach. They couldn't play. Their father had told them they had to study the sky and the ocean so they would not make the kind of mistake they made before.

"When you look at the sky," their father had told them, "face into the wind and look at the place where the sky meets the land or the ocean."

The day was peaceful, with the wind blowing gently from the ocean. Oomoo watched the sky and the ocean. From time to time, she looked at the killer whales. She wondered what that whale had thought, and why it hadn't attacked Usk. "You will never understand the whale," an old man of the village had told her.

That afternoon, everyone in the village gathered at Oomoo's tent. The people formed a great ring. They sang. Then Oomoo's father led Usk into the middle of the ring. Women brought him a large smoked fish—his favorite food. He gulped it down and wagged his head from side to side. Then Oomoo's father took blue paint and painted the outline of a whale on each side of Usk.

"Let this bear live under the sign of the whale," her father said. "Let no hunter shoot this bear or bother this bear. If this bear needs food, feed this bear. We owe much to this bear. Let us thank him."

The people from the village cheered and danced. Oomoo and Oolak danced with the others. They were very, very proud of their bear. They knew that they should not play with him because he was a bear, not a playmate. But they also knew that they owed their lives to that huge, white, playful bear.

D **Number your paper from 1 through 17.**

1. Things closer to the bottom of the pile went into the pile ▨.

Look at the pile in the picture.

2. Which object went into the pile **first?**

3. Which object went into the pile **last?**

Review Items

Write the name of each animal in the picture.

10. Which animal in the picture is the biggest?

11. Which animal in the picture is the smallest?

12. About how long are killer whales?

13. Compare the size of killer whales with the size of other whales.

14. What are clouds made of?

15. What kind of cloud does the
    picture show?

16. What happens to a drop of water
    at **B**?

17. The picture shows half a hailstone.
    How many times did the stone go
    through a cloud?

SPECIAL PROJECT

Make a wall chart that shows and tells about Eskimos.
- Make pictures of the things that they use and wear.
- Make pictures of the kinds of houses that they live in.
- Find out what mukluks look like. Make a picture of them.
- Find out another name for killer whales and another name for Eskimos.
- Find out what kind of food Eskimos eat in the wintertime.
- Find out what kind of food they eat in the summertime.
- Find out what kind of animal skins they use to make clothes.

Write the facts about Eskimos on the chart. You may want to write other facts about Eskimos.

A

1	2	3
1. Atlantic Ocean	1. armor	1. earliest
2. Bermuda Triangle	2. dinosaur	2. Triceratops
3. Andros Island	3. layers	3. killers
4. Africa	4. Tyrannosaurus	4. Mesozoic
5. engineer	5. skeleton	5. explaining

B # Layers of the Earth

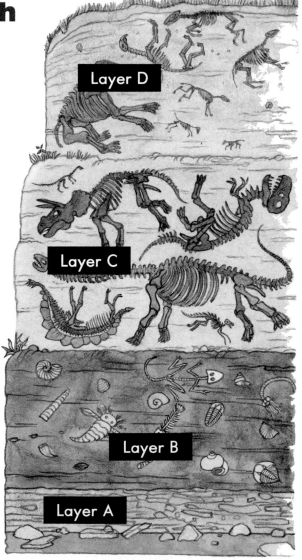

You learned a rule about piles. Which things went into the pile earlier? We use the rule about piles to figure out how things happened a long time ago.

Look at picture 1. It shows a large cliff. There are rows of stones and rocks and seashells. Each row is called a layer. The layers are piled up. That means the layers closer to the bottom of the pile came earlier.

Which layer went into the pile earlier, layer C or layer D?

When we look at the layers of rock, we find skeletons of animals and shells of animals. In layer B, we find strange fish and other animals that lived many millions of years ago. In layer D we find the skeletons of horses. Near the bottom of layer D, we find horses that are no bigger than dogs. Near

PICTURE 1

the top of layer D, we find horses that are as big as the horses of today.

When we look at layer C, we find the skeletons of some very strange animals. These are dinosaurs. Some of the dinosaurs were much bigger than elephants. Other dinosaurs had great spikes on their tails. No dinosaurs are alive today. The only place we find their bones is in one of the layers under ground. That is layer C. We can't find dinosaur bones in layer B. We can't find them in layer D.

The layers of ★ rock tell us a great deal about things that happened millions and millions of years ago. They tell us what it was like when the great dinosaurs walked on Earth. There were no horses, bears, elephants or rabbits. There were no mice or cats. But there were many animals. Most of them were probably cold-blooded.

Some dinosaurs ate big animals. These dinosaurs were huge killers that could move fast. The ones that are found near the top of layer C stood almost 20 feet tall.

When we move above layer C, we find the beginning of animals that we know—horses, cats, bears, pigs. No layers show skeletons of humans. But if these skeletons were in the picture, they would be at the very top of the pile, in layer D.

Here's another fact about the layers: When we dig a hole in any part of the world, we find the same layers. If we dig a hole in Africa or in Canada, we find skeletons of elephants near the top of the pile. We find dinosaurs in the next layer down.

The layer that has dinosaur skeletons is called the Mesozoic. The layer that came after the Mesozoic is the top layer. The top layer has no skeletons of dinosaurs. This layer is still being laid down. We live at the top of the top layer.

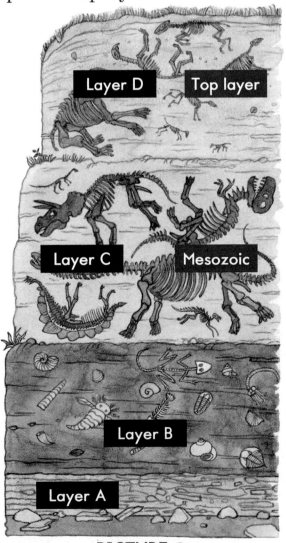

Layer D Top layer

Layer C Mesozoic

Layer B

Layer A

PICTURE 2

Skill Items

The smell attracted flies immediately.

1. What word means **right now**?
2. What word means **really interested** the flies?

Review Items

3. The sun shines ▆▆▆.

   • some of the time   • all of the time

4. Can you see the sun all day long and all night long?

5. If you can see the sun, is it **daytime** or **nighttime** on your side of the earth?

6. What is it on the other side of the earth?

7. The earth turns around one time every ▆▆▆ hours.

8. How many heat lines are hitting place X on the map?
9. Write the letter of the place that's the coldest.
10. Why is place T hotter than place X?

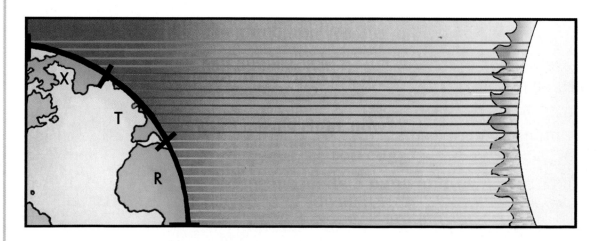

11. Which object went into the pile **first?**

12. Which object went into the pile **last?**

13. Which object went into the pile **earlier,** the bone or the book?

14. Which object went into the pile **earlier,** the shoe or the bone?

15. Which object went into the pile **just after** the book?

16. Which object went into the pile **just after** the bone?

17. Things closer to the bottom of the pile went into the pile ▭.

18. Write the letter of the storm clouds.

19. Write the letter of the clouds that may stay in the sky for days at a time.

20. Write the letter of the clouds that have frozen drops of water.

A

B

C

A

1	2	3
1. <u>Fl</u>orida	1. Andros Island	1. Mesozoic
2. <u>st</u>ormy	2. Bermuda Triangle	2. armor
3. <u>war</u>ning	3. Atlantic Ocean	3. Triceratops
4. <u>Ca</u>rla	4. Edna Parker	4. Tyrannosaurus
5. <u>ex</u>plaining		5. exciting
		6. squawking

B

Dinosaurs of the Mesozoic

You've read about the Mesozoic. What kind of animals lived in the Mesozoic? The picture shows two of the most important dinosaurs that lived in the Mesozoic.

The huge killer that lived late in the Mesozoic is named Tyrannosaurus.

Tyrannosaurus was about 20 feet tall, twice as tall as an elephant. The dinosaur with the horns and the armor is named Triceratops. Tyrannosaurus did not have an easy time killing Triceratops.

Edna Parker

Edna Parker was thirteen years old. She had been out on her father's ship before. But this was the first time that her father, Captain Parker, let Edna bring a friend along. This was going to be a great trip for Edna.

On other trips, Edna had a problem. She became bored. There was never anything for her to do on the ship after it left the harbor. Sometimes she would sweep up or help with the meals, but most of the time she just sat around and looked over the side of the ship at the swirling water. With Carla along, Edna would have fun.

• • •

☙ Captain Parker was explaining the trip to the two girls. He pointed to a map of Florida and the Atlantic Ocean as he spoke.

"We are starting from here," he said, pointing to the tip of Florida. "We are going to follow this dotted line to an island called Andros Island." Captain Parker continued, "That means we will pass through a place where hundreds of ships have sunk or been lost. It's called the Bermuda Triangle." Captain Parker continued, "Many sailors say the Bermuda Triangle is the most dangerous part of the ocean."

Carla's face seemed to drop.

"Hey," Captain Parker said, and smiled. "Nothing's going to happen in a big ship like this. We ☙ are very ★ safe. And this is not the stormy season."

Carla asked, "Why is the Bermuda Triangle such a dangerous part of the ocean?"

"Bad seas," the captain answered. "There are huge waves and storms that come up without any warning. And there are whirlpools."

Edna said, "You know what whirlpools are, don't you, Carla?"

"I think I know what they are," Carla replied.

Captain Parker said, "Let me explain. Did you ever watch water that was going down the drain? Sometimes it spins around and around and it makes the shape of an ice cream cone."

"I've seen those," Carla replied. "They suck water right down the drain."

"Yes," Captain Parker said. "Those are tiny whirlpools. The kind of whirlpools that you find in the Bermuda Triangle are just like those, except they are big enough to suck a ship down."

"Wow," Carla said.

Edna was trying to imagine a huge whirlpool.

Captain Parker said, "Well, girls, Andros Island is only 120 miles from here, so we should arrive there in less than a day. We should have a smooth trip. The weather looks good. I am going to look over some maps now. You girls may play on deck, but stay away from the sides of the ship. And stay away from the lifeboats."

"All right, Dad," Edna said, and the girls rushed onto the deck.

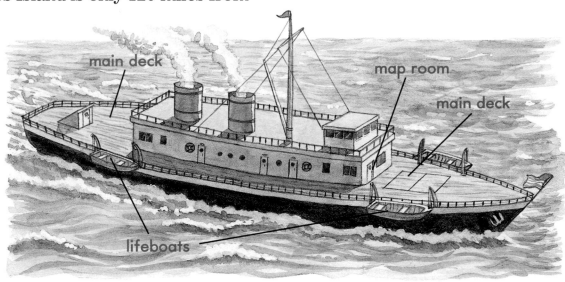

D Number your paper from 1 through 27.

Use these names to answer the questions:
Tyrannosaurus, Triceratops.

1. What is animal A?
2. What is animal B?

Skill Items

Use the words in the box to write a complete sentence.

immediately	restless	repeated	actually	moaned
attracted	careless	ordinary	gently	

3. She ▆▆ ▆▆ that ▆▆ mistake.
4. The smell ▆▆ flies ▆▆.

Review Items

Look at the map.

5. What's the name of the place shown by the letter C?

6. Which letter shows the coldest place?

7. Which letter shows the hottest place?

8. Which letter is farthest from the equator?

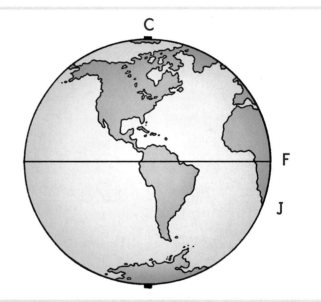

9. During which season do ice floes start?

10. During winter in Alaska, you can walk far out on the ocean. Tell why.

11. What kind of boats do Eskimos use in the summer?

12. Why don't they use those boats in the winter?

13. Which letter shows the part of the earth that receives more heat from the sun than any other part?

14. Which letter shows the part of the earth that receives less heat from the sun than any other part?

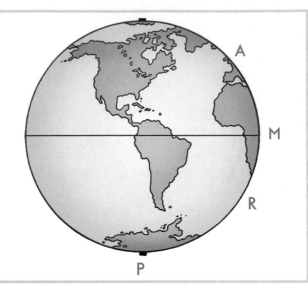

15. Which came **earlier** on Earth, dinosaurs or horses?

16. Which came **earlier** on Earth, strange sea animals or dinosaurs?

17. Write the letter of the layer that went into the pile **first.**

18. Write the letter of the layer that went into the pile **next.**

19. Write the letter of the layer that went into the pile **last.**

20. Which layer went into the pile **earlier,** B or D?

21. Which layer went into the pile **earlier,** A or D?

22. Write the letter of the layer where we would find the skeletons of humans.

23. Write the letter of the layer that has dinosaur skeletons.

24. Write the letter of the layer where we would find the skeletons of horses.

25. Write the letter of the layer we live on.

26. What's the name of layer C?

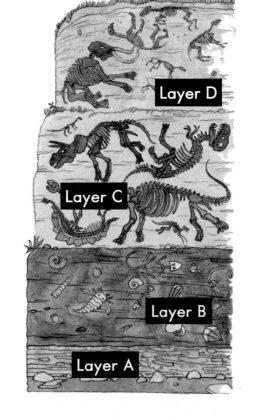

27. What kind of animals lived in the Mesozoic?

A

1
1. seagulls
2. elevator
3. surface
4. pirates
5. instant
6. handkerchief

2
1. first mate
2. mast
3. engineer
4. silent

3
1. galley
2. stern
3. touch
4. pretend
5. roughed

4
1. exciting
2. powered
3. squawking
4. sliced

5
1. hailstone
2. spyglass
3. tiptoe

B

Looking for Something to Do

Edna and Carla had dashed out of the map room. They had run to the stern of the ship, where they watched the seagulls that followed the ship. The girls watched the waves roll off the stern of the ship.

Then the girls ran to the galley. The cook was busy. They tried to talk to him, but the only thing he wanted to talk about was how much his new gold tooth hurt. After the girls spent about five minutes in the galley, they went to the engine room.

The engine room in a ship is the place where the ship's engine is. Some ships have engines that are as big as a school room. The engine of Captain Parker's ship was not that big. It was about the size of a small truck.

The engineer looked at the girls and said, "What do you think you're doing here?"

They told him that they were looking around. He replied, "If you want to stay here, I'll put you to work. So if you don't want to work, get out."

The girls left the engine room. They walked around the front deck. They thought about climbing the ladder that went up to the top of the mast. But that seemed too scary.

At last the girls sat down on the front deck near a lifeboat. They sat and they sat and they sat. The girls tried to talk about different things. Edna studied the water. Then she realized that she was doing the same kinds of things that she used to do when she went alone on these trips. She was sitting in the sun watching the water.

The sea was very calm, like a sheet of glass. The ship sliced through the water and left waves that moved out in a giant V as far as Edna could see.

There were beads of sweat on Carla's forehead. Carla said, "This Bermuda Triangle isn't as exciting as they say it is."

Edna nodded. "Yeah, this is boring."

For a moment, the girls were silent. Edna heard the squawking sound of the seagulls and the steady hum of the great engine that powered the ship. Then Carla said, "I wish we had our own boat. Then we could have some fun. I could be captain and you would be my first mate."

The girls looked at each other and smiled. Edna said, "Why don't we pretend that we have our own ship?"

Carla said, "I see a boat we can use for our game." She pointed to a lifeboat that was hanging at the side of the ship. It was ready to be lowered into the water in case of trouble.

Edna shook her head no. She said, "Remember what my dad told us? Stay away from the lifeboats."

"Oh, come on, Edna. We won't get in trouble if we are careful. We won't touch anything. We'll just sneak into the lifeboat and play for a while."

"No," Edna said slowly, looking at the lifeboat. Edna hadn't made up her mind to do it, but she looked around to see if any of the crew members could see them. She was just trying to figure out how hard it would be to sneak into the boat. No crew members were in sight.

"Come on," Carla said with a big smile. "Come on, Edna."

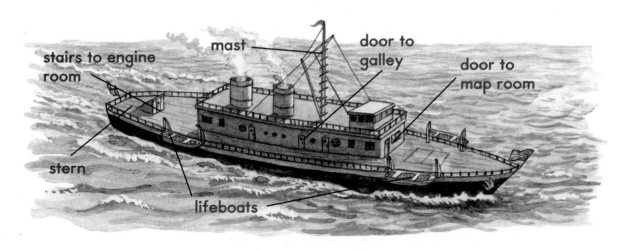

stairs to engine room

mast

door to galley

door to map room

stern

lifeboats

C Number your paper from 1 through 26.

Skill Items

Write the word from the box that means the same thing as the underlined part of each sentence.

they'd	spices	center	leaning
we'd	discovered	throne	hay

1. They put the table in the <u>middle</u> of the room.
2. The horses came running to get some <u>dried grass</u>.
3. <u>We would</u> rather play a game.

Review Items

Use these names to answer the questions:
Tyrannosaurus, Triceratops.
   4. What is animal K?
   5. What is animal L?

6. Captain Parker's ship passed through a place where hundreds of ships have sunk or been lost. Name that place.
7. Write the letters of the 3 things you find in the Bermuda Triangle.

   a. streams   c. huge waves   e. ice floes
   b. sudden storms d. whirlpools   f. mountains

8. When geese learn to fly, do they start in the water or on the land?
9. They run with their ▮▮▮▮ out to the side.

10. What's the name of the line that goes around the fattest part of the earth?

11. What's the name of the spot that's at the top of the earth?

12. What's the name of the spot that's at the bottom of the earth?

Choose from these words to answer each item:
- moon
- Florida
- sun
- equator
- geese
- poles
- Canada
- migration

13. The heat that the earth receives comes from the ▓▓▓▓.

14. The part of the earth that receives more heat than any other part is the ▓▓▓▓.

15. The parts of the earth that receive less heat than any other part are called the ▓▓▓▓.

16. Write the letters of the 2 kinds of places that are safe for geese.

   a. places with a few geese
   b. places with a few ducks
   c. places with many geese
   d. places with no geese or ducks

Write the name of each numbered object in the picture. Choose from these names:
- kayak
- spear
- Eskimo
- fishing pole
- sled
- sled dogs

23. Do ice floes make noise in the winter?

24. Why do ice floes make noise in the spring?

25. In which direction will you drift when you're in an ocean current?

26. In which direction will you drift when you're in a strong wind?

1
1. shallow
2. tearing
3. hind
4. practice
5. bow

2
1. spyglass
2. surface
3. instant
4. besides
5. lightning

3
1. elevator
2. forty
3. handkerchief
4. perhaps

4
1. bailing
2. roughed
3. glassy
4. tiptoed
5. pirates
6. sloshed

The Lifeboat

Carla and Edna were on the deck of Captain Parker's ship. Carla pretended to take out her spyglass and look around. "We're on an island," she said. "And there's our boat, pulled up on the beach." She pointed to the lifeboat. "I'm the captain and you're my first mate. So when I give an order, you carry it out."

Edna pulled off her shoes and socks and rolled up her pants to the knees. She tied a handkerchief around her head. She felt like a sailor now. "Yes sir, Captain, sir," she said as she stood up. The deck felt very hot on Edna's feet.

"Remember, we're on an island," Carla said. "We have to be very careful when we sneak into our boat. There are pirates on this island. Follow me."

Carla crouched down and tiptoed across the deck to the lifeboat. She climbed in the front. "The coast is clear," she said softly.

"Ouch, ouch, ouch," Edna whispered as she tiptoed across the deck. Edna jumped into the lifeboat. It rocked from side to side. It was held in the air by ropes that were attached to the bow and to the stern. Edna knew that you did something with the ropes to lower the boat into the water, but she wasn't sure how to do it. And she didn't want to find out.

For a moment, Edna had a bad feeling. They were doing something they shouldn't do. But then Edna explained things to herself. There wasn't anything else to do. None of the crew members would talk to them. And besides, they would be very careful.

Suddenly the boat dropped. Carla must have grabbed one of the ropes at the front of the boat or perhaps the rope just slipped. Edna didn't know. All she knew was that the boat was falling like a high-speed elevator. The ropes were making a howling sound as they ran through the wheels that had been holding the lifeboat. Edna wanted to yell something, but her voice wouldn't work.

The bow of the boat hit the water before the stern. Edna held on to the side of the boat as hard as she could. But when the boat hit the water, Edna went flying forward, bumping into ⭐ Carla. A huge wave broke over the front of the lifeboat and sloshed around in the bottom of the boat. The boat bounced in the waves that the large ship was making. Another wave broke over the side of the boat. For an instant, Edna was amazed at how loud the waves were. From the deck the ocean seemed almost silent. But now there were rushing sounds, splashing sounds, sloshing sounds. The waves from the stern of the big ship hit the lifeboat and almost turned it over.

Carla tried to stand up. She was waving her arms and yelling. Edna yelled, too. "Help!" "Stop!" "Here we are!" they yelled. The girls waved their arms. They continued to wave as the large ship became smaller, smaller, smaller. Then the girls stopped waving and continued to watch the large ship. Now it was only a dot on the glassy water.

Suddenly, as the girls watched the dot, a very cool breeze hit them from behind. The air suddenly had a different smell. The wind roughed up the surface of the water.

Edna turned around and looked up. Behind the lifeboat was a great storm cloud. It rose up and up. "Oh no," Edna said. Then her mind started to work fast. "Let's start bailing water out of this boat. We're in for a storm."

When the girls started bailing, there was about 5 inches of water in the bottom of the boat. The girls bailed and bailed. The waves got bigger and bigger. Now there was only about 3 inches of water in the boat, but the waves hitting the boat were very big and they were starting to splash over the side. The girls bailed and bailed and the waves splashed and splashed. Now there was about 4 inches of water in the boat.

The girls had to stop bailing when a terrible wind hit the boat. The waves were so large that Edna had to hang on to the side of the boat. She just kept hanging on and hoping that the storm would stop. But the waves were now over 20 feet high and the winds were moving forty miles per hour. The boat was going up and down the waves.

 Number your paper from 1 through 19.

Here are three events that happened in the story.
Write **beginning, middle** or **end** for each event.
1. The girls had to stop bailing when a terrible wind hit the boat.
2. The ropes were making a howling sound as they ran through the wheels that had been holding the lifeboat.
3. Carla pretended to take out her spyglass and look around.

Review Items
4. In which direction do geese fly in the fall?
5. What is this trip called?
6. Geese live in large groups called ▩▩▩.

7. Where are most wild geese born?

A   B   C

8. Write the letter of the clouds that may stay in the sky for days at a time.

9. Write the letter of the storm clouds.

10. Write the letter of the clouds that have frozen drops of water.

11. Which letter shows the place that has the warmest winters?

12. Which letter shows the place that is closest to the equator?

13. Which letter shows the place that is closest to a pole?

14. Is the North Pole or the South Pole closer to that letter?

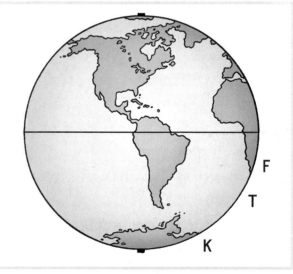

15. The earth makes a circle around the sun one time every ▓▓▓▓.

16. How many days does it take the earth to make one full circle around the sun?

17. During winter at the North Pole, how much does the sun shine?

• never   • all the time

18. During summer at the North Pole, how much does the sun shine?

• never   • all the time

19. Name 2 things that can make an ice chunk drift.

A

1

1. <u>thunder</u>
2. <u>shallow</u>
3. blinding
4. somehow
5. <u>lightning</u>

2

1. moaned
2. funnel-shaped
3. stumbled
4. aloud
5. tearing

B # Facts About Whirlpools

In today's story, you will read about a whirlpool. Here are facts about whirlpools:

- Whirlpools are made up of moving water.
- A whirlpool is shaped like a funnel.

Here is a funnel. It is wide on top and narrow on the bottom.

Here is a whirlpool. It is wide on top and narrow on the bottom.

- The water in a whirlpool spins around and around. Something caught in a whirlpool goes around and around as it moves down.

C A Giant Whirlpool

Now it was starting to rain. The small lifeboat was sliding up huge waves and then down the other side of the waves. Edna felt sick and dizzy.

Just then the boat reached the top of a wave, and Carla shouted, "I see land." She pointed.

The lifeboat slid down the wave and Edna could not see anything but water. Then the boat moved up, up, to the top of another wave. Now Edna could see what Carla had pointed to. But it wasn't land. It was a wave, much bigger than the other waves.

"Hang on," Edna shouted. "A giant wave is coming toward us."

For an instant, everything became bright as lightning shot through the sky. A boom of thunder followed. The huge wave was now very close to the boat. Edna looked up to the top of it. It was like a cliff of water with a white, foaming top.

Somehow, the boat moved up the huge wave—up, up, very fast. And now faster. The boat was moving so fast that Edna couldn't see what was happening. More lightning. Thunder. Edna had to close her eyes. She was dizzy. Dizzy.

The boat wasn't just moving up. It was moving around and around. The boat was moving so fast that Edna could hardly tell which direction was up and which direction was down. But she could see that the boat was on the top of a huge funnel-shaped cone of water. The boat was being sucked into a giant whirlpool.

Edna tried to say something, but her voice wouldn't work. She pointed down to the bottom of the whirlpool. It seemed to be hundreds of meters below the tiny boat.

The next things happened very fast. They happened so fast that Edna was never sure exactly what happened or why. First, there were large hailstones—hundreds of them. For an instant, Edna noticed them floating in the boat, which was quickly filling up with water. So much hail came down that everything seemed to be white. The hail was hitting the girls, but Edna couldn't even feel it. Suddenly, ★ there was a great flash and a great spray of water. The flash was blinding.

Later, Edna thought a lot about that flash and the splash. Later she talked to Carla about it. The girls figured out that the lightning must have hit the water right in front of their boat. The lightning must have hit with so much power that it sent the boat flying through the air. After the flash was the giant splash. That must have been the splash that the boat made when it came down. The boat must have landed far from the whirlpool.

The hail continued to fall for a few minutes. Then it stopped, and a steady rain began to fall. For hours, the rain came down. The wind died down and the waves became smaller and smaller. Finally the rain stopped. Without any warning at all, it stopped. The sea was calm again, and Edna was sick. Edna didn't want to talk. She didn't want to move. She was dizzy. She was lying near the back of the boat. The boat was half-filled with water now. Edna moaned, "Ooooh." She wasn't sure she knew where she was anymore.

Carla was in the front of the boat, talking to herself. "I don't believe this," she said over and over. "I don't believe this. I want to go home."

Edna looked over the side of the boat. But she didn't see deep blue water that seemed to go down forever. She saw shallow water and sand. The boat was now in water that was only about a meter deep. Slowly, Edna looked around. "Land," she said aloud. She pointed to a row of palm trees and a beach that was about half a mile away. "Land," she said again. She was standing up and stepping over the side of the boat.

"Land," she said and stumbled into the water. She fell down and got up and started to wade toward the trees. She wanted to be on land. She wanted to be on something that would not rock and bounce and make her dizzy. "Land," she said.

D Number your paper from 1 through 18.

Skill Items

Write the word from the box that means the same thing as the underlined part of each sentence.

hooves	tame	modern	tusks
charging	English	ancient	

1. We visited the <u>very, very old</u> city.
2. My pet goat is <u>not wild</u>.
3. The hunters wanted the elephant's <u>large, curved teeth</u>.
4. We visited a very <u>new</u> city.

Review Items

The rim of the volcano exploded.

5. What word means **made a bang and flew apart?**
6. What word means **a mountain formed from hot flowing rock?**
7. What word means **the top edge** of the volcano?

8. The earth is shaped like a ▩▩.

9. The ▩▩s are the coldest places on the earth and the ▩▩ is the hottest place on the earth.

10. At which letter would the winters be very, very cold?

11. At which letter would the winters be very, very hot?

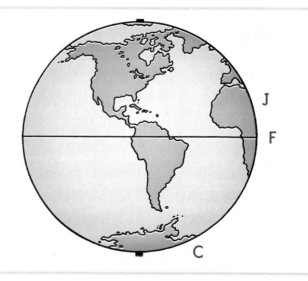

12. Write the letter of the earth that has the North Pole tilting away from the sun.

13. Write the letter of the earth that has the North Pole tilting toward the sun.

14. Write the letter of the earth that has darkness all around the North Pole.

15. Write the letter of the earth that has daylight all around the North Pole.

16. Write **A, B, C** and **D.** Then write the season each earth in the picture shows.

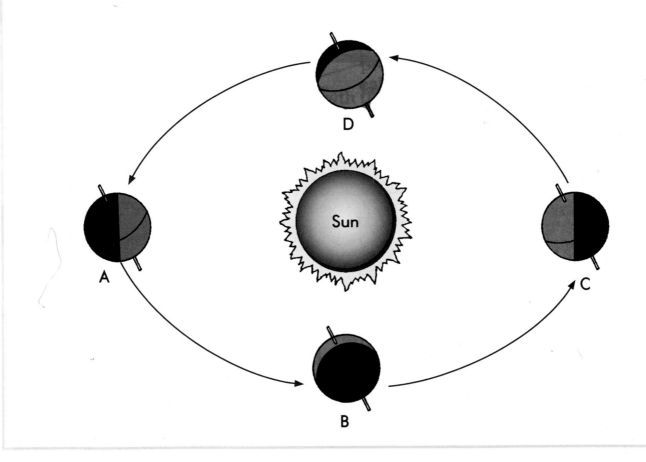

17. Are killer whales fish?

18. Tell if killer whales are **warm-blooded** or **cold-blooded.**

A

1
1. upright
2. overturned
3. anyone
4. aloud

2
1. tangle
2. gallons
3. ignore
4. strangest
5. bending
6. crowded

3
1. faint
2. hind
3. tearing
4. practice
5. terrible
6. driven
7. groove

B

A Long Night

Carla called to Edna, "Help me get this boat on shore." Carla was pulling the lifeboat toward shore. She was a long way behind Edna. Edna waited for her. Then the girls pulled the lifeboat onto the beach and turned it over. Many gallons of salt water spilled out and ran back to the ocean.

The sky was starting to clear. In the distance were heavy clouds, but the waves on the ocean were small. Behind Edna and Carla was a heavy jungle. A great tangle of trees and vines crowded down to the beach. From the jungle came the sounds of birds and other animals. The whole beach was covered with red sand. Edna had never seen sand like that before.

Edna walked a few feet from the overturned lifeboat and sat down on the soft, red sand beach. "I'm sick," she said.

"I'm sick, too," Carla said. She was lying down on the beach.

A few minutes later, Carla was sleeping. Edna closed her eyes. The world seemed to be spinning around and around. The beach seemed to be rocking. "Oh," she said aloud. She kept her eyes closed and tried to ignore the terrible rocking and spinning.

• • •

"BRRRRAAAAHHHH!"
Edna sat up, her eyes wide. It was night. At first she didn't know where she was.

"BRRRAAAHHH!"
"What's making that noise?" Carla asked.

Edna turned toward Carla's voice. It was so dark that Edna could hardly see her.

Suddenly, as Edna looked in Carla's direction, she saw something

moving out of the jungle. She heard it, too. It crashed through the vines and trees. There were breaking sounds and tearing sounds as small trees snapped and broke. Edna could see the faint outline of the trees being bent over and snapped down. Then she saw the faint outline of something else, something very large. An animal of some sort. "It can't be," Edna said aloud. The animal that she saw was too big. It was as big as some of the trees.

Edna didn't have much time to look at the animal because it stayed on the beach for only a few seconds. All Edna saw was a very faint outline. But she saw enough to know that she was looking at an animal like nothing she had ever

seen before. It was big. It seemed to have a huge head. And it seemed to walk upright, on its hind legs.

During the few seconds that Edna saw the animal, it seemed to throw its head back when it roared. Then it suddenly turned around and disappeared into the jungle. It left a trail of great crashing and bending sounds.

"What was that?" Carla asked.

"I don't know, but I'm scared," Edna answered.

"Yeah," Carla said. "I think we should go stay under the lifeboat."

"Good idea," Edna said.

So the girls crawled under the lifeboat and tried to sleep. But neither girl slept. One time, Edna was almost asleep when Carla moved her foot and made a noise. Edna sat up so suddenly that she hit her head on the inside of the lifeboat.

That was the longest night that Edna remembered. She kept waiting for the sky to become light. She wasn't sure which part would become light first, because she didn't know where east was. The first part to get light was over the jungle. Then it seemed that a year passed before it was light enough to see the ocean clearly. The sun was not up yet, but the birds were squawking and screaming in the jungle.

At last, Edna and Carla crawled out from under the lifeboat. The first thing they did was walk to where they had seen the outline of the huge animal. As soon as they got close to the spot, they saw the animal's huge footprints in the red sand.

When Edna looked at the footprints, she knew that there was an animal on this island that looked like no other living animal anyone had ever seen. It left footprints that were a yard long!

C Number your paper from 1 through 22.

Skill Items

Write the word from the box that means the same thing as the underlined part of each sentence.

speech	excited	screech	box
certain	armor	pouch	surface

1. She put her keys in the small bag.
2. The sharp sound of the peacock startled me.
3. I am sure about the answer to the question.

Use the words in the box to write complete sentences.

volcano	practiced	attracted	exploded
sense	immediately	strangely	

4. The smell ▮▮▮ flies ▮▮▮.
5. The rim of the ▮▮▮ ▮▮▮.

Review Items

6. What season is it at the North Pole when the North Pole tilts toward the sun?

7. What season is it at the North Pole when the North Pole tilts away from the sun?

8. Female animals fight in the spring to protect ▨.

9. Name 2 kinds of Alaskan animals that are dangerous in the spring.

10. Name 3 animals that are warm-blooded.

11. Name 3 animals that are cold-blooded.

12. What are clouds made of?

13. What kind of cloud does the picture show?

14. What happens to a drop of water at **B**?

15. Which object went into the pile **first?**

16. Which object went into the pile **last?**

17. Which object went into the pile **earlier,** the cup or the book?

18. Which object went into the pile **earlier,** the bone or the book?

19. Which object went into the pile **just after** the pencil?

20. Which object went into the pile **just after** the bone?

21. Whirlpools are made up of moving ▨.

22. A whirlpool is shaped like a ▨.

A

1
1. breath
2. shriek
3. leathery
4. immediately

2
1. clearing
2. dents
3. driven
4. practiced
5. terrible
6. terribly

3
1. sense
2. pond
3. club
4. thick
5. spread
6. stared

4
1. groove
2. grove
3. steam
4. stream
5. tail
6. trail

B

Footprints

There was a row of footprints in the red sand. The footprints of the animal were a yard long. Each footprint had three toes. The size of the footprints told Edna something about the size of the animal. The footprints made very deep dents in the sand. These deep dents told Edna something about how much the animal weighed.

Between the footprints was a deep groove in the sand. Carla asked, "What could make that deep trail?"

Suddenly Edna shouted, "A tail. I'll bet a tail did that. That animal is walking on its hind legs. It's dragging a heavy tail behind it. The tail makes the groove in the sand."

For a while, the girls walked around the footprints and didn't say anything. Then they looked toward the jungle. The animal had left a huge path through the jungle. On either side of this path were thick

vines and trees. But the path was almost clear. It looked as if somebody had driven a truck through the jungle and knocked down all the small trees and vines.

Edna said, "I don't think we should go into that jungle."

"Yeah, we shouldn't do it," Carla said. The girls were silent for a few moments. They just stood there and looked at the great path that led into the jungle. Then Carla said, "But we could follow that path for a little way. We don't have to go too far."

"I don't want to go in there," Edna said. But she wasn't telling Carla the truth. Part of her was frightened and wanted to run away. But part of her wanted to see what made those huge footprints. Her mind made pictures of that animal. In one of the pictures, the animal was chasing Carla and Edna. Edna was running as fast as she could, but the animal was getting closer and closer and . . .

"Come on," Carla said. "Let's go just a little way."

Now another part of Edna's mind was taking over. It wanted to see that animal. This part of Edna's mind was not terribly frightened. It made up pictures of Carla and Edna sneaking up on the animal. In these pictures, the animal did not see Edna and Carla. "This animal is not very smart," Edna

said to herself. "If it was a smart animal, it would have found us last night. Maybe it does not have a good sense of smell. Maybe it has poor eyes."

"Okay, let's follow the path," Edna said to Carla. "But just a little way."

Carla picked up a short, heavy branch. She practiced swinging it like a club. Edna picked up a branch too. They were easy to find in the path made by the animal.

So the girls started down the path into the jungle. They walked very slowly and carefully. They jumped each time a screech or a roar came from the jungle. They tried not to step on small branches that would make a cracking sound. Slowly, they moved farther into the jungle. Soon, Edna could not see the beach behind her. The trees over them blocked out the light.

"This is far enough," Edna said after she realized that the girls had gone over a hundred meters into the jungle.

"Shhh," Carla said, and pointed straight ahead. Edna could see a clearing. In the middle of it was a small pond. From the pond, steam rose into the air. The girls moved forward. Now Edna could see a small stream flowing into the pond. And she saw tall grass.

When the girls reached the edge of the clearing, Edna stopped. She noticed that the trees were very strange. She looked at a small tree on the edge of the clearing. "I saw a picture of a tree like this somewhere," she said. "But I can't remember where." She tried to remember. Suddenly, she did. And when she remembered, she wanted to run from the jungle as fast as she could. She had seen a picture of that tree in a book on dinosaurs. She had looked at the picture in the book many times. And she clearly remembered the tree. It was in a picture that showed Tyrannosaurus fighting with Triceratops.

Edna looked at the tree and remembered the huge footprints. "Oh no," she said aloud.

Review Items

1. When days get longer, is the North Pole tilting toward the sun or away from the sun?

2. When days get shorter, is the North Pole tilting toward the sun or away from the sun?

3. In April, the sun shines for more than ▮▮▮▮ hours each day in Alaska.

---

4. Which globe shows how the earth looks on the first day of winter?

5. Which globe shows how the earth looks on the first day of summer?

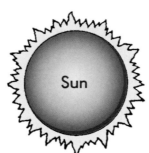
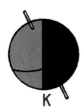

Use these names to answer the questions:
Tyrannosaurus, Triceratops.

6. What is animal X?

7. What is animal Y?

8. Which came **earlier** on Earth, dinosaurs or horses?

9. Which came **earlier** on Earth, strange sea animals or dinosaurs?

10. Write the letter of the layer that went into the pile **first.**

11. Write the letter of the layer that went into the pile **next.**

12. Write the letter of the layer that went into the pile **last.**

13. Which layer went into the pile **earlier,** B or C?

14. Which layer went into the pile **earlier,** A or C?

15. Write the letter of the layer where we would find the skeletons of humans.

16. Write the letter of the layer that has dinosaur skeletons.

17. Write the letter of the layer where we would find the skeletons of horses.

18. Write the letter of the layer we live on.

19. What's the name of layer C?

20. What kind of animals lived in the Mesozoic?

21. Captain Parker's ship passed through a place where hundreds of ships have sunk or been lost. Name that place.

22. Write the letters of the 3 things you find in the Bermuda Triangle.

a. streams	d. sudden storms
b. ice floes	e. mountains
c. huge waves	f. whirlpools

23. What happens to something that gets caught in a whirlpool?

Number your paper from 1 through 36.

1. What are clouds made of?
2. What kind of cloud does the picture show?
3. What happens to a drop of water at **B**?

4. The picture shows half a hailstone. How many times did the stone go through a cloud?

5. Which object went into the pile **first?**
6. Which object went into the pile **last?**
7. Which object went into the pile **earlier,** the rock or the pencil?
8. Which object went into the pile e**arlier,** the pencil or the knife?
9. Which object went into the pile **just after** the knife?
10. Which object went into the pile **just after** the rock?

11. Things closer to the bottom of the pile went into the pile ▮▮▮▮ .
12. Which came **earlier** on Earth, dinosaurs or horses?

13. Which came **earlier** on Earth, strange sea animals or dinosaurs?

14. Write the letter of the layer that went into the pile **first.**

15. Write the letter of the layer that went into the pile **next.**

16. Write the letter of the layer that went into the pile **last.**

17. Which layer went into the pile **earlier,** B or A?

18. Which layer went into the pile **earlier,** A or C?

19. Write the letter of the layer where we would find the skeletons of humans.

20. Write the letter of the layer that has dinosaur skeletons.

21. Write the letter of the layer where we would find the skeletons of horses.

22. Write the letter of the layer we live on.

23. What's the name of layer C?

24. What kind of animals lived in the Mesozoic?

Use these names to answer the questions:
Tyrannosaurus, Triceratops.

25. What is animal F?

26. What is animal G?

27. Write the letters of the things you find in the Bermuda Triangle.

       a. ice floes   d. streams

       b. mountains   e. huge waves

       c. whirlpools   f. sudden storms

28. Whirlpools are made up of moving .

29. A whirlpool is shaped like a ▇▇▇.

30. What happens to something that gets caught in a whirlpool?

31. Write the letter of the footprint made by the heaviest animal.

32. Write the letter of the footprint made by the lightest animal.

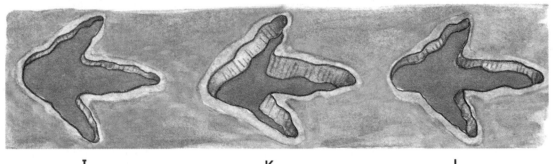

        J   K   L

Skill Items

For each item, write the underlined word or words from the sentences in the box.

> The smell <u>attracted</u> flies <u>immediately</u>.
>
> The <u>rim</u> of the <u>volcano</u> <u>exploded</u>.

33. Which underlined word refers to a mountain formed from hot flowing rock?

34. Which underlined word means **right now?**

35. Which underlined word means the **top edge?**

36. Which underlined word means **made a bang and flew apart?**

================ END OF TEST 3 ================

1
1. <u>half</u>-folded
2. <u>ea</u>gle
3. <u>for</u>got
4. <u>mon</u>ster

2
1. leathery
2. breaths
3. instantly
4. mouthful
5. immediately
6. lying

3
1. started
2. stared
3. sailed
4. slid
5. spread
6. attract

The Monster

Just as Edna was going to tell Carla about the tree in the book, a loud flapping sound came from the sky. A huge bird-like animal sailed down from above the jungle. It wasn't a bird because it didn't have feathers. It had large wings that looked like leather. The animal had large sharp teeth. As the animal got close to the ground, Edna could see that it was very big—bigger than an eagle. The animal flapped its leathery wings loudly as it landed in the middle of the clearing. When it landed, the girls could see it more clearly.

Carla whispered, "What is that thing?"

Edna said, "It's an animal that lived a hundred million years ago."

Edna and Carla stared at the animal. It was on a rock with its wings half-folded and its mouth open.

"Let's get out of here," Edna said.

The girls began to sneak down the path toward the beach. Suddenly, the ground shook and there was a terrible crashing sound. The ground shook again. Edna couldn't tell where the sound was coming from. She ran from the path and hid behind a vine-covered tree. Then she realized that the crashing sound was moving closer and closer. It was coming from the beach and moving down the path toward the clearing. A small tree crashed to the ground right in front of Edna. Above her was the form of a monster. It was standing in the path that Edna and Carla had followed. Edna could smell the animal. It gave off a smell something like garbage. Edna instantly recognized the animal. Tyrannosaurus.

The monster moved so quickly that Edna could hardly believe it. Like lightning, it turned its head one way and then another. Its mouth was open and it seemed to be smiling with teeth as big as knives. The huge, bird-like animal in the clearing spread its wings and started to flap them. Immediately Tyrannosaurus turned its head in the direction of the animal. An instant later, the monster was running toward the winged animal.

With each step, the ground shook. As Tyrannosaurus ran toward the clearing, its huge tail followed. It hit the tree that Edna was standing behind. The tree cracked. Edna went flying into the soft plants that covered the floor of the jungle. Before Edna could stand up, she heard noises from the clearing. There was a leathery flapping sound. Then there was a terrible crunching sound, like the sound of bones being crushed. There were three squawking sounds. Then there were more crunching sounds.

Edna got up and started to run. She ran down the path toward the beach. She made her legs move as fast as they could. And she kept telling them to move faster. She told herself, "Get out of here. Get out of here." She tripped and almost fell. "Don't fall," she told herself. "Run," she told herself. "Run and don't stop."

She wasn't thinking about the noise she made as she ran. She wasn't thinking that Tyrannosaurus might hear her. She wasn't thinking about anything but running. "Run," she told herself. "Don't slow down."

She noticed that there was a large snake on the path right in front of her. It was yellow and black, and it was at least three meters long. But she didn't even slow down. With a great leap she jumped over the snake and kept on running. When the girls had gone into the jungle, the path had seemed long. Now it seemed longer. It seemed as if it would never end. "Run," she said out loud between her breaths. "Run. Run."

Edna ran until she could see the beach ahead of her. Then her mind slowly began to work again. She stopped and turned around. There was nothing on the path behind her. Good. Good. Tyrannosaurus was making so much noise eating that flying animal that it couldn't hear Edna. Besides, Tyrannosaurus already had a meal. What would it want with a tiny animal like Edna? Edna wouldn't be much more than a mouthful for the monster. Edna was thinking now. She walked out onto the red sand of the beach.

She was out of breath. Now she began to realize how frightened she had been. She had been so frightened that she forgot about everything. She forgot about being careful. Suddenly, Edna turned all the way around. She had forgotten about Carla. Where was Carla?

Edna looked in all directions, but she couldn't see Carla.

C Number your paper from 1 through 20.

Skill Items

Here are three events that happened in the story.
Write **beginning, middle** or **end** for each event.
1. Edna went flying into the soft plants that covered the floor of the jungle.
2. A huge bird-like animal sailed down from above the jungle.
3. She had been so frightened that she forgot about everything.

Story Items

4. Write the letter of the footprint made by the lightest animal.
5. Write the letter of the footprint made by the heaviest animal.

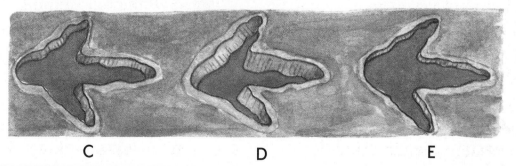

C   D   E

The picture shows marks left by an animal.

6. Which arrow shows the direction the animal is moving?

7. Write the letter of the part that shows a footprint.

8. Write the letter of the part that shows the mark left by the animal's tail.

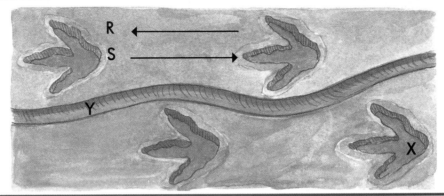

Review Items

9. About how long are killer whales?

10. Compare the size of killer whales with the size of other whales.

11. Are killer whales fish?

12. Tell if killer whales are **warm-blooded** or **cold-blooded**.

13. Name 2 things that can make an ice chunk drift.

14. In which direction will you drift when you're in an ocean current?

15. In which direction will you drift when you're in a strong wind?

16. What kind of boat do Eskimos use in the summer?

17. Why don't they use those boats in the winter?

18. Write the letter of the storm clouds.

19. Write the letter of the clouds that may stay in the sky for days at a time.

20. Write the letter of the clouds that have frozen drops of water.

A

B

C

A

1
1. cough
2. pour
3. volcano
4. neither
5. adventure
6. supplies

2
1. remains
2. shriek
3. reason
4. attract
5. safety

3
1. lying
2. laying
3. breathe
4. breath
5. pacing
6. packing

4
1. glanced
2. prancing
3. strangely
4. untangle

B

Looking for Carla

Carla was not in sight. That meant that Carla was still back there in the jungle. Edna took a couple of steps into the jungle. She stopped and looked down the path. She couldn't see anything. Part of her mind told her, "Don't go back there. You'll get killed." Then another part of her mind said, "You've got to help Carla. Go back."

For a moment Edna thought of calling to Carla. But then she realized that the sound of her voice would attract the monster.

Suddenly, she noticed that she was walking back toward the clearing. She had decided to try to help her friend.

She crouched over and kept near the side of the path. She was ready to duck behind a tree as soon as she spotted Tyrannosaurus. She couldn't hear anything except her breath and the sounds of her feet moving through the green plants. Step, step, step—she moved down the path.

She noticed a beautiful flower growing in the middle of the path. She noticed that the birds in the jungle were not squawking. "Why are they silent?" she asked herself.

She answered, "They probably flew away when Tyrannosaurus ran into the clearing."

Then once again she noticed how quiet it was. Step, step, step. Edna was nearly all the way back to the clearing when she heard Tyrannosaurus. She could smell the dinosaur, too, but she couldn't see it.

Edna ducked behind a tree on the side of the path. Now her mind started to think about the things that might have happened.

Maybe Tyrannosaurus had already found Carla and maybe Tyrannosaurus . . . "No," she told herself. "Don't think about things like that. Carla is all right."

Edna stayed behind the tree for a minute or two. Tyrannosaurus didn't seem to be moving toward her. So, slowly she snuck back onto the path and moved toward the sound of the breathing. Closer and closer. Then she saw Carla lying near the path. Her leg was tangled up in some vines. She was lying very still.

Part of Edna's mind said this: "Carla is not moving, so she is dead."

Another part of Edna's mind said this: "No. She is not dead, and she is not hurt. She is lying very still because Tyrannosaurus is very near and she doesn't want to move." Edna snuck up a little closer. Now she could see Tyrannosaurus. The dinosaur was at the edge of the clearing, looking in the direction of Carla. But the dinosaur was not standing still. It was pacing and turning its head from one side to another, as if it was looking for something.

Edna looked at Carla. She was all right.

On the far end of the clearing were the remains of the flying dinosaur. For some reason, Tyrannosaurus was not eating them.

Suddenly, Edna got an idea of how to save Carla. The plan was very dangerous, but Edna felt strangely brave. She felt that she had to try to help Carla. Edna's plan was to catch the dinosaur's attention. She would go into the jungle and make a lot of noise. Tyrannosaurus would come after the noise. When the dinosaur followed the noise, Carla would be able to free herself and run to safety.

Edna's heart was pounding. She knew that she would have to be very fast. She remembered how fast Tyrannosaurus moved through the jungle.

Suddenly, Tyrannosaurus turned around. Three Triceratops dinosaurs came into the clearing. They held their heads down as they moved toward Tyrannosaurus. Tyrannosaurus ran toward them and then stopped. It opened its mouth very wide and let out a terrible shriek.

"Now," Edna told herself. She ran toward Carla, who was already sitting up and trying to untangle her leg.

Edna grabbed the vines and tried to pull them free. It seemed to take forever. Carla didn't say anything. The girls tugged at the vines and tried to get Carla's leg free. The dinosaurs were very close to them.

C Number your paper from 1 through 22.

Skill Items

Write the word from the box that means the same thing as the underlined part of each sentence.

armor	gulped	shabby	docked
graph	mast	bailed	boots

1. He <u>quickly swallowed</u> the milk.
2. She got some new <u>mukluks</u>.
3. The animal's <u>hard covering</u> protects it from enemies.

The new exhibit displayed mysterious fish.

4. What word describes **things we don't understand?**
5. What word means **an arrangement of things for people to look at?**
6. What word means **showed?**

Review Items

7. How long ago did dinosaurs live on Earth?
   - 30 thousand years ago
   - 1 million years ago
   - 100 million years ago
8. In what season are animals most dangerous in Alaska?
9. During what season do female animals in Alaska have babies?
10. About how long are killer whales?
11. Compare the size of killer whales with the size of other whales.

Write the name of each animal in the picture.

12.

13.

15.

14.

16.

17.

18. Which animal in the picture is the biggest?

19. Which animal is the smallest?

20. The map shows a route. What state is at the north end of the route?

21. What country is at the south end of the route?

22. About how many miles is the route?

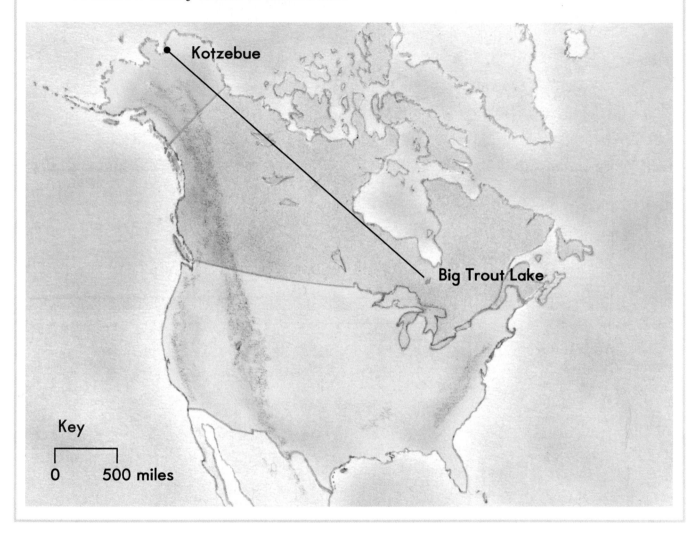

A

1	2	3
1. <u>however</u>	1. swift	1. quake
2. <u>explodes</u>	2. glanced	2. hardened
3. <u>underwater</u>	3. thud	3. explosion
4. <u>volcano</u>	4. pours	4. prancing
5. <u>coughing</u>	5. directed	5. divided

B

Volcanos and Earthquakes

You will be reading about volcanos and earthquakes. A volcano is a mountain that is made of hot melted rock. That rock comes from inside the earth.

The picture shows what a volcano would look like if it were cut in half and we could see the inside.

There is a layer of melted rock in the earth far below the volcano. The melted rock moves up to the surface of the earth. When the melted rock pours out onto the surface of the earth, the rock cools and becomes hard. More melted rock piles up on top of the hardened rock. The volcano keeps growing in the shape of a cone.

The volcano may pour out great clouds of smoke.

Sometimes a volcano explodes. Sometimes there are earthquakes around volcanos.

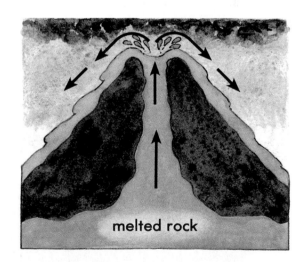

melted rock

C

Explosion

Carla and Edna were tugging at the vines that were tangled around Carla's leg. The vines were like thick, sticky ropes that wouldn't let go. Occasionally, Edna glanced up and looked at what was happening in the clearing. The three Triceratops dinosaurs were lined up, waiting for Tyrannosaurus. The giant Tyrannosaurus was prancing around with its mouth wide open. It would move toward the Triceratops dinosaurs and then it would back away. From time to time, it would let out a terrible shriek.

The leg is free! Take her hand and help her up. Now run. Keep an eye on her. Let her run in front of you. Push her on the back so that she runs faster. Is that as fast as she can run? Let's get out of here. Keep running. Look, there's the beach. Run. Right down to the edge of the water. Stop. Turn around. Look back. They're not coming after you. Safe. Safe.

The girls stood near the edge of the water for a few minutes, listening to the sounds that came from the jungle. The sounds told them that a terrible fight was going on. Tyrannosaurus would shriek from time to time. Then there would be a great thud. After a few minutes, the shriek of Tyrannosaurus turned into a cry. Just then the whole island seemed to shake.

The tops of the trees began to shake. They shook so hard that coconuts fell to the ground. The birds left the island. They were flying to the west. Suddenly the ground shook with such force that Edna fell down. The red beach moved up and then down. It rocked to one side and then to the other.

"Earthquake!" Carla yelled.

Some trees near the edge of the jungle fell over. As Edna sat up, she noticed a great cloud of smoke over the top of the island. "Volcano," she shouted.

The smoke boiled and billowed into the air with great speed. Within a few seconds, it had covered the whole eastern part of the sky. And still the smoke cloud was growing.

"Come on," Edna shouted. She ran  toward the boat. The beach suddenly shook. She stumbled, fell, and slid through the red sand. She got up and ran. The sky was now becoming dark, as the enormous cloud continued to grow.

The girls reached the boat and turned it over. They pushed it into the shallow water. When they were a few meters from the shore, a terrible quake shook the island. It made a large crack in the sand beach. That crack moved out into the water, right under the boat.

Suddenly, Edna noticed that the sand under her feet had disappeared. She slipped underwater. The currents were very swift and she felt her feet being pulled into the current.

Edna reached up and tried to grab something. Her hand grabbed a rope that was attached to the front of the boat. She held on to the rope with all her might. The currents were spinning her around, but she kept a tight grip on the rope. Slowly she pulled herself up to the boat. She came out of the water coughing.

As soon as she caught her breath, she called, "Carla, Carla!" She had salt water in her eyes, so she couldn't see well.

"I'm here," Carla answered.

Edna rubbed her eyes with one hand and looked in the direction of the voice. Carla was sitting in the boat. She helped Edna get into the boat. The sky was so dark now that it was almost like night.

Suddenly, there was a terrible explosion. The explosion had so much force that it seemed to press the air against Edna's face. This pressing feeling came before the sound of the explosion. The sound was like nothing that Edna had ever heard. It was so loud that her ears rang for hours. That explosion had so much force that it knocked down all the trees on the island.

The girls began to row away from the island. "Where are we going to go?" Carla asked.

"I don't know," Edna replied. "I don't know." She did know one thing, however. She knew that she didn't want to be near that island.

D Number your paper from 1 through 25.

Skill Items

Use the words in the box to write complete sentences.

displayed	adventure	exploded	reason
rim	glanced	mysterious	directed

1. The ▮▮▮ of the volcano ▮▮▮.
2. The new exhibit ▮▮▮ ▮▮▮ fish.

Review Items

3. What season is it at the North Pole when the North Pole tilts toward the sun?

4. What season is it at the North Pole when the North Pole tilts away from the sun?

5. In what season are animals most dangerous in Alaska?

6. During what season do female animals in Alaska have babies?

7. Things closer to the bottom of the pile went into the pile ▮▮▮.

8. Write the letter of the layer that went into the pile first.

9. Write the letter of the layer that we live on.

10. Which layer went into the pile later, A or B?

11. Write the letter of the layer where we would find the skeletons of humans.

12. Write the letter of the layer where we find the skeletons of dinosaurs.

13. Write the letter of the layer where we find the skeletons of horses.

14. What's the name of layer C?

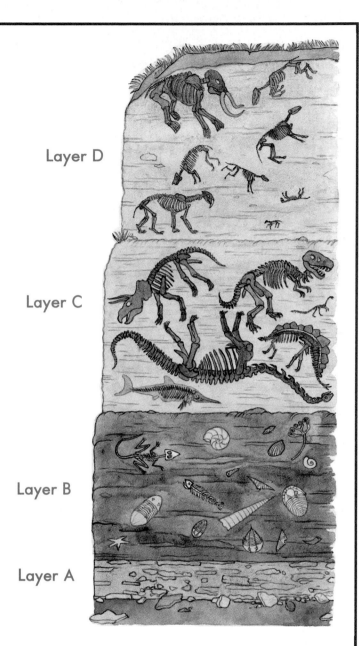

Layer D

Layer C

Layer B

Layer A

Use these names to answer the questions:
Tyrannosaurus, Triceratops.

15. What is animal R?

16. What is animal S?

17. What are clouds made of?

18. What kind of cloud does the picture show?

19. What happens to a drop of water at **B?**

20. The picture shows half a hailstone. How many times did the stone go through a cloud?

21. Which letter on the map shows Alaska?

22. Which letter shows Canada?

23. Which letter shows the main part of the United States?

24. Which 2 letters show where Eskimos live?

25. How warm is it during winter in Alaska?

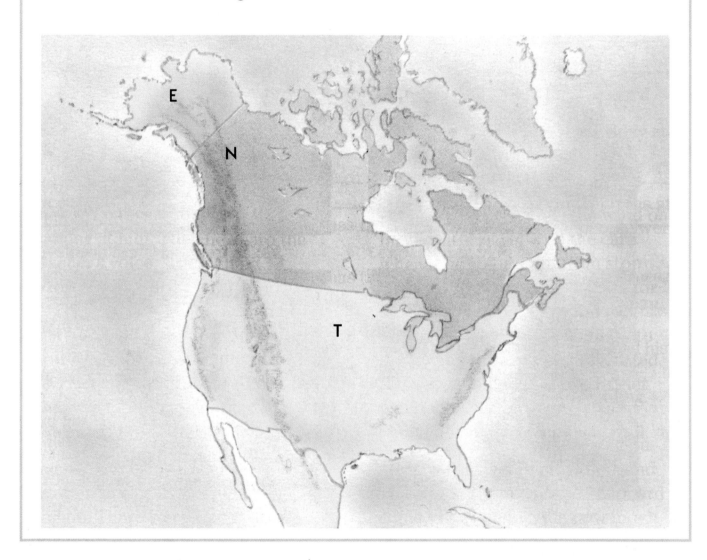

A

1	2	3
1. approach	1. <u>blisters</u>	1. throat
2. bandage	2. <u>adventure</u>	2. chew
3. laundry	3. <u>unreal</u>	3. nor
4. stomach	4. <u>neither</u>	4. rim
5. mysterious	5. <u>shadow</u>	5. beneath
6. Tuesday	6. <u>supplies</u>	6. honestly

B

Underlined Words

Some of the words in stories you will read must be spoken loudly. Here's the rule about words that must be spoken louder than other words: **The words that must be spoken louder are underlined.**

The following are sentences with underlined words. Say the underlined words in a loud voice. Say the other words in a soft voice.

a. That is <u>wrong</u>.
b. You are a <u>crook</u>.
c. I am <u>not</u> a crook.
d. I'm <u>tired</u> of reading.
e. My name is <u>Sam</u>.
f. <u>My</u> name is Sam, <u>too</u>.
g. This book is <u>hard</u>.
h. If you think <u>your</u> book is hard, try reading <u>this</u> book.
i. You sure like to <u>talk</u>.

C

Back in the Lifeboat

The lifeboat was floating on a bright, shining sea. The sea was so calm that it looked almost as if it was made of glass. When Edna looked down, she could see different colors. Where the water was not very deep, the color was green. Deeper spots were blue, with the deepest spots dark blue. The sun pounded down on the girls. Edna had blisters on her hands from rowing, but she was not rowing now. She was just sitting. In the far distance, a billowing cloud rose high into the sky. Edna could no longer see the island.

As she sat there in the lifeboat, she realized that they didn't have supplies. There were no other islands in sight. The boat seemed to be drifting in a current, and the current was taking the boat to the west. But how long would it be before the girls spotted another island? What would they do if they didn't find land soon? Edna was already starting to feel thirsty. She tried not to think about it, but when she swallowed, she noticed that her throat was dry.

Neither Edna nor Carla had said anything for a long time. The adventure they had on the island was so unreal that Edna didn't know what to say.

Suddenly, Edna noticed that the boat was drifting faster. When she looked to the west, she got a very sick feeling. In the distance, she could see the rim of a whirlpool.

The boat was moving toward it, speeding faster and faster, through the green water.

The rushing sounds got louder and louder. Now the boat was moving over the rim of the whirlpool. "Hang on," Edna shouted, as she grabbed on to the side of the boat. She hung on with all her might. The boat sped around and around and around. Edna looked up at the sky. The clouds seemed to be spinning around and around. The boat was going ⭐ deeper and deeper into the whirlpool.

Now Edna could see a great cone of water above the boat. The boat was spinning so fast that its force pressed Edna against the bottom of the boat. She felt sick and dizzy. She squeezed her eyes closed as tightly as she could. Then the sounds seemed to fade away and everything went dark.

. . .

Heat. Terrible heat. "Where am I?" Edna said aloud. Then she realized that she was lying in the bottom of the lifeboat. The sun was beating down on her face. The boat was not moving. As she sat up, she realized that there was some water in the bottom of the boat. The water was very warm.

Edna looked over at Carla. "Are you okay?" Edna asked.

Carla looked very sick. "I think so," she said. "What happened?"

"I don't know," Edna answered. "We were in a whirlpool. That's the last thing I remember. Are we dead?"

"I don't think we're dead," Carla replied. "But I don't remember how we got out of the whirlpool. I passed out."

"I passed out, too," Edna said. Slowly, she turned around and looked at the ocean. It was perfectly calm. She didn't see any signs of whirlpools. And she didn't see any billowing clouds that marked the island. "We must be far from the island," Edna said.

Edna looked over the side of the boat, into the water. It was very dark blue. She could see some fish swimming around beneath the boat. They seemed to like staying in the shadow of the boat. As Edna looked at the fish, she remembered something she had once read. Fish have a lot of fresh water in them. If you chew on raw fish, you can squeeze the water out. Edna didn't like the idea of chewing on raw fish, but she knew that without water, she and Carla would not last for more than a few more hours in the hot sun.

D Number your paper from 1 through 23.

Skill Items

Write the word or words from the box that mean the same thing as the underlined part of each sentence.

shriek	breath	swift	armor
skeletons	an instant	a sense	tangle

1. The animal <u>bones</u> were near the big old tree.
2. He was afraid for <u>a moment</u>.
3. The runner was <u>very fast</u>.

Review Items

4. Write the letters of the 3 things you find in the Bermuda Triangle.

      a. sudden storms   d. mountains

      b. whirlpools   e. streams

      c. ice floes   f. huge waves

5. Write the letter of the footprint made by the heaviest animal.
6. Write the letter of the footprint made by the lightest animal.

      R   S   T

7. How long ago did dinosaurs live on Earth?

- 10 million years ago
- 100 million years ago
- 100 thousand years ago

8. Two things happen to melted rock when it moves down the sides of a volcano. Name those 2 things.

9. What is it called when the earth shakes and cracks?

10. The earth makes a circle around the sun one time every ▇▇▇.

11. How many days does it take the earth to make one full circle around the sun?

12. Is it easier to fly alone or with a large flock?

13. Flying near the back of a large flock is like riding your bike ▇▇▇.
   - with the wind
   - against the wind

14. During winter at the North Pole, how much does the sun shine?
   - never
   - all the time

15. During summer at the North Pole, how much does the sun shine?
   - never
   - all the time

Write the name of each animal in the picture.

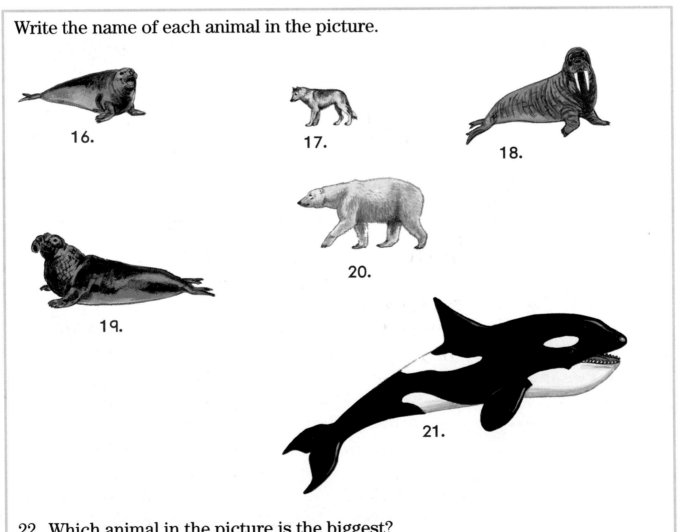

16.

17.

18.

19.

20.

21.

22. Which animal in the picture is the biggest?

23. Which animal is the smallest?

A

1
1. actually
2. exhibit
3. museum
4. Leonard
5. character
6. embarrassed

2
1. underwater
2. overboard
3. somehow
4. automobile

3
1. directed
2. divided
3. bandages
4. approached
5. sandwiches
6. honestly
7. handful

1. Monday
2. laundry
3. yesterday
4. mysterious
5. stomach
6. Tuesday
7. possible

B

Saved

Edna realized that she and Carla needed water. Without it, they would not last for more than a few more hours. Edna moved to the front of the boat and started to look for fishing gear. But then she noticed a slim line of smoke in the distance. It wasn't the billowing smoke that came from the island. "A ship," Edna said as she stood up. "I think there's a ship over there." She pointed.

Carla stood up. "You're right. I can see it, and I think it's coming in this direction."

The next hour seemed longer than any hour Edna ever remembered. Edna didn't do anything but watch the approaching ship. She felt that if she stopped watching it, it would disappear. As it got closer, she recognized the ship. "That's Dad's ship," she shouted. "They're coming back for us."

.   .   .

The crew members helped Edna and Carla onto the deck of the ship. Captain Parker put his arms around the girls. Then Edna started to cry.

She didn't want to cry. During the whole adventure, she hadn't cried. But now, as her dad hugged her, she couldn't help it. Tears started to run down her cheeks. "Dad," she said. She was so glad to be back, and she was ashamed for not paying attention to what her father had said.

"I'm glad we found you," Captain Parker said. "Now let's get you taken care of."

Both girls had blisters on their hands from rowing. They were both badly sunburned. And they were very hungry and thirsty. But within an hour, they were fixed up. Now the girls had burn cream on their noses. They had little bandages on their hands. And they had full stomachs. Edna drank three glasses of juice. She ate two sandwiches. And she almost finished a huge piece of pie. But she couldn't make it through that pie. She pushed herself away from the table and stood up. "I'm full," she said.

"I'd like to talk with you girls," Captain Parker said. The girls followed him to the map room. Captain Parker told them to sit down. "All right," he said. "What happened?"

"I know we shouldn't have been playing around with the lifeboat," Carla said. "But I'm the one to blame. Edna didn't ★ want to do it. It was my idea."

"Just tell me what happened," Captain Parker said. So the girls told the whole story: how the boat fell into the water, how they got sucked into the whirlpool, how they found the mysterious island, and what happened on the island. After the girls had finished telling about the second whirlpool, Carla said, "I don't know how we got out of the whirlpool, but we did, somehow. Then the next thing we knew, your ship was coming back toward us."

"That's some story," Captain Parker said. "Do you honestly think all those things happened?"

"Oh yeah," Edna said. "We're not making it up. It really happened, the whole thing."

Then Carla said, "Don't you believe us?"

Captain Parker smiled. "From the way you tell the story, I think <u>you</u> believe it. But I'm not sure it really happened that way."

"It <u>did</u> happen, Dad," Edna said. "It really did. Everything we told you is <u>true</u>."

"Well then, tell me this," Captain Parker said. "What day of the week was it when you went overboard?"

"Monday," Edna said.

"And you spent a night on the island. Is that correct?"

"Yes," Edna agreed.

Captain Parker said, "So what day would that make today?"

"Today is Tuesday," Edna said.

Captain Parker opened a door and said to a crew member, "Tell these girls what day today is."

The man looked a little puzzled. "Monday," he said.

"Monday?" Edna said. "No, that was yesterday. Today is Tuesday."

The young crew member smiled and said, "What is this, some kind of joke?"

Captain Parker said, "No, everything is all right. Thank you."

Carla said to Edna, "It can't be Monday."

"But it is Monday," Captain Parker said. "You may have had too much sun out there. But it has only been five hours since you left the ship."

"But it really happened, Dad," Edna said.

Later that afternoon, Edna was taking her wet clothes to the laundry room. As she approached the laundry room, she checked the pockets of her pants. She turned one pocket inside out and suddenly she stopped. About a handful of wet red sand fell onto the deck of the ship. If the adventure hadn't happened, how did that sand get into her pocket?

Edna never found the answer to that question.

C Number your paper from 1 through 22.

Skill Items

Here are three events that happened in the story.
Write **beginning, middle** or **end** for each event.

1. In the distance was a slim line of smoke.
2. Captain Parker opened a door and talked to one of the crew members.
3. Later that afternoon, Edna was taking her wet clothes to the laundry room.

She automatically arranged the flowers.

4. What word means **without thinking?**
5. What word means that she put things where she wanted them?

Review Items

6. Captain Parker's ship passed through a place where hundreds of ships have sunk or been lost. Name that place.
7. Two things happen to melted rock when it moves down the sides of a volcano. Name those 2 things.

8. The picture shows marks left by an animal. Which arrow shows the direction the animal is moving?
9. Write the letter of the part that shows the mark left by the animal's tail.
10. Write the letter of the part that shows a footprint.

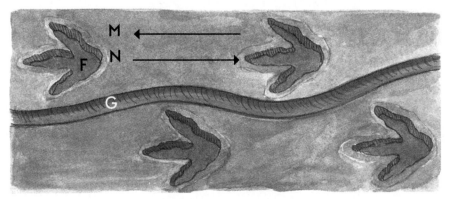

11. The earth makes a circle around the sun one time every ▮▮▮▮.

12. How many days does it take the earth to make one full circle around the sun?

13. How many heat lines are hitting place R on the map?

14. How many heat lines are hitting place A?

15. How many heat lines are hitting place M?

16. Write the letter of the place that's the hottest.

17. Write the letter of the place that's the coldest.

18. Write the letter of the place that has the warmest winters.

19. Write the letter of the place that's farthest from the equator.

20. Why is place M hotter than place R?

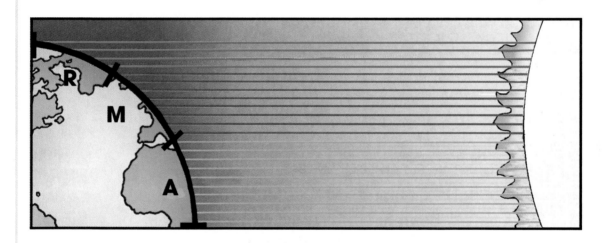

21. During winter at the North Pole, how much does the sun shine?

  • never   • all the time

22. During summer at the North Pole, how much does the sun shine?

  • never   • all the time

SPECIAL PROJECT

For today's lesson, you will do a project on dinosaurs. You will make a wall chart that shows some of the great dinosaurs.

Dinosaurs lived during the Mesozoic. The Mesozoic was divided into three parts: The early Mesozoic, the middle Mesozoic and the late Mesozoic. Tyrannosaurus lived in the late Mesozoic.

Make your chart show three layers. In the bottom layer, show pictures of some dinosaurs that lived in the early Mesozoic. Try to find at least two dinosaurs from the early Mesozoic. Write facts about the dinosaurs that you show on your chart. Tell each dinosaur's name, what it ate and how big it was.

Do the same thing for the dinosaurs of the middle Mesozoic. Find at least four dinosaurs. One of them may be Apatosaurus, which was much, much bigger than Tyrannosaurus or Triceratops. Put their pictures in the middle layer of the chart. Write facts that tell their names, what they ate and how big they were.

Do the same thing for the dinosaurs of the late Mesozoic. Find facts and pictures for at least four dinosaurs.

A

1
1. arrange
2. magazine
3. material
4. Esther
5. electricity
6. expression

2
1. possible
2. everyone
3. grandmother
4. automobile
5. display
6. exhibit

3
1. embarrassed
2. darted
3. actually
4. hurrying
5. outing
6. pencils
7. crazier

4
1. invent
2. pace
3. character
4. Leonard
5. museum
6. speech

B

Inventing

You live in a world that is filled with things that are made by humans. In this world are cars and airplanes and telephones and books. There are chairs and tables and stoves and dishes. There are thousands of things that you use every day.

Each of these things was underlined. That means that somebody made the object for the first time. The person who made the first automobile invented the automobile. The person who made the first television invented the television. Remember, when somebody makes an object for the first time, the person invents that object. The object the person makes is called the invention. The first airplane was an invention. The first telephone was an invention.

Everything that is made by humans was invented by somebody. At one time, there were no cars, light bulbs or glass windows. People didn't know how to make these things, because nobody had invented them yet.

Most of the things that you use every day were invented after the year 1800. Here are just some of the things that people did not have before 1800: trains, trucks, cars, airplanes, bicycles, telephones, radios, televisions, movies, tape recorders, computers, electric appliances like washing machines, toasters, refrigerators or dishwashers.

C Grandmother Esther

The year was 1980. Leonard was 12 years old. He was at the museum with his grandmother. Going places with Grandmother Esther was fun, but it was also embarrassing. It was embarrassing because Grandmother Esther had a lot to say, and she talked in a very loud voice. She talked the loudest and the longest about inventing. So when Leonard went to the museum with Grandmother Esther, he was ready to hear a lot of loud talk about inventing.

In the museum, they spent a little time looking at the displays of wild animals and the dinosaurs. Leonard wanted to spend more time here, but Grandmother Esther kept hurrying Leonard along. She would say, "Let's keep moving or we won't see all the things we want to look at in the other parts of the museum."

Leonard knew what parts of the museum his grandmother was talking about—the displays of the first automobiles, the first airplanes, the first computers and other things, such as the first radios.

So Grandmother Esther swept Leonard through the display of Egypt 4 thousand years ago. She darted through the exhibit of the cave people and through the display of horses. She slowed her pace as the two approached the display of the first airplanes.

As they walked through the large doorway of the exhibit hall, she announced, "Here is where we see the work of the most important people in the world—the inventors."

Leonard listened to his grandmother's speech about inventors. He nodded and very quietly said, "Yes." He was hoping that she might talk more softly if he talked softly, so he spoke in a voice that was almost a whisper. But it didn't work. Grandmother Esther's voice echoed across the large display hall.

"Without inventors there would be nothing," she said. Other people were starting to look at her and Leonard. Leonard could feel his ears getting hot from embarrassment.

"Where would we be today without inventors?" she asked herself loudly. Then she answered her own question: "We would have no planes because nobody would invent them. We would have no electric lights, no radios. We would not be able to build buildings like this one. We would still be living in <u>caves</u>!"

Grandmother Esther said the word **caves** so loudly that a guard at the other end of the exhibit hall turned around and stared at her. She marched to the display of the first airplane and pointed to it. "This was a great invention," she announced. "The two men who invented it knew that a machine could fly through the air. But other people didn't believe them. They said the inventors were <u>crazy</u> for working on a flying machine. But the inventors didn't give up. They invented a machine that actually flew. Once others saw that it was possible for machines to fly, they began inventing better flying machines. They invented faster machines and bigger machines. Look at them!" She waved her arm in the direction of the other airplanes on display. Nearly everyone in the hall looked at the rows of planes.

Grandmother Esther marched down the center aisle of the display. In a great voice, she said, "But none of these later planes would be possible without the first one. And the first one would not have been possible without the inventors—those brave men who didn't listen to other people but who knew that we don't have to stand with our feet stuck in the mud. We can <u>fly</u> with the <u>birds</u>!"

The sound of her voice echoed through the hall. Then, one of the people who had been listening to her began to clap. Then others clapped. Soon there was a loud sound of clapping. Even the guard was clapping. Leonard was very embarrassed, but he didn't want to be the only one not clapping. So he clapped, too. He said to himself, "My grandmother is a real character."

D Number your paper from 1 through 18.

Skill Items

Write the word from the box that means the same thing as the underlined part of each sentence.

adventure	enormous	however	hardened
approached	displayed	mysterious	glanced

1. The ice cream <u>became hard</u> in the freezer.
2. He went to school, <u>but</u> he was sick.
3. She <u>looked quickly</u> at the sign.

Use the words in the box to write complete sentences.

actually	exhibit	directed	automatically
character	displayed	divided	arranged

4. The new ▆▆▆ ▆▆▆ mysterious fish.
5. She ▆▆▆ ▆▆▆ the flowers.

Review Items

6. Which letter shows the place that has the warmest winters?

7. Which letter shows the place that is closest to the equator?

8. Which letter shows the place that is closest to a pole?

9. Is the North Pole or the South Pole closer to that letter?

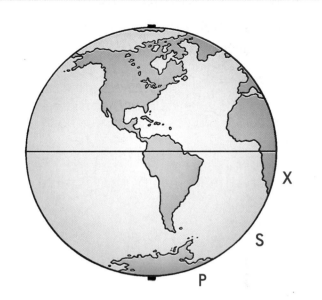

10. Write the letter of the earth that has the North Pole tilting away from the sun.

11. Write the letter of the earth that has the North Pole tilting toward the sun.

12. Write the letter of the earth that has darkness all around the North Pole.

13. Write the letter of the earth that has daylight all around the North Pole.

14. Write **A, B, C,** and **D.** Then write the season each earth in the picture shows.

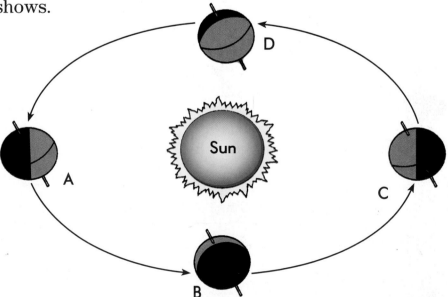

15. Two things happen to melted rock when it moves down the sides of a volcano. Name those 2 things.

16. What is it called when the earth shakes and cracks?

17. Most of the things that we use everyday were invented after the year ▮▮▮▮.

    - 1900
    - 2000
    - 1800

18. Write the letters of the 5 things that were not invented by anybody.

    a. horses
    b. buildings
    c. flowers
    d. snakes
    e. shoes
    f. bushes
    g. doors
    h. cows
    i. wagons
    j. hats

1
1. sharp-minded
2. exhibit
3. hard-boiled
4. myself

2
1. outdoors
2. railroad
3. stairway
4. understand

3
1. arranged
2. crazier
3. choked
4. stuffed
5. coughed
6. expression

4
1. material
2. electricity
3. magazine
4. ceiling
5. invention
6. inventors

B Grandmother Esther's Inventions

Leonard and his grandmother had been in the museum all morning. Now they were sitting outdoors, on the wide stairway that led from the museum. Grandmother Esther was pulling things from her lunch bag and setting them on the stair. And she was still talking. Leonard thought that she would never stop.

"Yes," she said, "I was an inventor myself." Leonard had heard this story many times. He could say the whole thing as well as she could.

"Yes," she repeated. "But things were different back then. Nobody wanted to listen to a woman inventor. Everybody used to think that inventors were a crazy bunch anyhow. But they thought that a woman inventor had to be even crazier than the other inventors. So nobody listened to me. And so some great inventions were never made."

She took a bite from a hard-boiled egg. Leonard thought she might stop talking while she ate, but she talked with her mouth full. "Yes," she said. "I actually invented the first water bed years before anybody else did. But you couldn't get good material back then. So it

leaked a little bit, and everybody said it was a crazy idea."

She continued, "I also invented the folding bicycle. You could fold it up and carry it with you. Just because there were a few little problems with it, people thought it was crazy. But I could have fixed those problems. With just a little more work, I could have made a bike that wouldn't fold up when you were riding it."

Leonard wanted to invent things, too. But what could he invent? Almost without thinking, he said, "Well, the trouble with being an inventor is that everything has already been invented."

Grandmother Esther started to cough. While she was still coughing, she said, "Leonard, what kind of talk is that?" She pointed to the large hall behind her. "Think of how the world looked to people a hundred years ago. They said, 'We've got horse carts and buildings. We have railroads and ⭐ ships. We must have everything. There is nothing more to invent.' But a few sharp-minded people could see that people didn't have everything."

Leonard realized that she was right. The people who lived in caves thought that everything had been invented. They didn't know about radios and automobiles and planes and television.

Grandmother Esther was still talking as she ate her sandwich. "The inventor sees things that are not there yet. The inventor thinks about how things could be. Everybody else just sees things as they are now."

Leonard nodded his head. For a moment he thought about what she said. Then he asked, "But how do you think about things that haven't been invented? What do you do, just think of make-believe things?"

She coughed and then she shouted, "Make-believe? Inventors don't deal in make-believe. They deal in what people <u>need</u>. That's where the invention starts. The inventor looks around and notices that people have trouble doing some things. The inventor sees a <u>need</u> that people have." Grandmother Esther stuffed the rest of her sandwich in her mouth. In an instant, she continued talking. "After the inventor sees a need, the inventor figures out how to meet that need."

"I don't understand," Leonard said.

She pointed back toward the exhibit hall and said, "The two men who invented the airplane saw a need. They saw that people could get places faster if they could fly in a straight line rather than going around on roads. They said to themselves, 'Let's make something that will let people go places faster.' So they invented a flying machine."

She continued, "The person who invented the car saw a need. That person saw that horses were a lot of work. People spent a lot of time feeding them and taking care of them. With a car, people would save a lot of time. With a car they could also go faster from place to place."

She pointed her finger at Leonard. "Remember, if you want to be an inventor, start with a need. Then figure out how to meet that need."

C Number your paper from 1 through 21.

Review Items

1. Write the letters of the 3 things you find in the Bermuda Triangle.

   a. huge waves   c. streams   e. ice floes
   b. mountains   d. whirlpools   f. sudden storms

2. The picture shows half a hailstone. How many times did the stone go through a cloud?

3. What is a person doing when the person makes an object for the first time?

4. The person who makes an object for the first time is called an ▨▨▨▨.

5. The object the person makes is called an ▨▨▨▨.

6. Write the letters of the 2 kinds of places that are safe for geese.

    a. places with a few ducks

    b. places with no geese or ducks

    c. places with a few geese

    d. places with many geese

7. Write the letter of the layer that went into the pile **first.**

8. Write the letter of the layer that went into the pile **next.**

9. Write the letter of the layer that went into the pile **last.**

10. Which layer went into the pile **earlier,** B or C?

11. Which layer went into the pile **earlier,** D or C?

12. Write the letter of the layer where we would find the skeletons of humans.

13. Write the letter of the layer that has dinosaur skeletons.

14. Write the letter of the layer where we would find the skeletons of horses.

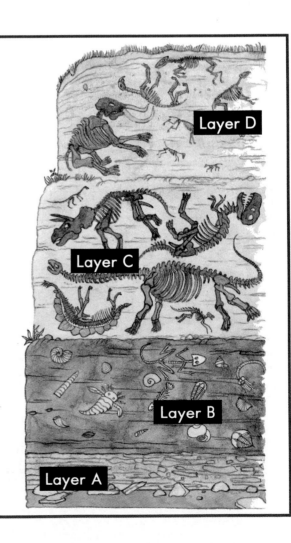

Layer D

Layer C

Layer B

Layer A

15. When days get longer, is the North Pole tilting **toward the sun** or **away from the sun?**

16. When days get shorter, is the North Pole tilting **toward the sun** or **away from the sun?**

17. In April, the sun shines for more than ▮▮▮ hours each day in Alaska.

---

18. Which globe shows how the earth looks on the first day of winter?

19. Which globe shows how the earth looks on the first day of summer?

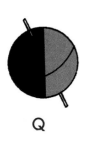

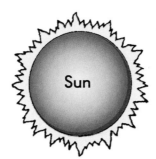

---

20. How long ago did dinosaurs live on the earth?
    - a hundred years ago
    - a hundred million years ago
    - a million years ago

Study Item

21. Today's story mentions the two men who invented the first airplane. Look in a book on airplanes, in an encyclopedia or on a computer and see if you can find out the names of these two men.

A

1	2
1. invisible	1. chuckled
2. suggest	2. ceiling
3. protection	3. repeated
4. explanation	4. magazine
5. vocabulary	5. expression
6. automatically	

B

Trying to Discover Needs

Leonard tried to think like an inventor, but the job was a lot harder than Leonard thought it would be. At first, Leonard had a lot of trouble trying to figure out things that people might need. He tried to remember what Grandmother Esther had said. "Start with a need," she had said. "Then figure out how to meet that need." But figuring out what people need was a big problem.

Leonard started out by asking people, "What do you need?" First, he asked his father. "Say, Dad, I'm thinking of inventing some things. What do you need?"

His dad was reading a paper. He looked up at Leonard and smiled.

"Well," his dad said as he put the paper down. "Well," he repeated. "Let me see." He looked up at the ceiling. "Let me see." Leonard's dad chuckled. "I could use more money. Maybe you can invent a tree that grows money."

Leonard smiled. Then he waited.

His dad said, "It would be nice to have less traffic on the road. Maybe you could invent a way to take traffic off the road."

Leonard didn't even smile over his dad's last idea. "Come on, Dad," he said. "I'm not kidding around. I need some ideas about things I might be able to invent. But I have to start with a <u>need</u>."

"Well, let me see," his father said, and looked down at the paper again. "There are probably a lot of things that people need. I just can't think of one right now."

"Okay," Leonard said. "Thanks anyhow." To himself, he was saying, "My dad just doesn't have the mind of an inventor."

Next, Leonard talked to his mother. "Mom," he said, "I need ideas for inventions." He explained his problem to her. She was working at her desk.

"Oh, dear," she said. "Every time I go somewhere I can think of a million things that would make good inventions. Let me see . . . " She rubbed her chin and looked off into space.

"Let me see," she repeated. "Oh, yes," she said after a few moments. "I would like to have something that automatically made up the grocery list. You know, when the refrigerator gets low on milk, the ⭐ word **milk** automatically goes on the list. Or when we run out of peanut butter, **peanut butter** goes on the list."

"Yeah," Leonard said. "That sounds pretty good. But how would that work?"

His mother looked at him with a puzzled expression. "Leonard," she said, "I'm not the inventor. You asked if I knew of something that should be invented. You didn't ask me how to invent it. If you want to know how to invent it, go ask your grandmother."

So Leonard asked his grandmother. He first explained his mother's idea. Then he said, "But I don't know how to invent that kind of list."

Grandmother Esther was reading a car magazine. She looked up over her glasses and shook her head no. She said, "Your mother has had that crazy idea about the list for twenty years. She must have tried to get me to invent that list fifty times. And I must have told her five thousand times that I don't know how to invent a list that automatically writes down things when you get low on them. But every time I turn around, here she is again, talking about that same invention. I think your mother's problem is that she hates to go grocery shopping and she doesn't like to make up grocery lists. Now I'm not saying that it's impossible to invent something that would make up lists. I'm just saying that you're looking at one inventor who doesn't know how to do it."

"Okay," Leonard said. "Thanks anyhow." As he left the room, Grandmother Esther was looking at her magazine, talking to herself. She was saying, "Again and again and again I kept telling her, I don't know how to do it. But she kept coming back with the same idea, that silly list writer."

During the week that followed, Leonard talked to nearly everybody about things they thought should be invented. At the end of the week, he didn't have any good ideas for inventions. But he had discovered something. People just don't seem to be very good at telling about things that they need. Leonard said to himself, "Maybe the hardest part of being an inventor is finding something to invent."

C Number your paper from 1 through 24.

Skill Items

They were impressed by her large vocabulary.

1. What word means they thought her vocabulary was very good?
2. What word refers to all the words a person knows?

Review Items

3. The men who invented the first airplane saw a need. What need?

4. Write the letter of the footprint made by the heaviest animal.
5. Write the letter of the footprint made by the lightest animal.

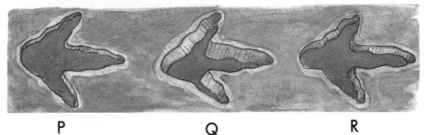

P   Q   R

The picture shows marks left by an animal.

6. Which arrow shows the direction the animal is moving?

7. Write the letter of the part that shows a footprint.

8. Write the letter of the part that shows the mark left by the animal's tail.

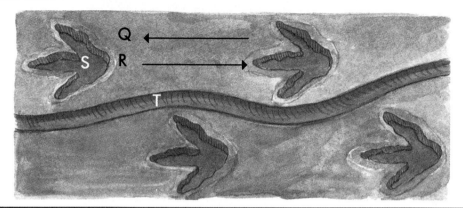

9. Geese live in large groups called ▨▨▨.

10. Where are most wild geese born?

11. In which direction do geese fly in the fall?

12. What is this trip called?

13. The ▨▨▨s are the coldest places on the earth, and the ▨▨▨ is the hottest place on the earth.

14. Which letter shows the part of the earth that receives more heat from the sun than any other part?

15. Which letter shows a part of the earth that receives less heat from the sun than any other part?

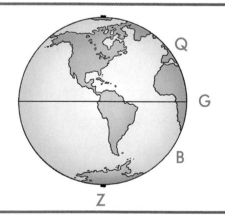

16. If you can see the sun, is it **daytime** or **nighttime** on your side of the earth?

17. What is it on the other side of the earth?

18. The earth turns around one time every ▨▨▨ hours.

19. Write the letter of the earth that shows the person in daytime.
20. Write the letter of the earth that shows the person 6 hours later.
21. Write the letter that shows the person another 6 hours later.
22. Write the letter that shows the person another 6 hours later.

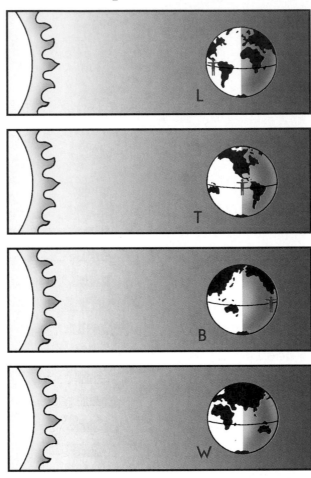

23. Write the letters of the 2 kinds of places that are safe for geese.

       a. places with many geese

       b. places with a few geese

       c. places with a few ducks

       d. places with no geese or ducks

Study Item

24. The two-wheeled bicycle is not very old. It was probably hard for somebody to get the idea of a two-wheeled bicycle because it seemed impossible for somebody to move along on two wheels without falling over. Find out when James Starley invented his two-wheeled *Ariel* bicycle.

1
1. assignment
2. solution
3. arithmetic
4. empty
5. electricity

2
1. collar
2. checker
3. muddy
4. pedal
5. subtract
6. invisible

3
1. Frank
2. mess
3. Rita
4. Sarah
5. towels
6. suggested

Bad Ideas

Leonard had tried asking people about things that they thought he could invent. But the people he asked weren't very good about giving him good ideas. One of Leonard's friends, Frank, suggested inventing a vacation that lasted all year long. Another friend, Teddy, wanted a machine that made ice cream from dirt. Ann wanted something to put on her teeth so she would never have to brush them.

Rita wanted a pair of wings so she could fly. Sarah wanted something that would make her invisible. Freddie wanted a bicycle that you didn't have to pedal. You'd just sit on the thing and it would take you places. All these people had ideas about things that they wanted, but most of these ideas were dreams.

"Dreams are a problem," Grandmother Esther told Leonard. He had just told her that he was thinking about giving up the idea of being an inventor. And he had told her why. "Yes, dreams are a problem," she repeated. "Here's why, young man. There are dreams that are wishes. And there are dreams that an inventor has. The line between these dreams is not always clear." Grandmother Esther continued, "Think of the men who invented the first plane. They had a dream, a crazy dream. They wanted to fly. Men with legs who had stood on the ground from the time they were born wanted to fly with the birds. That was a dream as crazy as the dream of becoming invisible or the dream of making ice cream from dirt. And I can't help you out. You'll have to find out which dreams are

just empty wishes and which dreams may turn into inventions."

"Okay," Leonard said and left the room.

Grandmother Esther was talking to herself about dreams. "Where would we be without dreams? The inventor must have them. And who is to say that a dream is crazy? It was a crazy dream to have lights that ran by electricity or machines that could add and subtract. It was a crazy dream to . . . "

Leonard was ready to forget about being an inventor. But then something happened that changed the way he looked at the

problem. As he walked into the kitchen, he noticed that he had mud on the bottom of his shoes. He hadn't noticed it before. Now it was too late. He had made tracks all over the house. If only he had noticed that his shoes were dirty. For a moment, he felt very dumb for tracking mud all over the house. He could almost hear what his mother was going to say: "You should always check your shoes before coming into the house."

Leonard tiptoed over to the outside door and took off his muddy shoes. He got some paper towels and started to clean up the mess. Then, when he had almost cleaned the last footprint on the kitchen floor, an idea hit him. It hit him so hard that it put a smile on his face. Just like that, he knew how to think like an inventor. He said out loud, "I need a shoe checker. I know I need it because when I don't have one, I don't do a good job of checking my shoes."

A shoe checker wasn't a bad idea for an invention. But the idea wasn't the most important thing to Leonard. The way he got the idea was the important thing. He didn't do something well. Then he figured out that he needed something to help him do it well.

That's how to figure out things to invent. You don't ask people. You do things. And when you do them, you pay attention to problems that you have. Each of the problems that you have tells you about something that you could invent to solve the problem.

Leonard's mother walked into the kitchen and saw Leonard smiling. "This is the first time I've seen you have a good time while you clean up a mess," she said.

"That's because I like this mess," Leonard said.

His mother shook her head. "He must take after his grandmother," she said to herself.

C Number your paper from 1 through 20.

Skill Items

Here are three events that happened in the story.
Write **beginning, middle** or **end** for each event.

1. Leonard's mother walked into the kitchen and saw Leonard smiling.
2. Grandmother Esther was talking to herself about dreams.
3. One of Leonard's friends, Frank, suggested inventing a vacation that lasted all year long.

Use the words in the box to write complete sentences.

impressed	arranged	honestly	stuffed
repeated	automatically	stomach	vocabulary

4. She ▮▮ ▮▮ the flowers.
5. They were ▮▮ by her large ▮▮.

Review Items

6. The first thing you do when you think like an inventor is find
   a ▨.

7. What's the next thing you do?

8. Geese live in large groups called ▨.

9. Where are most wild geese born?

10. In which direction do geese fly in the fall?

11. What is this trip called?

Choose from these words to answer items 12—14:
- moon
- Florida
- sun
- equator
- geese
- poles
- Canada
- migration

12. The heat that the earth receives comes from the ▨.

13. The part of the earth that receives more heat than any other
    part is the ▨.

14. The parts of the earth that receive less heat than any other part
    are called the ▨.

15. The sun shines ▨.

   - some of the time
   - all of the time

16. Can you see the sun all day long and all night long?

17. Things closer to the bottom of the pile went into the pile ▨.

18. Write the letter of the storm clouds.

19. Write the letter of the clouds that may stay in the sky for days
    at a time.

20. Write the letter of the clouds that have frozen drops of water.

A   B   C

Number your paper from 1 through 18.

1. How long ago did dinosaurs live on Earth?

2. Each picture has 2 arrows that show how the melted rock moves. Write the letter of the picture that shows 2 correct arrows.

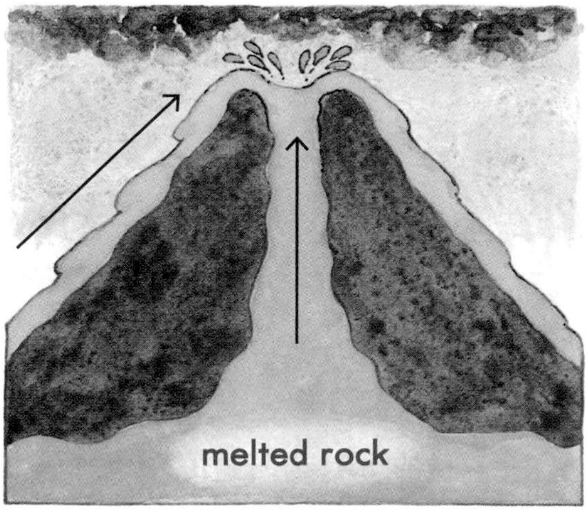

A

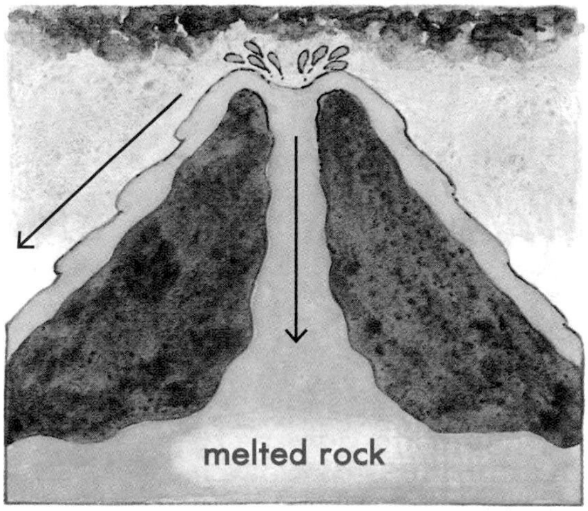

B

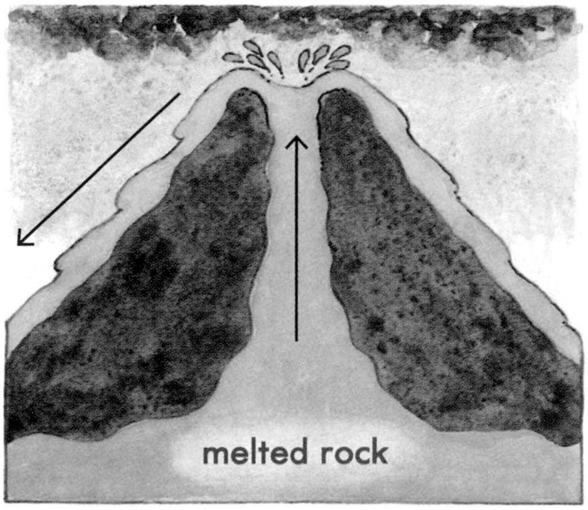

C

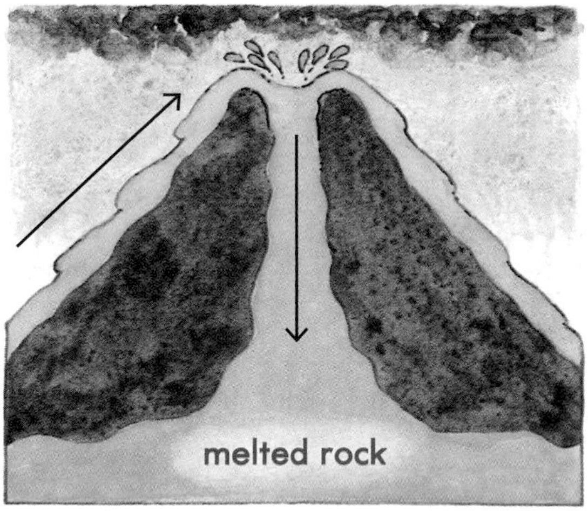

D

3. Two things happen to melted rock when it moves down the sides of a volcano. Name those 2 things.
4. What is it called when the earth shakes and cracks?
5. What is a person doing when the person makes an object for the first time?
6. The person who makes an object for the first time is called an ______.
7. The object the person makes is called an ______.

8. Most of the things that we use every day were invented after the year ▮▮▮▮.

      • 2200   • 1800   • 1600

9. Write the letters of the 5 things that were invented by somebody.

a. radios	f. trains
b. trees	g. shoes
c. killer whales	h. birds
d. desks	i. dirt
e. ice	j. computers

10. The men who invented the first airplane saw a need. What need?

11. The first thing you do when you think like an inventor is find a ▮▮▮▮.

12. What's the next thing you do?

Skill Items

For each item, write the underlined word or words from the sentences in the box.

> She <u>automatically</u> <u>arranged</u> the flowers.
>
> They were <u>impressed</u> by her large <u>vocabulary</u>.
>
> The new <u>exhibit</u> <u>displayed</u> <u>mysterious</u> fish.

13. What underlining means **showed**?

14. What underlining describes things we don't understand?

15. What underlining refers to all the words a person knows?

16. What underlining means that she put things where she wanted them?

17. What underlining means **an arrangement of things for people to look at?**

18. What underlining means they thought her vocabulary was very good?

END OF TEST 4

A

1
1. example
2. energy
3. device
4. respond

2
1. whenever
2. shopkeeper
3. earmuffs
4. bedtime
5. bathtub

3
1. impressed
2. forgetting
3. explanation
4. buzzer
5. automatically

4
1. mentioned
2. sternly
3. matching
4. protection
5. unfolded
6. bakery

5
1. collar
2. difficult
3. hood
4. plastic
5. raise
6. vocabulary

B

A Plan for Inventing

Thinking like an inventor was difficult for Leonard until he figured out this plan: He did different things. And he noticed each time he had a problem. When he noticed a problem, he knew that he had a need. He needed something that would solve that problem. The thing he needed to solve the problem was an invention.

After Leonard worked out his plan for finding needs, he tried to do all kinds of things. He washed the car, washed the windows, and washed the dog. He washed the floors and the walls and the dishes.

He helped his dad fix a table. He helped the man who lived next door change a tire on his car.

All the time Leonard did these things, his mind was working. He tried to see where he had problems. For three weeks he did things and noticed the problems that he had. And at the end of three weeks, he had a big list of things that he might invent. Some of the ideas were pretty good.

Leonard had found out that he wasn't very good at cracking raw eggs, and he thought of an invention that would crack egg shells. Leonard had found out that he was always forgetting to hang up his clothes when he took them off at night. Then his mother would come in and say, "Leonard, Leonard, look at your clothes, all over the place." Leonard figured out that what he needed was a tape that would come on just before bedtime. The voice on the tape would say, "Leonard, Leonard, hang up your clothes. Don't just drop them under your nose."

Leonard had a problem each time it rained. Leonard hated umbrellas, so he never took one with him. But then he would be caught in the rain without an umbrella. He would get soaked.

He thought of a way to meet his need for some protection from the rain. Why not invent a coat that has a special hood? When the hood is not being used, it looks like a big collar. But when the hood is unfolded, it becomes a little umbrella.

Leonard discovered that he had a great problem when he tried to wash his dog. The problem was that Leonard got all wet. If he tried to wash the dog in the bathtub, the dog would jump out in the middle of the bath and shake. The room would then be covered with water. Leonard would then have to spend a lot of time cleaning up the mess. If Leonard washed the dog outside, the problem was not as great, but Leonard still got soaked.

He thought of an invention to meet this need. The invention was a large plastic box with holes in it. First you would fill a tub with water.

Then you'd put the dog in the tub. Next, you'd put the plastic box over the tub. The dog would stick its head out through one of the holes. You could reach through the other holes and wash the dog and you wouldn't get wet while you were washing the dog. "Not bad," Leonard said to himself when he got this idea. "Not bad at all."

Leonard made pictures of some of his ideas. He showed them to the members of his family and he explained how they worked. His father said, "Leonard, I'm impressed."

Leonard's mother said, "Leonard, those are very good ideas. But did you ever think of inventing a machine that would automatically write out the things that you need at the grocery store?"

When Leonard's mother mentioned the list-making machine, Grandmother Esther said, "Stop talking about that crazy invention. Leonard seems to have some good ideas here. They show that the boy has been thinking like an inventor. Now he needs to stop thinking and start inventing." She looked sternly at Leonard.

Leonard smiled and said, "But I still don't know which thing I should invent."

"They're all pretty good," his father said.

His mother said, "I like the machine that makes up a list of things to buy."

Leonard said, "I'm not sure I've found the right idea yet."

Leonard shook his head. He was becoming very tired of trying to be an inventor.

C Number your paper from 1 through 13.

Review Items

1. What are clouds made of?
2. What kind of cloud does the picture show?
3. What happens to a drop of water at **B?**

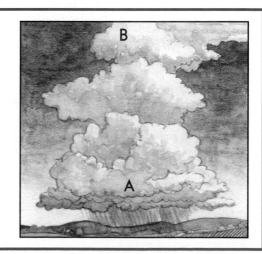

4. At which letter would the winters be very, very hot?

5. At which letter would the winters be very, very cold?

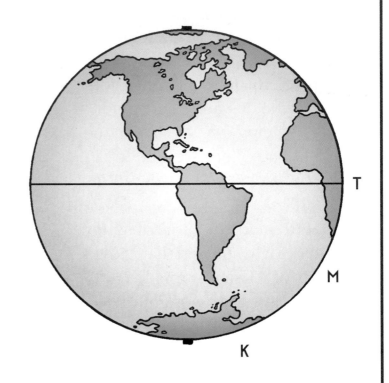

6. Female animals fight in the spring to protect .

7. Name 2 kinds of Alaskan animals that are dangerous in the spring.

8. Name 3 animals that are cold-blooded.

9. Name 3 animals that are warm-blooded.

10. Which object went into the pile **first?**

11. Which object went into the pile **earlier,** the book or the pencil?

12. Which object went into the pile **just after** the knife?

13. What kind of animals lived in the Mesozoic?

A

1
1. <u>in</u>terest
2. <u>a</u>side
3. <u>Gra</u>ndma
4. <u>en</u>ergy

2
1. <u>ex</u>ample
2. <u>ex</u>pect
3. <u>ex</u>cuse
4. <u>cle</u>ver

3
1. counter
2. kneeling
3. blocking
4. traced
5. serves

4
1. beam
2. dance
3. respond
4. she'd
5. target

B

The Electric Eye

Leonard was walking to school. Grandmother Esther was on her way to her exercise class. The exercise class was held near Leonard's school, so she was walking with him. Whenever she walked, she talked, and talked, and talked. And when she talked about inventing, she talked very loudly. Leonard knew that she wasn't shouting at him. He knew that she wasn't mad when she pointed her finger and raised her voice. He knew these things. But the other people who were walking along the street didn't know. They stopped and stared at Grandmother Esther.

To them, it must have seemed that she was yelling at Leonard.

Leonard was very embarrassed, but he didn't know what to say. As she talked, Leonard thought about an invention he needed. What about a pair of thick earmuffs? If he wore them, he wouldn't be able to hear her. No, that wouldn't work. She'd just talk louder. What about a buzzer? The buzzer could buzz louder when she talked louder. If she wanted the buzzer to stop, she'd have to talk softly.

"Now there's an invention," she said, pointing to something. She and Leonard were in front of a bakery.

The window was filled with things that looked so good to eat that Leonard tried not to look at them. Grandmother Esther seemed to be pointing at the door. "Yes, a very simple invention, but a very clever one."

"What invention is that?" Leonard asked.

"The electric eye, of course," she said. Leonard didn't know what she was talking about. "The electric what?" he asked.

"The electric eye. Don't tell me you don't know what an electric eye is."

Before he could respond, she opened the door to the bakery. She pointed to a tiny light that was on one side of the door, about half a meter from the floor. "There it is," she said. "The electric eye."

"What does it do?" Leonard asked.

"It tells the shopkeeper that you're 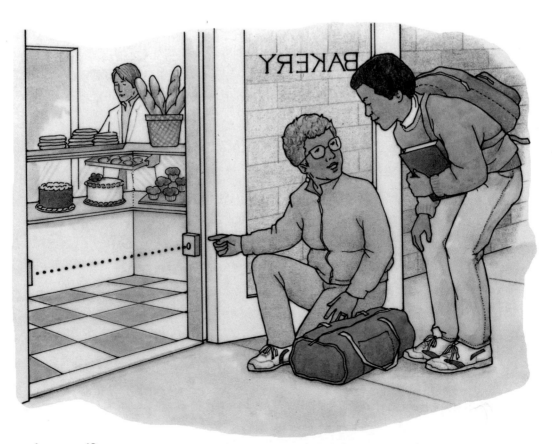 coming into the shop. Watch." She held her hand in front of the little beam of light that came from the electric eye. As soon as she did that a buzzer sounded in the back of the bakery. "That's just what happens when you walk into the store."

She explained how the electric eye worked. The beam of light went from one side of the door to the other. As long as the beam reached a little target on the other side of the door, nothing happened. But when something got in the way of that beam of light and kept it from reaching the target, the buzzer sounded. She explained that the buzzer kept sounding as long as the beam was broken. So when somebody walked in the door, the body would stop the beam of light from reaching the target. When the body stopped the beam, the buzzer sounded. That buzzer told the shopkeeper that somebody was going through the door.

Grandmother Esther was kneeling in front of the doorway as she explained how the beam worked. Several people were trying to get into the bakery. They waited as she explained the electric eye. The shopkeeper was standing behind the counter, looking at her. When she finished her explanation of the electric eye, she said, "This is a good example of a clever invention. The electric eye is a simple invention, but it has many, many uses."

One of the people who was trying to get into the store said, "Very interesting."

The other person said, "Yes, very interesting."

The shopkeeper said, "Excuse me, could you stand aside and let these people come in?"

Leonard said, "Come on, Grandma, you're blocking the doorway."

And Grandmother Esther said, "Of course, the electric eye is not as great an invention as the airplane or the electric light. But the electric eye serves many needs."

The shopkeeper said, "Yes, it does."

Leonard said, "Come on, Grandma, I've got to go to school."

 Number your paper from 1 through 24.

Skill Items

> **He responded to her clever solution.**

1. What word means **reacted?**
2. What word means **very smart?**
3. What word refers to solving a problem?

Review Items

4. When geese learn to fly, do they start in the water or on the land?
5. They run with their ▮▮▮▮ out to the side.

6. The earth is shaped like a ▇▇▇.

7. The hottest part of the earth is called the ▇▇▇.

- desert   - equator   - pole

8. What's the name of the spot that's at the bottom of the earth?

9. What's the name of the spot that's at the top of the earth?

10. What's the name of the line that goes around the fattest part of the earth?

11. What season is it at the North Pole when the North Pole tilts **away from** the sun?

12. What season is it at the North Pole when the North Pole tilts **toward** the sun?

Write the name of each numbered object in the picture. Choose from these names:

- kayak   - spear   - Eskimo
- fishing pole   - sled   - sled dogs

19. In what season are animals most dangerous in Alaska?

20. During what season do female animals in Alaska have babies?

21. About how long are killer whales?

22. Compare the size of killer whales with the size of other whales.

23. Are killer whales fish?

24. Tell whether killer whales are **warm-blooded** or **cold-blooded**.

1	2	3
1. clearer	1. tone	1. assignment
2. device	2. arithmetic	2. drawings
3. supper	3. stinks	3. enter
4. outfit	4. solution	4. sour
	5. giggled	5. practicing
		6. realizing

A Good Idea

The next evening, after supper, it happened. Leonard had no warning that it would happen. But it did. Everything in his mind suddenly came together and he had the idea for a great invention.

Here's how it happened: After supper, he went to his room to get a pencil. He was going to make some more drawings of ideas for inventions. When he started back to the kitchen, Grandmother Esther hollered at him, "Turn off the light in your room. Remember to save energy."

Leonard turned around, went back to his room, turned off the light, and stood there in the dark room. He felt the idea coming into his head. It got bigger and clearer and . . . "Hot dog!" he shouted. He shouted, "What an idea for an invention! Hot dog!"

He ran into the kitchen. "I've got it. What an idea! This is the best idea anybody ever had for an invention!"

His mother smiled. "I'll bet it's a machine that makes up a list of things you need at the store."

"Stop talking about that stupid machine," Grandmother Esther yelled from the other room. She ran into the kitchen. She was wearing her exercise outfit.

Grandmother Esther asked, "What's your idea, Leonard?"

Leonard said, "Let me explain how it's going to work. It's dark outside. And it's dark in the living room of your house. But when you walk through the door to the living room, the light goes on automatically. The light stays on as long as you're in the living room. But when you leave the living room, the light goes off."

Leonard's mother shook her head. "That sounds far too difficult."

Grandmother Esther said, "It sounds difficult to you because you don't know how the electric eye works."

"The electric eye?" Leonard's mother asked.

Leonard said, "Here's how it works, Mom. There's a little beam of light that goes across the doorway to the living room. When you enter the room, you break the beam. When you break that ⭐ beam, the light turns on. Then when you leave the room, you break the beam and the light goes off."

"Oh, my," Leonard's mother said. He could tell from her tone of voice that she didn't understand what he said.

"Good thinking," Grandmother Esther said, and slapped Leonard on the back. "That's a fine idea for an invention, a fine idea."

"Thank you," Leonard said.

Grandmother Esther made a sour looking face. Slowly she said, "There's one big problem with being a good inventor. You have to think of all the things that could go wrong."

"What could go wrong?" Leonard asked.

Grandmother Esther explained. "When you break the beam one time, the light goes on. When you break the beam the next time, the light goes off. When you break the beam the next time, the light goes on."

"Right," Leonard said.

"That's the problem," Grandmother Esther said. "What if two people walk into a dark room? When the first one goes into the room, the light will go on. Now the second person goes into the room. What happens to the light?"

"It goes off," Leonard said very sadly. He shook his head. "Now both people are in the dark, and my invention stinks."

"Wrong!" Grandmother Esther shouted. "Both people are in the

dark, but your invention does not stink. Every invention has problems. An inventor has to look at these problems and try to solve them. But you must remember that inventing something is more than just getting an idea. You must work on that idea until it is a good idea. Then you must take that good idea and make it into a good invention. Just because there's a problem doesn't mean that you give up. You've got a great idea."

Leonard's mother said, "I have a great idea for an invention. It's a machine that . . ."

"Not now," Grandmother Esther said. "We're close to a <u>real</u> invention."

Leonard said, "I'll just have to think about the problem and try to figure out how to solve it."

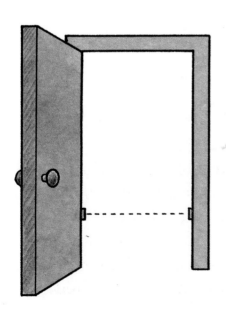

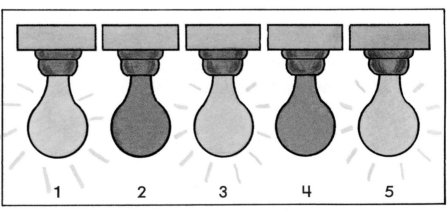

C Number your paper from 1 through 24.

Skill Items

Use the words in the box to write complete sentences.

device	outfit	solution	entered
impressed	mentioned	responded	vocabulary

1. They were ▨ by her large ▨.
2. He ▨ to her clever ▨.

Review Items

Here's how an electric eye at a store works.

3. When somebody walks in the door, the body stops the beam of light from reaching the ▨.
4. When the body stops the beam, what does the device do next?
5. What does that tell the shopkeeper?

6. Write the letter of the layer that went into the pile first.
7. Write the letter of the layer that went into the pile next.
8. Write the letter of the layer that went into the pile last.
9. Write the letter of the layer that we live on.
10. What's the name of layer C?

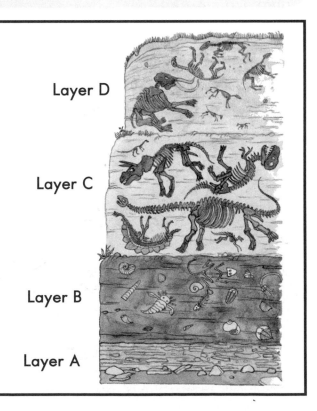

Layer D

Layer C

Layer B

Layer A

11. Name the country that is just north of the United States.

12. Which letter shows where the United States is?

13. Which letter shows where Canada is?

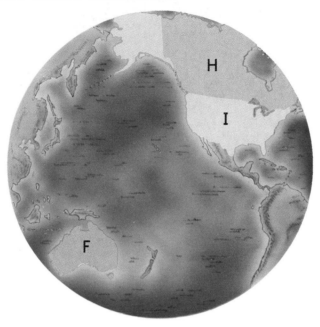

14. The picture shows half a hailstone. How many times did the stone go through a cloud?

15. What's the name of geese that are all white?

16. What's the name of geese that are gray and white and black?

17. What color are all geese when they are born?

18. How old are geese when they mate for the first time?

19. After male and female geese mate, how long do they stay together?

20. Most geese live for about ▨▨▨ years.

21. When geese learn to fly, do they start in the water or on the land?

22. They run with their ▨▨▨ out to the side.

23. How many poles are there?

24. The farther you go from the equator, the ▨▨▨ it gets.
   • hotter   • colder   • fatter

1	**2**	**3**
1. <u>bathroom</u>	1. entering	1. shaft
2. <u>one-way</u>	2. drums	2. whether
3. <u>homework</u>	3. practicing	3. drew
4. <u>outfit</u>	4. realizing	4. goose

B

One Way

Leonard said to himself, "Figure out how to solve that problem." It was a real problem. Every time the beam is broken, the lights change. If they are on, they go off. So if somebody is in a room with the lights on and somebody else comes into the room, the beam is broken and the lights go off.

He was on his way to school. He walked past the bakery. For a moment he remembered how embarrassed he had been when Grandmother Esther blocked the people who were trying to come into the store.

From time to time his mind would notice other things around him, but most of the time it was busy with the problem. "Think."

Then Leonard realized that he was looking at a sign. "One way," the sign said. And it had an arrow. "One way." Although Leonard didn't figure out the answer to his problem at that moment, he had a very strange feeling, as if he were very close to the answer. Leonard said, "My device has to know which way you are going. It has to know if you are entering the room or leaving the room." Leonard crossed the street. Then he stopped and said out loud, "But one electric eye can't tell whether you're coming in or going out."

Two boys who were walking to school giggled and pointed at Leonard. When Leonard saw them pointing, he realized how crazy he must have looked as he talked to himself.

Later that day in school, Leonard was supposed to be doing his arithmetic homework. He liked arithmetic and he was good at it, but he couldn't seem to work on it that day. He kept thinking of the problem and the one-way sign. Without realizing what he was doing, he drew the sign on his paper.

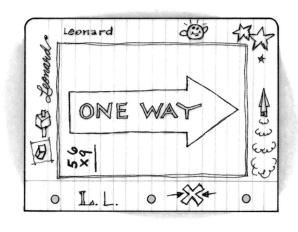

He studied the arrow. He traced it with his pencil three or four times. Then he traced over the letters in the sign. Then he put two dots next to each other on the shaft of the arrow. Suddenly, he felt goose bumps all over his face and down his back. He almost jumped out of his seat. "Wow!" he shouted. "I've got it!"

Everybody in the class was looking at him. He could feel his face becoming very hot. He cleared his throat and coughed. Then he looked down at his paper. He could still feel the eyes of everybody in the room looking at him. Then he heard the teacher's voice. "Is anything wrong, Leonard?"

Leonard looked up. "No, no. I just figured out the solution to a problem I've been working on."

The teacher said, "I'm glad to see that you are so excited about solving your arithmetic problems, but when you work out the solution to the next problem, try to be a little more quiet about it."

• • •

After school that day, Leonard ran home. It felt great to run. Sometimes when he ran he felt heavy, but as he went home that afternoon, he felt very light and very fast. He could feel the wind on his face. He raced with the cars when they started out from stop signs. He could stay with them for more than half a city block.

When he got home, he ran into the house. "Grandma!" he shouted. "I've got it!" Grandmother Esther was practicing on her drums. Leonard's mother was in the hall. She was wearing earmuffs.

Lesson 44   **215**

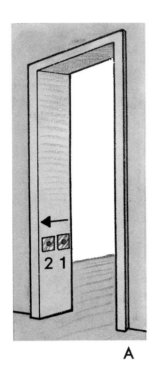
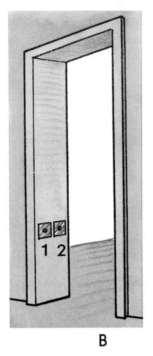
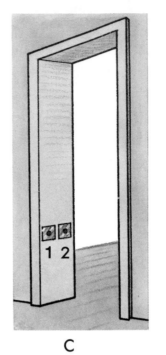
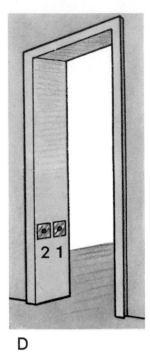

| A | B | C | D |

Leonard told Grandmother Esther how to solve the problem. "On the side of the door we put two electric eyes, not one." Leonard continued, "The electric eyes are side by side. When somebody goes through the door, they will break one beam first, then the second beam. If the outside beam is broken first and the inside beam is broken next, the person is moving <u>into</u> the room."

Leonard continued to explain, "If the inside beam is broken first and the outside beam is broken next, the person is moving out of the room. We make the electric eye device turn on the light if somebody goes <u>into</u> the room and turn off the light if somebody goes out of the room."

C Number your paper from 1 through 26.

Story Items

1. In today's story, what was Leonard doing that made two boys on the street giggle and point at him?
2. What did Leonard do when he figured out the solution?
3. Where was he?
4. When Leonard got home, his mother was wearing earmuffs. Why?
5. How many electric eyes will Leonard need on each doorway?
6. How many beams will go across the doorway?

7. Leonard's first invention had problems. Let's say two people walk into a dark room. What happens to the light in the room when the first person enters?

8. What happens to the light when the second person enters?

Review Items

9. Which came earlier on Earth, dinosaurs or horses?

10. Which came earlier on Earth, strange sea animals or dinosaurs?

11. What's the name of the place shown by the letter C?

12. Which letter shows the hottest place?

13. Which letter shows the coldest place?

14. Which letter is farthest from the equator?

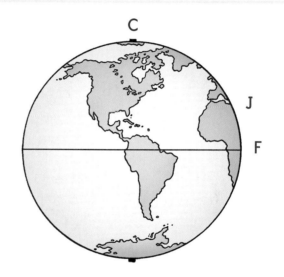

15. What are clouds made of?

16. What kind of cloud does the picture show?

17. What happens to a drop of water at **B**?

18. Most geese live for about ▆▆▆ years.

19. How old are geese when they mate for the first time?

20. After male and female geese mate, how long do they stay together?

---

21. Which letter shows the place that is closest to the equator?

22. Which letter shows the place that is closest to a pole?

23. Is the **North Pole** or the **South Pole** closer to that letter?

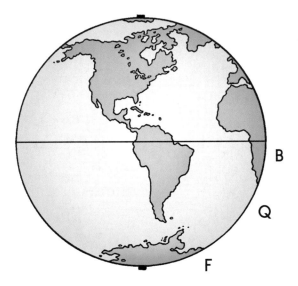

24. Name 2 things that can make an ice chunk drift.

Study Items

Grandmother Esther talked about what a great invention the electric light bulb is. The man who invented it was named Thomas Alva Edison.

25. Find out when he invented the electric light bulb.

26. Find out 2 other things that he invented.

A

1	2	3
1. diagram	1. secret	1. snappy
2. lawyer	2. rapped	2. sighed
3. purchase	3. shame	3. company
4. attorney	4. booming	4. patent
5. permission		
6. electrical		

B

Another Problem

"That's a great solution," Grandmother Esther said. Leonard had just explained his idea. Instead of one electric eye on the side of the door, he would use two of them. When somebody walked into the room, the body would break one beam before the other beam. If the outside beam was broken first, the person was moving into the room. If the inside beam was broken first, the person was moving out of the room.

Leonard explained, "As soon as I saw that arrow on the one-way sign, I knew that I was close to the solution."

"Good job," Grandmother Esther said and rapped out a snappy drum roll. Grandmother Esther continued, "But there is still one problem."

"Oh, no," Leonard said. "Not another problem."

Grandmother Esther hit the biggest drum. Then she said, "Your machine can tell whether somebody comes into the room or goes out of the room. And your machine turns off the lights when somebody leaves the room."

Then she said, "But what would happen if three people were sitting in the room reading and one of them left the room?"

Leonard sighed and said, "The light would go off."

Leonard felt dumb for not seeing this problem before his grandmother pointed it out. The electric eye device that he had imagined couldn't count. It couldn't tell if one person was in the room or if ten were in the room. The only thing Leonard's device knew how to do was to turn the lights on if somebody came into the room and turn them off if somebody left the room. But the device didn't know how many people were in the room.

Grandmother Esther said, "Your invention has to know how to count people in the room." Then she made a long drum roll and ended it with a terribly loud boom. "So, make it count," she said.

"How do I do that?" Leonard asked.

She responded, "What if you had a counter on your device? When a person went into the room, the counter would count one. When the next person went into the room, the counter would count again—two. With a counter, your device would know how many people are in the room. ⭐ It wouldn't shut off the lights until the last person left the room."

For a few moments, Leonard thought about what she said. Then he said, "I get it. The lights wouldn't go off if there were still some people in the room." Then he added, "But I don't know how to make the device count."

"Think, think, think," she said and began to tap on the smallest drum. "Think, Leonard, think," she repeated.

Leonard knew that she wasn't going to tell him any more about how to make the device count, so he left the room and began to think.

For nearly the rest of the day, Leonard's mind kept hearing his grandmother say, "Think, think, think." But the problem was much harder for Leonard than she made it sound. He thought and thought.

Just before supper, he went into the bathroom. He filled the sink with water and washed his hands. When he started to let the water out of the sink, he got the idea. The water would keep going out of the sink until the sink was empty. The water kept going out until there was <u>zero</u> water in the sink. That was the secret. "Count to zero," he said out loud.

He ran to his room and got some paper. Then he made a little drawing that showed how the device could count. Look at the drawing that he made.

Leonard ran into the kitchen. Grandmother Esther was starting to eat her salad. He showed her the drawing and explained. "The device can tell each time somebody goes into the room and each time somebody goes out. So we make a counter that counts <u>forward</u> each time somebody goes into the room. If four people go into the room, the counter counts one, two, three, four. Each time somebody leaves the room, the counter counts <u>backward</u>. So if three people leave, the counter counts backward: three, two, one. But the lights don't go off until the counter counts back to zero."

Leonard continued to explain, "When the last person leaves the room, the counter counts back to zero. Now the lights go off."

Grandmother Esther jumped out of her chair, threw her arms around Leonard, and gave him a kiss.

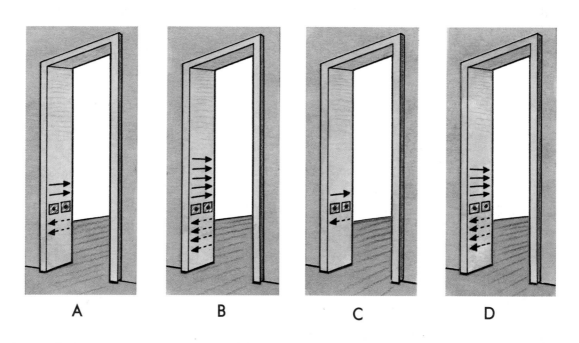

A   B   C   D

C Number your paper from 1 through 25.

Story Items

1. How many electric eyes did Leonard use for his invention?
2. How many beams went across the doorway?
3. If a person moves into a room, which beam will be broken first— the inside beam or the outside beam?
4. Which beam will be broken next?

5. The solid arrows show how many times people went into the room. How many people went into the room?

6. The dotted arrows show how many people left the room. How many people left the room?

7. Are the lights on in the room?

8. How many more people would have to leave the room before the lights go off?

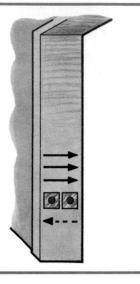

Skill Items

Here are three events that happened in the story.
Write **beginning, middle** or **end** for each event.

9. The water kept going out until there was zero water in the sink.

10. Leonard told Grandmother Esther that the one-way sign helped him figure out a solution.

11. Leonard told his Grandmother Esther how the counter on his device would work.

The patent attorney wrote an agreement.

12. What do we call a lawyer whose special job is getting patents for new inventions?

13. What word means **lawyer?**

14. What word means a **promise made by people?**

15. What word names a license for somebody to be the only person who can make a product?

Review Items

16. How many days does it take the earth to make one full circle around the sun?

17. The earth makes a circle around the sun one time every .

18. How many heat lines are hitting place E on the map?

19. How many heat lines are hitting place G?

20. How many heat lines are hitting place J?

21. Which letter on the map shows Canada?

22. Which letter shows Alaska?

23. Which letter shows the main part of the United States?

24. Which 2 letters show where Eskimos live?

25. How warm is it during winter in Alaska?

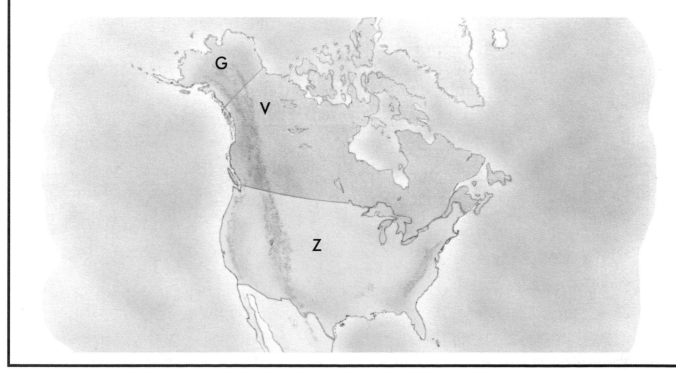

A

1
1. business
2. manufacturer
3. disappointed
4. flood
5. turner-off-er

2
1. model
2. patent
3. purchase
4. supply
5. automatic

3
1. electrical
2. connected
3. diagrams
4. lawyers
5. announcer

4
1. owe
2. attorney
3. company
4. permission

B

Leonard's Model

It's easy to say that the invention will count things, but it's a much harder job to build a device that counts. Grandmother Esther was a big help for this part of the job. She knew a lot about electricity. Grandmother Esther got books for Leonard that showed him where to buy electric eyes and how to hook electric wires up to make the electric eyes work. These books also showed where to purchase electric counters. After Leonard and his grandmother decided which type of electric eyes they wanted, she made a few phone calls, took Leonard with her in her jeep, and bought the supplies that they needed to build a model of his invention.

"Now remember, Leonard," she said as they left the electrical supply store. "You owe me ninety dollars. When you start making money from your invention, just remember that I'm giving up my fishing trip so that you can build your invention."

"You shouldn't give up your fishing trip, Grandmother," he said. "I'll get the money."

"I'm kidding you," she said. "I'd much rather invent something than go fishing any time." She started up the jeep and made the engine roar loudly. Suddenly, the jeep jumped forward, snapping Leonard's head back. And off they went to their home.

Leonard and his grandmother built a model of the electric eye device. The model was a little room with a doorway that was about one meter tall. There was a light bulb connected to the top of the doorway.

To show how the model worked, Leonard used a large teddy bear and large dolls. Leonard moved these objects through the doorway. An object would break the outside beam first, then the inside beam. As soon as the first object broke both beams, the light went on. Leonard would move more objects through the doorway and the light would stay on.

Then Leonard would begin to move the objects the other way. The light would stay on until the last object went back through the doorway. Then the light would go off.

"This device works!" Leonard shouted after he and his grandmother had tested it four times.  "It works. We've invented an automatic light turner-off-er!"

But Leonard's work was not finished. He had a model of the invention, and that model worked. But now he had to protect his invention. An invention needs protection from people who copy it and say that it is their invention. To protect an invention, the inventor gets a patent. When an invention is patented, the only person who can make copies of that invention is the inventor. If other people want to make copies of it, they have to get permission from the inventor. The inventor may tell somebody that it is all right to make copies of the invention. But the inventor doesn't usually <u>give</u> somebody this right. The inventor <u>sells</u> the right. The inventor may say this to the person who wants to make copies: "Each time you make a copy, you must give me so much money." Maybe the person has to pay five dollars for each copy that is built. Maybe the inventor sells the whole patent to a company that wants to make copies of the invention. If the invention is good, the inventor may make a lot of money from that invention.

But the first step is to get a patent. Without a patent, the inventor has no protection against people who want to make copies of the invention. Getting a patent is very difficult. There are special lawyers who do nothing but get patents for inventors. These lawyers are called patent attorneys. Grandmother Esther explained patents and patent attorneys to Leonard. Then she phoned a patent attorney and told her that Leonard wanted to patent his invention.

Leonard and his grandmother had three meetings with the patent attorney. The attorney answered hundreds of questions. Leonard and Grandmother Esther made diagrams of the invention for her.

When they finally finished their meetings with the patent attorney, Grandmother Esther said, "Now you owe me another three thousand dollars. If your invention doesn't start making some money, I'll have to give up my flying lessons."

"You're great, Grandma," Leonard said. "You're just great."

"Oh, stop it," Grandmother Esther said and slapped Leonard on the back.

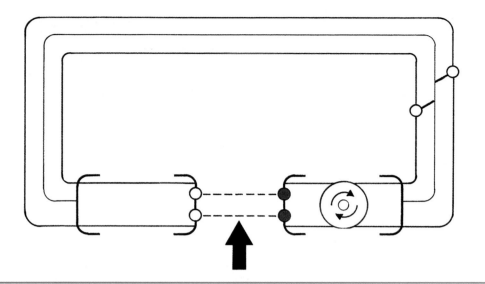

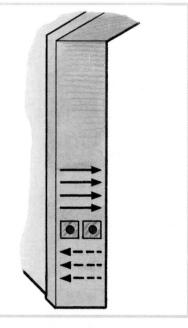

C Number your paper from 1 through 25.

Use the words in the box to write complete sentences.

agreement	sighed	solution	patent	flood
diagram	responded	secret	attorney	

1. He ▣ to her clever ▣.
2. The ▣ ▣ wrote an ▣.

Review Items

3. The solid arrows show how many times people went into the room. How many people went into the room?

4. The dotted arrows show how many times people left the room. How many people left the room?

5. Are the lights on in the room?

6. How many more people would have to leave the room before the lights go off?

Answer these questions about the counter on Leonard's device:

7. Every time somebody goes into the room, what does the counter do?

    • + 1   • - 1   • - 0

8. Every time somebody goes out of the room, what does the counter do?

    • + 1   • - 1   • - 0

9. What number does the counter end up at when the last person leaves the room?

10. What happens to the lights when the counter gets to that number?

For each picture, tell if the lights in the room are **on** or **off.** The solid arrows show people going into the room. The dotted arrows show people leaving the room.

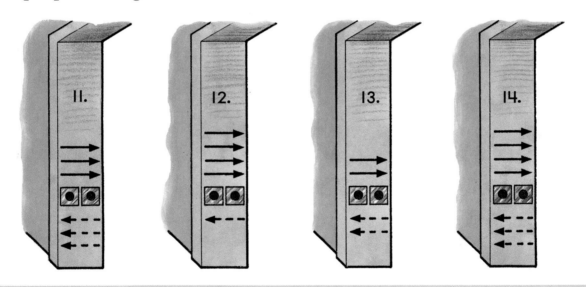

15. Two things happen to melted rock when it moves down the sides of a volcano. Name those 2 things.

16. What is it called when the earth shakes and cracks?

17. The earth makes a circle around the sun one time every ▮▮▮▮.

18. How many days does it take the earth to make one full circle around the sun?

19. Is it easier to fly alone or with a large flock?

20. Flying near the back of a large flock is like riding your bike ▓▓▓▓.

    - against the wind
    - with the wind

21. During winter at the North Pole, how much does the sun shine?

    - all the time
    - never

22. During summer at the North Pole, how much does the sun shine?

    - all the time
    - never

23. When days get shorter, is the North Pole tilting **toward** the sun or **away from** the sun?

24. When days get longer, is the North Pole tilting **toward** the sun or **away from** the sun?

25. In April, the sun shines for more than ▓▓▓ hours each day in Alaska.

A

1	2	3
1. <u>basket</u>ball	1. disappointed	1. cloth
2. <u>loud</u>speaker	2. announcer	2. Friday
3. <u>note</u>book	3. smoking	3. prize
4. <u>mean</u>time	4. manufacturers	4. business
	5. charges	5. cost
		6. forth

B

An Invention Fair

Leonard had found out a lot about inventing things. He found out that you have to start with a need. Then you get an idea for an invention that meets that need. Then you have to build a model of the invention and show that it works. Once you have a model, you must go to a patent attorney and get a patent for your invention. If your invention is the first one of its kind, you'll get a patent. Once you have a patent, you have protection for that invention. Nobody can make copies of the device that you have patented. You can give other people permission to make copies of the invention, but you can charge them for the right to make the copies.

But Leonard was not finished learning about inventions. Once you have patented an invention, you must sell it to somebody who is in the business of making things. Businesses that make things are called manufacturers. Grandmother Esther explained, "There are different ways that we can get in touch with manufacturers. We can take our model and go visit manufacturers who make things for houses. We can call them on the phone and see if they are interested in our invention. We can take out an ad in a magazine that manufacturers read." She shook her head no. Then she smiled and continued. "But there's a better way. We can put our invention in an invention fair."

"What's an invention fair?" Leonard asked.

His grandmother explained. "An invention fair is a place where inventors and manufacturers get together. The inventors bring their inventions. The manufacturers go to

WORLD'S LARGEST INVENTION FAIR

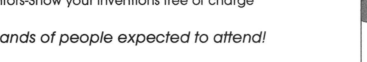

1st prize...$20,000   **2nd prize...$10,000**   **3rd prize...$5,000**

Special prizes for clever inventions will also be awarded
Starts Friday at noon and runs all day Saturday
Inventors-Show your inventions free of charge

Thousands of people expected to attend!

the fair to see if they want any of these new inventions. At the fair there are prizes for the best inventions."

"How soon can we enter an invention fair?" Leonard asked.

Grandmother Esther tossed a magazine to Leonard. It was opened to a large ad. The top of the ad announced, "World's Largest Invention Fair!" The rest of the ad told about the prizes and the fair. The first prize was twenty thousand dollars. The second prize was ten thousand dollars. And the third prize was five thousand dollars. There were also special prizes for inventions that were clever.

The fair would start on Friday at noon. Then it would run all day Saturday. It didn't cost inventors anything to show their inventions at the fair. ⭐ Thousands of people were expected to visit the fair.

Leonard read the ad three times. Each time he read it, the fair sounded greater and greater.

"Can we win?" Leonard asked his grandmother.

"First prize," she said, smiling. "First prize."

Leonard slowly stood up. "You mean we can get twenty thousand dollars for our invention?" Leonard could not even imagine how much money that was. He once saved one hundred dollars. But that wasn't even close to one <u>thousand</u> dollars. As Leonard started to think about twenty thousand dollars, he became a little dizzy. "Twenty thousand dollars," he said over and over.

• • •

The invention fair took place in a huge hall. Leonard and his grandmother got there early in the morning. The fair opened at noon. Before noon, the inventors had to set up their displays. No inventor could get into the hall before that morning because there had been a basketball game in the hall the evening before. So the inventors were lined up at the door the next morning, ready to set up their displays. Some of them complained about the basketball game. An old man standing near Leonard and his grandmother told them that it would take him six hours to set up his display and he didn't know how he would have it ready when the fair opened. The old man said, "I'll just have to keep working on it while the fair is going on."

The doors opened and the inventors went into the hall. Other large doors opened and trucks moved into the hall. Men jumped from the trucks and began setting up rows and rows of tables. The men covered the tables with blue cloth. Every now and then a voice came over the loudspeaker and made

announcements. One announcement was, "No smoking in the hall." Another announcement told the inventors where their tables were. Each inventor had a blue piece of paper that had a letter and a number on it. The announcer explained to the inventors that all slips that had the letter A would be in the first aisle, that the Bs would be in the next aisle, that the Cs would be in the next aisle, and so forth. Here's what it said at the top of Leonard's slip: F16.

As Leonard and his grandmother walked to the aisle, Leonard said, "This is the biggest hall I've ever seen in my life."

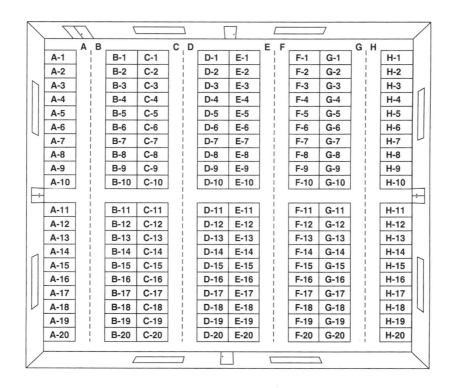

C Number your paper from 1 through 26.

Story Items

Write the words that go in the blanks to tell about the steps Leonard took to invent the electric eye device.

1. He started with a ▨.

       • solution   • need   • light

Then he got an idea for an invention.

2. Then he built a ▨ of the invention to show it worked.

3. Then he got a ▨ to protect his invention.

4. What are businesses that make things called?

5. What plan did Grandmother Esther have for getting in touch with these businesses?

- an invention fair
- a magazine
- a lawyer

6. What was first prize at the invention fair?

7. What was second prize?

8. What did Grandmother Esther think they would win?

9. On what day did the fair start?

10. At what time did the fair start?

11. The invention fair was held in a great ▨▨▨.

12. Why couldn't the inventors set up their displays the night before the fair?

Review Items

13. Things closer to the bottom of the pile went into the pile ▨▨▨.

14. What does an inventor get to protect an invention?

15. Special lawyers who get protection for inventions are called ▨▨▨.

- doctors
- patents
- patent attorneys

16. If other people want to make copies of an invention, they have to make a deal with the ▨▨▨.

17. What does the inventor usually make those people do?

18. The solid arrows show how many times people went into the room. How many people went into the room?

19. The dotted arrows show how many times people left the room. How many people left the room?

20. Are the lights on in the room?

21. How many more people would have to leave the room before the lights go off?

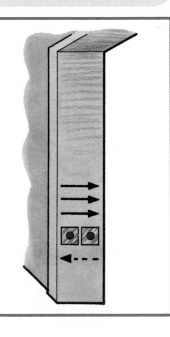

22. Write the letter of the earth that has the North Pole tilting away from the sun.

23. Write the letter of the earth that has the North Pole tilting toward the sun.

24. Write the letter of the earth that has darkness all around the North Pole.

25. Write the letter of the earth that has daylight all around the North Pole.

26. Write **A, B, C** and **D**. Then write the season each earth in the picture shows.

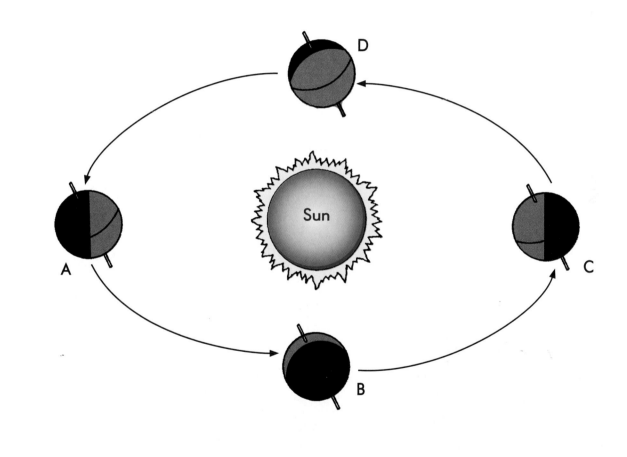

A

1
1. hesitated
2. during
3. applause
4. operator
5. introduced
6. excellent

2
1. interrupted
2. praised
3. flood
4. notebooks
5. disappointed
6. wandering
7. nudged

B # The Manufacturers at the Fair

Leonard was very disappointed when the fair opened at noon. He expected to see thousands of people pour into the hall. He imagined that there would be crowds of people looking at his display. But when the fair opened at noon, only a very few people came into the hall.

Only three of the people who came into the hall stopped at Leonard's exhibit. As soon as one of them stopped, Leonard showed how the device worked. For his display he had brought the little room with the doorway. He moved his dolls and stuffed animals into the room. Then he moved them out. He showed how the device worked and explained how the light stays on until everybody has left the room.

But none of the people who stopped at the display that afternoon seemed to be very impressed. Two of them nodded and said, "Very interesting." Then they walked down the F aisle to the next exhibit. The third person who stopped at Leonard's display was a slim woman wearing a gray coat. She didn't say anything. She just looked, listened, nodded her head, and walked away.

Grandmother Esther told Leonard that these people were manufacturers. "They don't seem very interested in the invention," Leonard said.

His grandmother said, "Smart manufacturers will never let you know that they're interested in your invention. They know that you'll want more money for your invention if they're very interested. So they'll act as if they're not very interested.

Don't let them fool you. The ones that seem the most interested are the ones who will never want to buy your invention."

"Another thing," his grandmother continued. "A smart manufacturer will try to stay far away from your display. Here's why. The manufacturer doesn't want a crowd to gather in front of your display. The more people who show that they are interested in your invention, the more money the manufacturers will have to pay for your invention. Remember, manufacturers want good inventions, but they don't want to pay any more money than they have to. So they're going to do everything they can to make you think that they're not interested."

After supper, great crowds of people flooded the hall. During most of the evening there was a group of people around Leonard's invention. The people smiled and praised Leonard for his invention.

Grandmother Esther explained, "The people who flood the fair after supper are not manufacturers. These are people who have other jobs. But they want to look at the new inventions. They're coming to the fair after work. The manufacturers have been at this fair since it opened. Being at the fair is part of their job."

"You're really smart, Grandmother," Leonard said.

Grandmother Esther said, "Those people you saw wandering

around here this afternoon are the real manufacturers. They're the important ones."

When the fair closed at ten that night, Leonard was very tired. "I never talked so much in my whole life," he explained to his grandmother.

The fair continued on the next day, Saturday. There weren't many people looking at the exhibits early in the morning. Grandmother Esther explained, "Most of the people you see here now are manufacturers. If you watch some of them, you'll see that they're writing things in little notebooks." Leonard watched two people, but neither person wrote anything. Then he spotted the slim woman in the gray coat. She was walking down the G aisle. When the woman got to the end of the aisle, she took out a little book and wrote something. Then she walked to the E aisle and talked to two men. She talked only for a moment. Then the men went one way and she went another way.

"This is really interesting," Leonard said.

Around 11 o'clock that morning, Grandmother Esther said, "Now the manufacturers will have to start making their deals with the inventors."

"Why do they have to make their deals now?" Leonard asked.

Grandmother Esther explained. "First of all, they want to make their deals before the prizes are announced this evening. If the manufacturers think that an invention will win a prize, they know that they can make a much better deal before it gets the prize. Once an invention is a first-prize invention, the inventor can get much more money for the invention."

Leonard said, "But Grandmother, why don't the manufacturers wait until later this afternoon before making deals with the inventors?"

Grandmother Esther said, "Here's the first reason. There will be many people here this afternoon. That means the inventors will be busy explaining their inventions. The second reason is that the manufacturers need at least three hours to make their deals with the inventors."

C Number your paper from 1 through 25.

Skill Items

> **The applause interrupted his speech.**

1. What word means **broke into?**
2. What word means **the clapping?**

Review Items

3. Write the letters of the 3 things you find in the Bermuda Triangle.

   a. ice floes   c. whirlpools   e. huge waves

   b. sudden storms   d. streams   f. mountains

---

4. Write the letter of the footprint made by the heaviest animal.
5. Write the letter of the footprint made by the lightest animal.

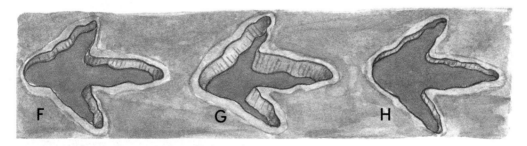

---

6. The picture shows marks left by an animal. Which arrow shows the direction the animal is moving?
7. Write the letter of the part that shows a footprint.
8. Write the letter of the part that shows the mark left by the animal's tail.

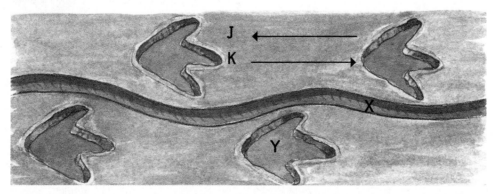

Write the name of each animal in the picture.

9.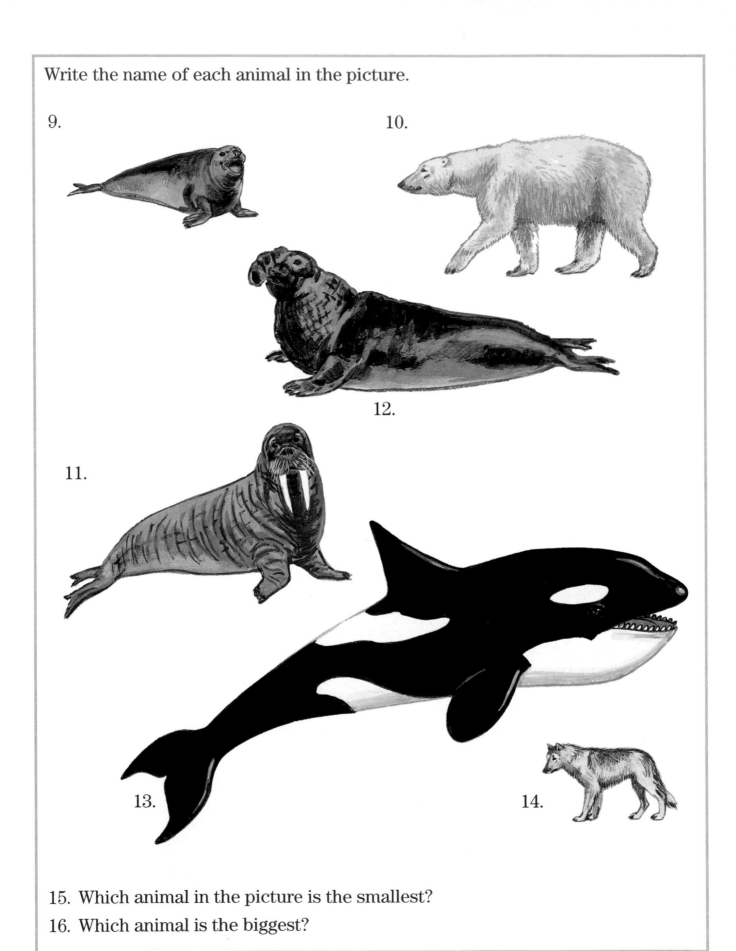

10.

12.

11.

13.

14.

15. Which animal in the picture is the smallest?

16. Which animal is the biggest?

17. Which globe shows how the earth looks on the first day of summer?

18. Which globe shows how the earth looks on the first day of winter?

H

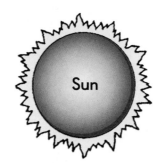

Sun

J

19. During which season do ice floes start?

20. During winter in Alaska, you can walk far out on the ocean. Tell why.

21. Do ice floes make noise in the winter?

22. Why do ice floes make noise in the spring?

23. In which direction will you drift when you're in an ocean current?

24. In which direction will you drift when you're in a strong wind?

25. The ▮▮▮▮s are the coldest places on the earth and the ▮▮▮▮ is the hottest place on the earth.

A

1	**2**	**3**	**4**
1. during	1. products	1. bald	1. stage
2. elbow	2. nudged	2. boss	2. spotlight
3. hurry	3. interrupted	3. eleven	3. paused
4. involve	4. introduced	4. kindergarten	4. judge
5. meantime	5. reasons	5. information	5. deciding
6. remind	6. shorter	6. businesslike	

B

Deals

Grandmother Esther had just given two reasons why the manufacturers would try to make deals with inventors before noon. The first reason was that the inventors would be very busy at their displays during the afternoon. The second reason was that it would take time for the inventor and the manufacturer to make a deal.

Just as she finished telling Leonard about what would happen, Leonard noticed that the slim woman in the gray coat was walking toward Leonard's display. She was with a man who was shorter than she was. They stopped at the display next to Leonard's and smiled as they looked at it.

Grandmother Esther whispered, "Leonard, they're going to try to make a deal with us. Let me do all the talking.

❀ The man and woman approached Leonard's display. They stopped. They didn't smile. They just stood there. "Hello," Leonard said at last.

The woman said, "Do you have a patent on this device?"

"Yes," Leonard replied.

The woman said nothing for a few moments. Then she said, "I'm with ABC Home Products." The woman continued, "I don't think many people would be interested in an invention like yours. But I may be able to talk my boss into working out a deal. But that deal must not involve a lot of money."

Grandmother Esther pointed to the large clock in the center of the hall. "It's already after eleven o'clock," she announced loudly. "This afternoon we're 🌸 going to be very busy. This evening we're going to win first prize and there will be many manufacturers who are interested in this invention. If you want to make a deal, you'd better start talking about a lot of money and you'd better start right now."

The woman's eyes opened wide. For a moment she didn't seem to know what to say. Then she turned to the man who was with her. He said, "ABC Home Products is a good company to be with. We have a very good name and very good products. That should be important to any inventor."

"We're in no hurry to make a deal," Grandmother Esther said. Then she said, "In fact, I would just as soon wait until after the prizes are announced this evening."

"But what if you don't win first prize?" the man said. "There are some very exciting ⭐ inventions at this fair. I've looked at ten inventions that could take first prize."

"Well, that's fine," Grandmother Esther said. "You just go and make a deal for one of those inventions. But if you want to talk to us, you can always wait until after we win first prize."

The woman in the gray coat nudged the man with her elbow. The man said, "We're going over to talk to the man we work for. Maybe we'll be back in a few minutes."

The man and woman left. Leonard watched them. They walked very fast toward the C aisle, where another man was standing. In the meantime, three men who had been standing at the head of the F aisle approached Leonard's display. A tall bald man walked up and introduced himself and the two men who were with him. Then he smiled and said, "It's just a shame that our company can't buy your device. I think it's very clever. But we've got too many inventions already. That's a real shame."

One of the other men said to the tall bald man, "Do you think that we might be able to take this invention if we didn't have to pay very much for it?"

The bald man said, "Well, I don't know. I just hadn't thought of that."

The third man said, "I'll bet that we could probably talk our boss into taking it if we didn't have to pay more than a few hundred dollars for it."

The bald man said, "That's an idea I hadn't thought of. Maybe you're right. Maybe we could do that."

Grandmother Esther said, "Who do you think we are, a couple of kindergarten children? You're not going to steal this invention. You're going to tell us the name of the company you're with. You're going to

give us your business card. You're going to tell us your best deal. And then we're going to see if that deal is better than the deal ABC Home Products wants to make."

"But Grandma," Leonard said. He was going to remind her that ABC Home Products had not told about the deal they wanted to make.

She interrupted Leonard and said, "I know what you're thinking, Leonard. You want to go with ABC Home Products. But we have to give these other manufacturers a chance, too."

A Number your paper from 1 through 25.

Skill Items

Use the words in the box to write complete sentences.

company	applause	owed	patent	connected
attorney	prize	agreement	interrupted	

1. The ▮▮ ▮▮ wrote an ▮▮.
2. The ▮▮ ▮▮ his speech.

Review Items

3. What are clouds made of?

4. What kind of cloud does the picture show?

5. What happens to a drop of water at **B?**

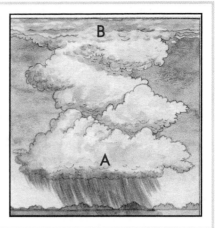

6. What is a person doing when the person makes an object for the first time?

7. The person who makes an object for the first time is called an ▆▆▆.

8. The object the person makes is called an ▆▆▆.

9. What are businesses that make things called?

10. Geese live in large groups called ▆▆▆.

11. Where are most wild geese born?

12. In which direction do geese fly in the fall?

13. What is this trip called?

Choose from these words to answer each item:
- moon
- Florida
- sun
- Canada
- equator
- geese
- poles
- migration

14. The heat that the earth receives comes from the ▆▆▆.

15. The part of the earth that receives more heat than any other part is the ▆▆▆.

16. The parts of the earth that receive less heat than any other part are called the ▆▆▆.

17. Which letter shows the part of the earth that receives **more** heat from the sun than any other part?

18. Which letter shows a part of the earth that receives **less** heat from the sun than any other part?

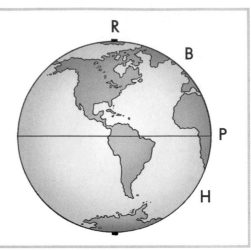

19. If you cannot see the sun, is it **daytime** or **nighttime** on your side of the earth?

20. What is it on the other side of the earth?

21. The earth turns around one time every ▬▬ hours.

22. Write the letter of the earth that shows the person in daytime.

23. Write the letter of the earth that shows the person 6 hours later.

24. Write the letter that shows the person another 6 hours later.

25. Write the letter that shows the person another 6 hours later.

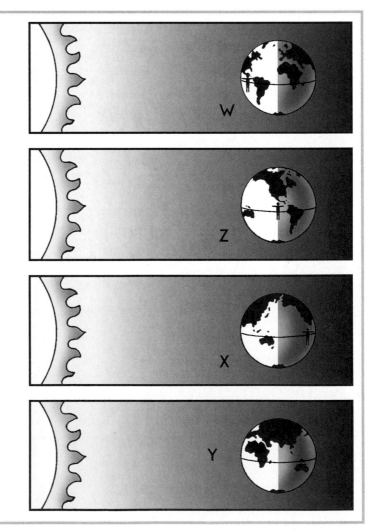

Number your paper from 1 through 34.

Here's the rule about an electric eye: **Each time the beam of light is broken, the light changes.**
1. The light is off. The beam is broken 2 times. Is the light **on** or **off** at the end?
2. The light is off. The beam is broken 5 times. Is the light **on** or **off** at the end?
3. The light is off. The beam is broken 8 times. Is the light **on** or **off** at the end?

4. How many electric eyes did Leonard use for his invention?
5. How many beams went across the doorway?

The picture shows two electric eye beams on the side of doors. The number **1** shows the beam that is broken first. The number **2** shows the beam that is broken next. Write the letter of the correct arrow for each doorway.

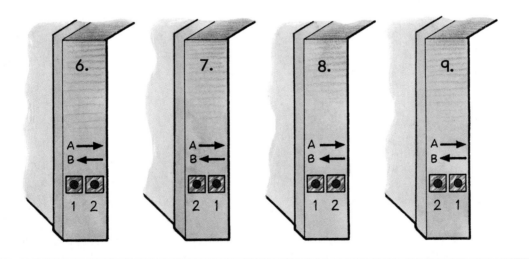

Answer these questions about the counter on Leonard's device:

10. Every time somebody goes into the room, what does the counter do?

    • + 1   • - 1   • + 0

11. Every time somebody goes out of the room, what does the counter do?

    • + 1   • - 1   • + 0

12. What number does the counter end up at when the last person leaves the room?

13. What happens to the lights when the counter gets to that number?

---

14. The solid arrows show how many times people went into the room. How many people went into the room?

15. The dotted arrows show how many times people left the room. How many people left the room?

16. Are the lights on in the room?

17. How many more people would have to leave the room before the lights go off?

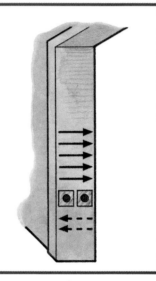

For each picture, tell if the lights in the room are **on** or **off.** The solid arrows show people going into the room. The dotted arrows show people leaving the room.

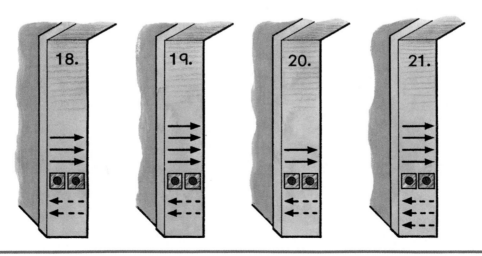

18.   19.   20.   21.

22. What does an inventor get to protect an invention?

23. Special lawyers who get protection for inventions are called ▓▓▓.

24. What are businesses that make things called?

Write the words that go in the blanks to tell about the steps you take to invent something.

25. You start with a ▓▓▓.

- light
- solution
- need

Then you get an idea for an invention.

26. Then you build a ▓▓▓ of the invention to show how it works.

27. Then you get a ▓▓▓ to protect your invention.

Skill Items

For each item, write the underlined word from the sentences in the box.

> The <u>patent attorney</u> wrote an <u>agreement</u>.
> The <u>applause</u> <u>interrupted</u> his speech.
> He <u>responded</u> to her <u>clever</u> <u>solution</u>.

28. What underlining means **reacted?**

29. What underlining means **lawyer?**

30. What underlining means **a promise made by people?**

31. What underlining means **the clapping?**

32. What underlining means **very smart?**

33. What underlining names a lawyer whose special job is getting patents for new inventions?

34. What underlining refers to solving a problem?

END OF TEST 5

A

1
1. young
2. guess
3. student
4. judges
5. remained
6. information

2
1. agreement
2. businesslike
3. offer
4. spotlight
5. excellent

3
1. deciding
2. dimmed
3. flatly
4. paused
5. hesitated
6. concluded

4
1. applause
2. item
3. stage
4. operator
5. key

B # The First-Prize Winner

The woman in the gray coat came back to Leonard's display with two men. The other group of men had just left. The woman's voice was very flat and businesslike when she said, "I will make one offer. We will pay you ten thousand dollars in cash for your invention and one dollar for every copy that we sell."

Leonard listened to the offer and could hardly believe what he heard. He wanted to shout out, "Yes, we'll take it!"

But his grandmother said, "I'll make you one offer. You will pay us fifteen thousand dollars in cash and two dollars for every device that you sell."

"Can't pay that much," the woman said flatly. "Here's the best I can do. Ten thousand dollars and two dollars for every copy we sell."

Grandmother Esther said, "Write it down and sign it. You've got a deal."

Leonard jumped up and shouted, "We did it!"

Suddenly the woman in the gray coat smiled. She looked very nice when she smiled. She held out her hand and Leonard shook it. Her voice seemed to change and she sounded very pleasant. "I think this will be a very good deal for all of us."

At two o'clock in the afternoon, Leonard and his grandmother were signing papers. Grandmother Esther had called their patent attorney and the attorney had come down to read the agreement. The attorney said that it looked good. So Leonard and his grandmother signed the papers.

The afternoon went by very fast. Large crowds of people gathered in front of Leonard's display. A lot of people who watched how the invention worked shook hands with Leonard and said things like this: "That's a good energy saver." "We could use a device like that in our house."

That evening at 8:30 the lights in the hall were dimmed. A large spotlight came on and a beam of bright blue-white light fell on a man who stood on a small stage. "It's time for the prizes," he announced. People from all over the hall began to crowd close to the stage.

"Should we go over there, Grandmother?" Leonard asked.

"Of course," she replied. "We want to be right there when they announce the winner of the first prize."

So ⭐ they walked over near the stage. The man explained, "It was a very, very hard job deciding on a first-prize winner. There were many excellent inventions. The first and second prize winners were so close that it might have been a good idea to give them both first prize. But . . ." he hesitated and raised one hand. "Ladies and gentlemen. The winner of the first prize is . . ." The man paused again. "The winner is Ronald Hogan and his automatic list-writer."

"What?" Grandmother Esther shouted. "We win first prize!"

Some of the people standing near Leonard turned around and looked at Grandmother Esther. The man on the stage continued, "For those of you who didn't see Mr. Hogan's great invention, I'll explain how it works. It fits on the side of your refrigerator. You give this machine information about what should be in the refrigerator. When the refrigerator gets low on anything, the machine automatically writes the name of that item on a list."

"Let's go home," Grandmother Esther said to Leonard. "This is like a bad dream."

"No, Grandma," Leonard said. "Let's stick around. Maybe we'll get one of the other prizes."

The man on the stage called Mr. Hogan to the stage and gave him a check for twenty thousand dollars. Grandmother Esther said, "This is enough to make you sick."

Then the announcer said, "Ladies and gentlemen, the second prize winner lost to the list-writer by only a hair." The man continued, "This prize goes to Leonard Mathis for his automatic light operator. Leonard, come on up here and get your check for ten thousand dollars."

People were clapping like crazy. The spotlight swung over and the beam was on Leonard. His grandmother was pushing him. "Go on. Get your prize."

He grabbed her arm. "You're coming with me," he shouted. He had to shout, because the applause was so loud.

"No," she said and tried to push him away.

"You come, or I'm not going up there," he said.

So she went with him. They stood on the stage. The light was almost blinding. The man asked Leonard some questions and he answered them. But he could hardly remember what was happening. The next thing he knew, he was holding a check, and people were clapping again.

C Number your paper from 1 through 22.

Skill Items

Here are three events that happened in the story.
Write **beginning, middle** or **end** for each event.

1. The next thing Leonard knew, he was holding a check and people were clapping again.
2. That evening at 8:30, the lights in the hall were dimmed.
3. The woman in the gray coat came back to Leonard's display with two men.

Review Items

Use these names to answer the questions:
Tyrannosaurus, Triceratops.

4. What is animal **D?**
5. What is animal **E?**

Write the words that go in the blanks to tell about the steps you take to invent something.

6. You start with a ___.
   - solution
   - electric eye
   - need

   Then you get an idea for an invention.
7. Then you build a ___ of the invention to show how it works.
8. Then you get a ___ to protect your invention.

9. Why don't smart manufacturers act interested in the inventions that they want? **Write the letter of the answer.**

        a. because they want to pay more for the invention
        b. so they don't have to pay as much for the invention
        c. because they are at the fair all day long

10. Write the letter of the best deal for an inventor.

11. Write the letter of the best deal for a manufacturer.

        a. 5 thousand dollars and 5 dollars for every copy sold
        b. 8 thousand dollars and 5 dollars for every copy sold
        c. 12 thousand dollars and 5 dollars for every copy sold

12. Write the letters of the 2 kinds of places that are safe for geese.

  a. places with no geese or ducks   c. places with many geese
  b. places with a few geese   d. places with a few ducks

13. The map shows a route. What state is at the north end of the route?

14. What country is at the south end of the route?

15. About how many miles is the route?

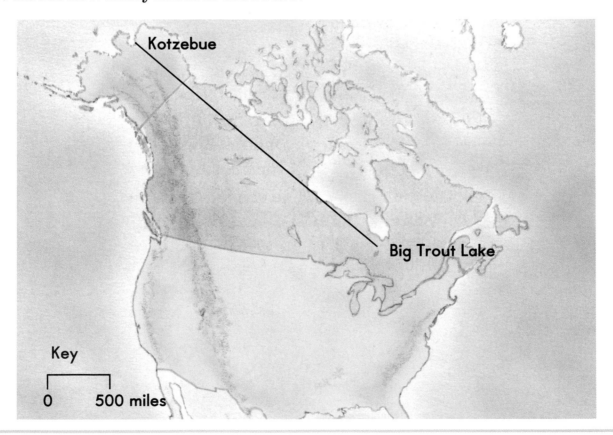

Kotzebue

Big Trout Lake

Key

0   500 miles

16. Name 3 animals that are warm-blooded.

17. Name 3 animals that are cold-blooded.

18. Write the letter of the storm clouds.

19. Write the letter of the clouds that may stay in the sky for days at a time.

20. Write the letter of the clouds that have frozen drops of water.

A

B

C

Study Items

Look in the Yellow Pages of your phone book to find out 2 things.

21. Find out if there are any electric-equipment manufacturers. The word **manufacturer** may be written like this in the Yellow Pages: **mfr.** If the Yellow Pages list any electric-equipment manufacturers, write down the name of one manufacturer. That would be the kind of company that would make copies of Leonard's invention.

22. Also look up the names of stores that might sell the copies that are manufactured. These are stores that would be listed under a heading like this: **Electric Equipment and Supplies—Retail.** The name **retail** tells you that you can buy things at that store. Write the name of an electric-equipment-and-supply retail store.

A

1	2	3	4
1. solar system	1. key	1. suppose	1. Pacific Ocean
2. Jupiter	2. headline	2. Wendy	2. San Francisco
3. Uranus	3. fancy	3. chosen	3. million
4. dwarf	4. student	4. booklet	4. Mercury
5. report	5. appear	5. gray-haired	5. Neptune
6. parents	6. young	6. planet	6. Pluto

B

Facts About Japan

In a few lessons, you're going to read a story that takes place in Japan.

Here are some facts about Japan:

Japan is a country that is west of the United States.

The United States is on one side of the Pacific Ocean and Japan is on the other side of the Pacific Ocean. The map shows that if you flew west from San Francisco, you would cross the Pacific Ocean and reach Japan.

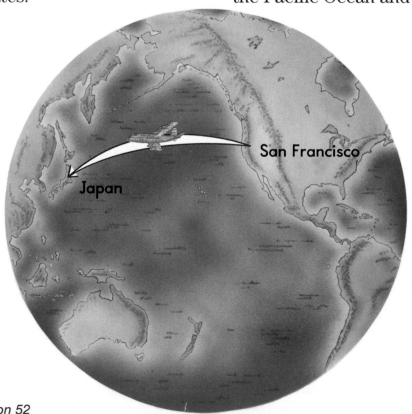

San Francisco

Japan

Japan is much smaller than the state of Alaska.

About 127 million people live in Japan.

Japan manufactures many products that are used in the United States and Canada. Some of Japan's more famous products are automobiles, TVs, and CD players.

C # Your Turn

Three months had gone by since the invention fair, but Leonard was still not used to the idea that he was really an inventor. He still had trouble thinking about the money that he had won for second prize in the fair. But he sure felt good.

He noticed that a lot of kids in school wanted to be his friend now. And he noticed that he didn't seem to have as much free time as he used to have. Nearly every day he talked on the phone to somebody at ABC Home Products. The people at ABC Home Products were making up ads that told about the invention. They gave it a fancy name: Mr. Light Saver.

For their ads, they had pictures of a funny-looking man who had a head that was a lightbulb. Mr. Light Saver told how he would save fuel, save electricity and save money. ABC Home Products had sent Leonard copies of the ads that were going to appear in the newspapers.

Mr. Light Saver turns lights on and off **AUTOMATICALLY.**
No more leaving lights on.
No more running around turning them off.
No more wasted money. Instead, big savings.
Do your part to save energy.
See your ABC Home Products dealer today and ask about the low-cost plan for putting Mr. Light Saver in your home.
Look in the Yellow Pages under **Electrical Equipment and Supplies—Retail.**

Walk in and lights go on.
Walk out and lights go off.

SAVE THOSE ENERGY DOLLARS BY PUTTING **MR. LIGHT SAVER** IN EVERY ROOM OF YOUR HOUSE.

 **new** from ABC HOME PRODUCTS

Leonard kept these ads in a notebook. He also kept copies of newspaper reports on the invention fair. The best newspaper report filled almost one whole page of the newspaper. It came out the day after the fair.

At the top of this report was a headline: "Young Student Wins Prize for Invention." Beneath the headline was another headline: "Leonard Mathis Gets Check for Ten Thousand Dollars for his Clever Energy Saver."

Leonard had four other reports in his notebook. They told how he invented the device, how his grandmother helped him, and what he planned to do with the money. One report told about Grandmother Esther.

Leonard had money in the bank. He had paid back the money that Grandmother Esther paid to the patent attorney and to the electrical supply store. ⭐ Leonard wanted to pay Grandmother Esther more than he owed her, but she wouldn't take it. "You're the one who did the hard work on this invention," she told him. "All I did was keep you going in the right direction."

Everybody was happy, even Leonard's parents. They were proud of Leonard. His mother was happy for another reason. She bought one of the first list-writers that came out.

She said, "Now grocery shopping is easy."

But Leonard noticed one problem she had when she went shopping. Here's what happened: Leonard was with his mother at the grocery store. They were going back to the car with the groceries when Leonard noticed the problem. He and his mother were each carrying two large bags. His mother approached the trunk of the car. She wanted to put the bags into the trunk. But she had a problem. She needed to use her hands to get her key out and open the trunk. But her hands were busy hanging on to the bags of groceries. She said, "Oh my," and put the bags down while she hunted for her keys.

Leonard said to himself, "Here's a problem. That means there is a need that could be filled with an invention." He looked at the back of the car. Then he walked over to the car and set the grocery bags down. The car was dusty. He drew two little circles in the dust. One circle was on each side. Then he looked at his mother, smiled, and said, "I have figured out an invention that will solve your problem."

Now it is your turn to think like an inventor. See if you can figure out the device that Leonard was thinking about when he told his mother that he could solve her problem with an invention.

D **Number your paper from 1 through 29.**

1. The arrow on the map goes from San Francisco to ▮▮▮▮.

2. Which ocean does the arrow cross?

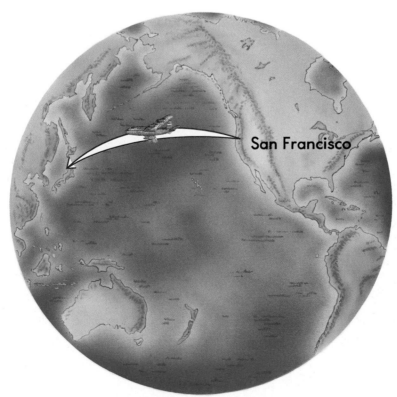

San Francisco

3. Which is bigger, Alaska or Japan?

4. Is Japan a **state** or a **country?**

5. How many people live in Japan?

- 127 million
- 127 thousand

6. Write the letters of 3 types of products that are used in the United States and manufactured in Japan.

a. furniture

b. TVs

c. books

d. Mr. Light Saver

e. CD players

f. cars

g. rugs

Skill Items

She selected a comfortable seat.

7. What word tells that the seat **felt** pleasant?

8. What word means **chose?**

Review Items

The solid arrows show people going into the room. The dotted arrows show people leaving the room. For each picture, tell if the lights in the room are **on** or **off.**

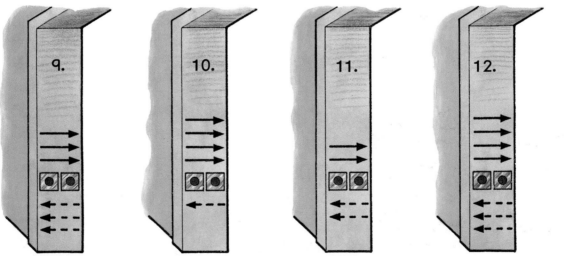

13. What runs an electric eye?

14. What kind of boat do Eskimos use in the summer?

15. Why don't they use those boats in the winter?

Write the words that go in the blanks to tell about the steps you take to invent something.

16. You start with a ▬▬.

        • need   • device   • solution

    Then you get an idea for an invention.

17. Then you build a ▬▬ of the invention to show it works.

18. Then you get a ▬▬ to protect your invention.

19. Write the letter of the best deal for an inventor.

20. Write the letter of the best deal for a manufacturer.

    a. 15 thousand dollars and 4 dollars for every copy sold

    b. 15 thousand dollars and 8 dollars for every copy sold

    c. 15 thousand dollars and 5 dollars for every copy sold

21. If an invention wins a prize, would a manufacturer have to pay more money for it?

22. About how long are killer whales?

23. Compare the size of killer whales with the size of other whales.

24. Are killer whales fish?

25. Tell if killer whales are **warm-blooded** or **cold-blooded.**

26. Which letter shows the place that has the warmest winters?

27. Which letter shows the place that is closest to the equator?

28. Which letter shows the place that is closest to a pole?

29. Is the **North Pole** or the **South Pole** closer to that letter?

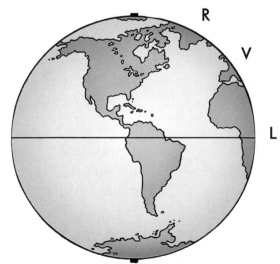

A

1	2	3	4
1. comfortable	1. concluded	1. Mars	1. final
2. dwarf planet	2. selected	2. Pluto	2. magnetic
3. solar system	3. lettered	3. Jupiter	3. nervous
4. cover	4. guessed	4. Saturn	4. section
5. score		5. Mercury	5. twenty-five
6. spaceship		6. Neptune	6. written
		7. Venus	
		8. Uranus	

B Facts About the Solar System

The story that you will read tells about going to different parts of the solar system. Here are facts about the solar system:

- The solar system is made up of the sun and nine planets.
- Most of those planets have moons.
- Earth, the planet that we live on, is one of the nine planets in the solar system.
- The sun is in the middle of the solar system.
- The sun is the only part of the solar system that is burning.
- The sun gives heat and light to all the planets of the solar system.

So our Earth gets heat and light from the sun.

Picture 1 shows the sun and the nine planets. The arrows show that the planets move around the sun. The planet with the dotted arrow is our Earth.

Here are the names of the planets: Mercury Venus, Earth, Mars, Jupiter, Saturn, Uranus, Neptune, Pluto.

Mercury is closest to the sun. Pluto is farthest from the sun. Pluto is different from the other planets. It is called a **dwarf planet** because of its size.

Picture 2 shows that the sun is much larger than any planet. The sun is one hundred times larger than Earth. But Earth is not the largest planet.

The largest planet is Jupiter. Which planet is next-largest?

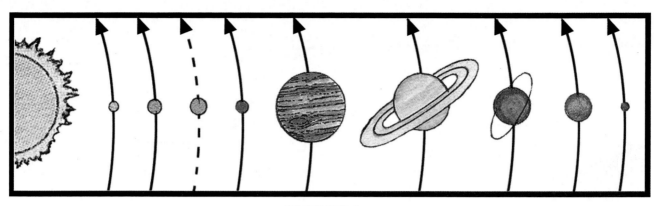

PICTURE 1

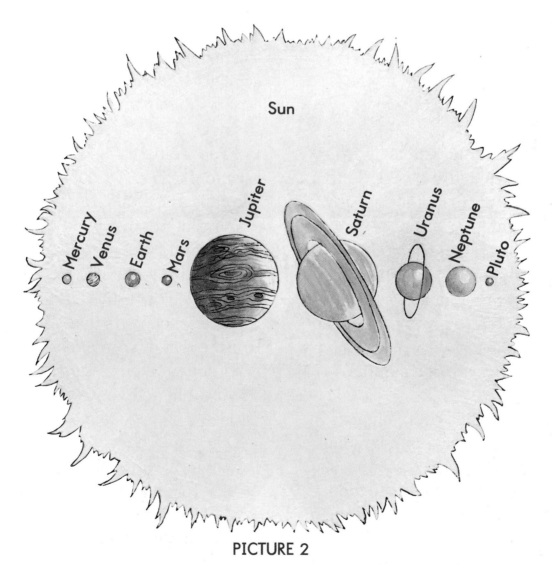

PICTURE 2

An Important Test

Wendy Chan's hand shook as she picked up the pencil. This test was the most important one she had ever taken. She didn't even want to think about what would happen if she failed it. Instead, she kept telling herself: "If you do well on this test, you will go on a trip across the solar system."

A woman with gray hair was standing in front of the room. Wendy was seated with about thirty other students. The students had come from different parts of Canada. Only ten students would be selected to go on the trip. Those would be the students with the highest test scores.

The gray-haired woman in front of the room smiled and said, "I think that you are all ready for this test. Am I correct?"

"Yes," the students agreed. Some of them laughed. They knew what would be covered in the test and they all wanted to go on the trip. So they had done just what Wendy had done for the past three months—studied.

She had studied every night, every Saturday, every Sunday. She had thought about the test when she ate, and she had even dreamed about the test. She kept thinking about one date—the date of the test. That was the most important date in her life—November 5, 2230. Yes, she was ready for the test—really ready.

The gray-haired woman explained. "I suppose that you know these rules as well as I do, but let's go over them one more time. The test will take four hours. You'll have a five-minute break at the end of each hour. You may not talk about the test during these breaks, but you may walk around or get something ⭐ to drink. The questions on the test will cover facts about our planet and the other planets in the solar system. It will also cover facts about the spaceships that we use to travel through the solar system."

The woman paused and smiled again. "I know that not all of you will be chosen for this trip. And I'm sorry that not everybody can go. But I would like to remind you that even if you don't go, this test has made you a smarter person. You have learned facts that you can use for the rest of your lives."

For a moment, Wendy felt like crying. She felt very sorry for students who would not be able to go on the trip. The woman concluded by saying, "Good luck to all of you. You're a fine group of students."

She was right. Only the best students from different parts of

Canada were selected to take the test.

The gray-haired woman said, "All right. You may begin the test. Open your test booklets and start."

Wendy turned her booklet over and opened it to item 1. The item showed a map of the world. The instruction said, "Label the lettered parts on this map."

"That's easy," she said to herself, and quickly wrote in the name for each letter.

1. Label the lettered parts on this map.

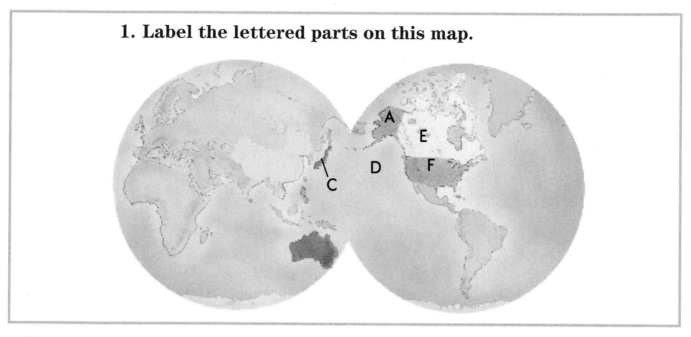

Wendy looked at item 2. That item appears below.

2. What kind of animals are in the picture? _____

In what country are most wild ones born? _____

What is a group of these animals called? _____

How long do most of them live? _____

Wendy wrote answers to the questions and moved to the next item. She read the item and started to feel a little sick. She couldn't remember the answer. She knew that if she missed more than one or two items on this whole test, she would not go on the trip.

Here was that item: Which planet has more moons, Jupiter or Saturn?

D Number your paper from 1 through 20.

Story Items

1. What kind of animals are in the picture?
2. In what country are most wild ones born?
3. What is a **group** of these animals called?
4. How long do most of them live?

Skill Items

Use the words in the box to write complete sentences.

interrupted	business	selected	applause
praised	excellent	comfortable	wandering

5. The ▮▮ ▮▮ his speech.
6. She ▮▮ a ▮▮ seat.

Review Items

7. The solid arrows show how many times people went into the room. How many people went into the room?

8. The dotted arrows show how many times people left the room. How many people left the room?

9. Are the lights on in the room?

10. How many more people would have to leave the room before the lights go off?

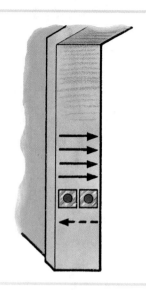

11. The arrow on the map goes from San Francisco to ▓▓▓▓.

12. Which ocean does the arrow cross?

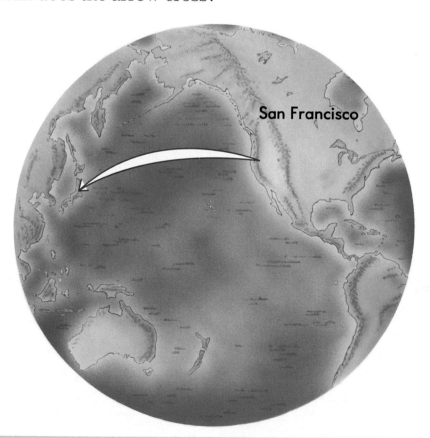

13. What does an inventor get to protect an invention?

14. Special lawyers who get protection for inventions are called ▮▮▮.

15. If other people want to make copies of an invention, they have to make a deal with the ▮▮▮.

16. What does the inventor usually make those people do?

17. Which is bigger, Alaska or Japan?

18. Is Japan a **state** or a **country?**

19. How many people live in Japan?

- 127   • 127 million   • 127 thousand

20. Write the letters of 3 types of products that are used in the United States and manufactured in Japan.

a. furniture   e. CD players

b. Mr. Light Saver   f. cars

c. books   g. rugs

d. TVs

A

1
1. message
2. improvement
3. magnetic
4. equipment

2
1. eighteen
2. hundred
3. thirty
4. twenty-five
5. twelve

3
1. day-dreaming
2. section
3. comfortable
4. latest
5. snack

4
1. streak
2. traveler
3. final
4. written
5. nervous
6. uncovered

5
1. office
2. certainly
3. spaceship
4. worried
5. correctly

B Past, Present and Future

- Things that are happening now are in the present time.
- Things that <u>will</u> happen are in the future time.

Look at the dates on the time line.

Some dates on the time line are in the past and some are in the future.

What is the present year?

What is the earliest year shown on the time line?

What is the future year that is closest to the present year?

What is the future year that is farthest in the future?

Touch each year on the time line and tell if it's in the past or in the future.

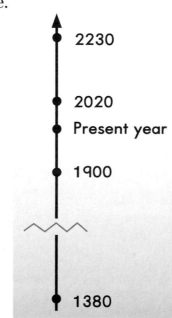

2230

2020
Present year

1900

1380

The Test Questions

Wendy started to feel sick because she couldn't remember the answer to the question. Then she said to herself, "Well, figure out the answer."

So she thought. And she remembered:

"Jupiter has 63 moons.
Saturn has 47 moons."

Wendy wrote the answer to the question. She knew it was correct.

The next items on the test asked facts about different places in the world. Here are the items:

> **If you went west from San Francisco, what is the name of the country you would reach first?**

> **If you go west from the United States, what ocean do you cross?**
>
> **Which is larger in size, Japan or Alaska?**
>
> **Which has colder winter temperatures, the United States or Canada?**
>
> **In which direction would you go from Canada to reach the main part of the United States?**

Wendy answered the questions quickly.

The next question asked about spaceships. The item showed a picture of Traveler Four, the latest spaceship. The instructions said, "Label the lettered parts."

Here's what Wendy wrote:

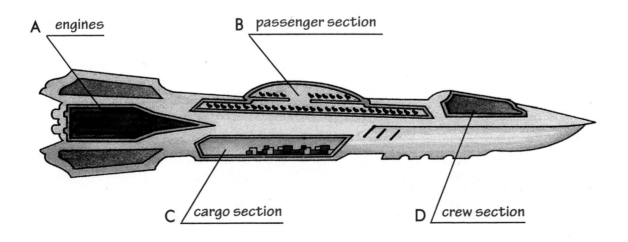

A engines
B passenger section
C cargo section
D crew section

There were more items about Traveler Four. Here are those items and Wendy's answers:

How long is Traveler Four? 405 feet
How much weight can Traveler Four carry? 600 thousand pounds
How many people are in the crew? 30
How many passengers does Traveler Four hold? 200
How fast can Traveler Four travel? 1 thousand miles per second

---

After Wendy answered the last question about Traveler Four, she thought about that ship. Imagine moving through space at the speed of one thousand miles per second. At that speed, you could go across the United States in two-and-a-half seconds. You could go around the world in only twenty-five seconds. You could go from Earth to the moon in only four minutes.

Wendy's mind moved away from the test. It began imagining what it must be like to be in Traveler Four. Imagine sitting in a comfortable passenger section that holds two hundred passengers. Imagine sitting there, eating a snack and talking to the person next to you as you streak through space at one thousand miles each second. The idea was so strange and impossible and exciting that Wendy could feel goose bumps forming on her arms. Imagine going from Earth to Jupiter in only four-and-a-half days.

In that time, the spaceship would travel almost 400 million miles. Imagine!

Suddenly, Wendy said to herself, "If you want to go on that trip, you'd better do a good job on this test. So stop day-dreaming and start working."

Wendy went back to the test. The next questions asked about the planets in the solar system. The questions asked how much they weighed, how fast they turned around, how long it took them to circle the sun, how many moons they had and how far from the sun they were. These questions were easy for Wendy. She knew many facts about the planets. Of course, she knew the most about the planet Earth. But the planet that interested her most was Jupiter. Wendy found it interesting because it was the biggest planet in the solar system.

Make sure that you know the
answers to these questions:

How fast does Traveler Four travel?
1 thousand miles per second

How long would it take Traveler Four to go across the United States?
two-and-a-half seconds

How long would it take Traveler Four to go to the moon?
4 minutes

How long would it take Traveler Four to go to Jupiter?
four-and-a-half days

How far is it from Earth to Jupiter?
400 million miles

D Number your paper from 1 through 20.

Story Items

1. How many moons does Jupiter have?
2. How many moons does Saturn have?
3. If you went west from San Francisco, what country would you reach first?
4. If you go west from the United States, what ocean do you cross?
5. Which is **larger** in size, Japan or Alaska?
6. Which has **colder** winter temperatures, the United States or Canada?
7. In which direction would you go from Canada to reach the main part of the United States?

Review Items

8. Here's the rule: **People who don't show interest in an invention are manufacturers.**
   - Person A walked by the display without saying anything.
   - Person B watched the display and then praised Leonard on his wonderful invention.
   - Person C talked to Leonard for 15 minutes about the invention.
   - Person D listened to what Leonard had to say and then said, "Thank you," and walked away from the display.

Write the letters of the 2 manufacturers.

Write the words that go in the blanks to tell about the steps you take to invent something.

9. You start with a ______.
   - solution
   - need
   - light

   Then you get an idea for an invention.
10. Then you build a ______ of the invention to show how it works.
11. Then you get a ______ to protect your invention.

12. Why don't smart manufacturers act interested in the inventions that they want? **Write the letter of the answer.**
    a. because they want to pay more for the invention
    b. because they are at the fair all day long
    c. so they don't have to pay as much for the invention

13. Name the planet we live on.
14. What's in the middle of the solar system?
15. Name the only part of the solar system that's burning.
16. Is Earth the planet that is closest to the sun?
17. The sun gives ______ and ______ to all the planets.

18. Which planet is largest?
19. Which planet is next-largest?
20. How many times larger than Earth is the sun?
    - 2 thousand
    - 1 hundred
    - 1 thousand

55

A

1	2	3
1. Tokyo	1. <u>classroom</u>	1. certainly
2. oxygen	2. <u>failure</u>	2. underlined
3. guest	3. <u>message</u>	3. correctly
4. pressure	4. <u>office</u>	4. improvement
5. adult	5. <u>spaceship</u>	5. worried
6. guy	6. <u>Sidney</u>	

B

Waiting for a Letter

Wendy's fingers were sore from writing. She had spent most of the last four hours writing answers to test items. Now she was reading over her answers a final time. The woman with gray hair walked to the front of the room. "All right," she said. "The time is up. Stop writing. Turn your test booklet over. Make sure that your name is on it. And pass it forward."

Suddenly, Wendy felt very frightened. Had she answered all the questions correctly? There were a couple of items that she wasn't sure about. She wasn't sure how fast Traveler Three went or when it was built.

Wendy knew many facts about Traveler One, Traveler Two and Traveler Three. Traveler One held two hundred passengers, but it was a very slow ship compared to Traveler Four. Traveler One could go only one mile per second. Traveler One took almost twelve years to go from Earth to Jupiter. Traveler Four could make the same trip in four-and-a-half days.

Traveler Two could go faster than Traveler One. Traveler Three could go faster yet. But Wendy wasn't sure how fast Traveler Three could go. She had written that it could go 45 miles per second, and she hoped her answer was right.

"You'll be getting a letter within a few weeks," the gray-haired woman said. The woman continued, "Your letter will tell you either that you have been selected to go on the trip or that you haven't been selected." Then the woman said, "I found out just this morning where the trip will go. If you're selected, you'll go to the planet Jupiter and spend nearly a week there."

Wendy listened to the words, but she didn't feel excited. She still felt worried about answering the questions correctly.

The woman continued, "I know that the letter will disappoint most of you." The woman said, "Just remember that you have had a chance to learn a great deal, and you certainly should not feel like a failure if you aren't selected."

Wendy turned around and looked at the faces of the other students in the room. Some were smiling. Most were serious. The girl directly behind Wendy looked very sad. "What's wrong?" Wendy asked.

"I blew it," she said, "I just blew it. I thought I knew this stuff, but my mind seemed to go blank and I . . ." She covered her face with her hands.

Wendy turned around and put her hand on the girl's shoulder. "Hey," she said. "Maybe you did better than you think."

"Yeah," the girl said and uncovered her face. She tried to smile.

The woman in the front of the room said, "Good luck and thank you."

Everybody stood up and started talking at the same time. A lot of students were asking questions like, "What was the answer to the question about the mountains in Japan?"

Wendy turned to the girl who had been sitting behind her. Wendy said, "What's your name?"

"Sidney Miller," she said.

"Listen," Wendy said. "When they send the list of people who are going on the trip, I'll look for your name. Maybe we'll both make it."

"Thanks," Sidney said.

● ● ●

The mail usually came to Wendy's house about 11 each ⭐ morning. By 11:15, Wendy's math class was over, so she ran to the phone and called her home. For the last five days, she had called home at 11:15 each morning. "Hi, Mom," she would say each day. She didn't have to tell her mother why she was calling. Her mother would say, "It hasn't come yet."

"Oh," Wendy would say. Each time her mother told her that the letter hadn't come, Wendy felt glad and sad. She felt sad because she hadn't found out whether she was going on the trip. She felt a little glad because she didn't want the letter to come if it said she wasn't going.

Then on November 19, Wendy's math teacher walked over to her desk just before the class was over. He bent over and said that there was an important message for her, and she should go to the office.

She felt so nervous that she hardly remembered leaving the classroom and going down the hall to the office. She was almost in a dream. The phone felt very heavy. She quickly moved it to her ear. "Mom," she said.

"You did it, honey," her mother said. "You're going."

C Number your paper from 1 through 22.

Skill Items

Without gravity, they were weightless.

1. What word means that something has no weight?

2. What word names the force that pulls things back to Earth?

Review Items

3. What is a person doing when the person makes an object for the first time?

4. The person who makes an object for the first time is called an ▭.

5. The object the person makes is called an ▭.

6. How many times larger than Earth is the sun?

     • 1 hundred   • 1 thousand   • 10 thousand

7. What does an inventor get to protect an invention?

8. Special lawyers who get protection for inventions are called ▨▨▨.

The picture shows two electric eye beams on the side of doors. The number **1** shows the beam that is broken first. The number **2** shows the beam that is broken next. Write the letter of the correct arrow for each doorway.

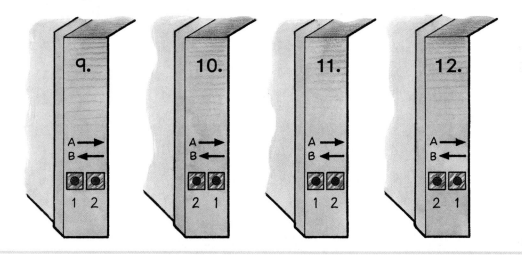

13. Which is smaller, Alaska or Japan?

14. Is Japan a **state** or a **country?**

15. How many people live in Japan?

     • 127   • 127 million   • 127 thousand

16. How old are geese when they mate for the first time?

17. After male and female geese mate, how long do they stay together?

18. Most geese live for about ▨▨▨ years.

Look at the map.

19. Which letter shows Big Trout Lake?

20. Which letter shows Crooked Lake?

21. Write the name of the lake that's farther north.

22. What country is the **X** in?

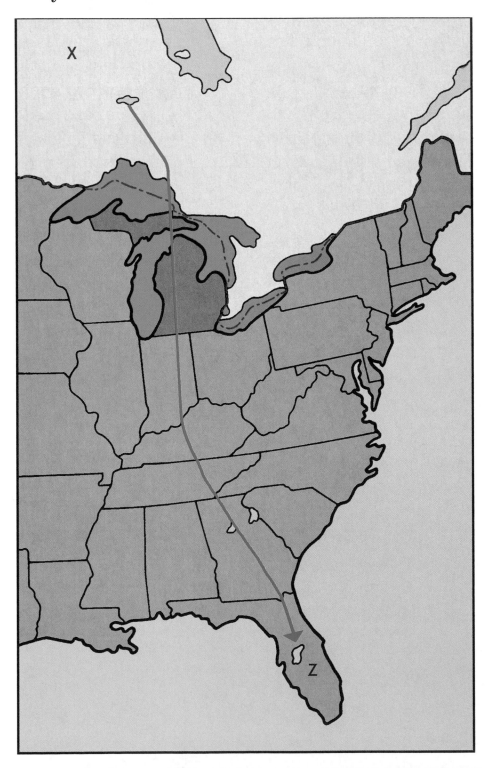

A

1	2	3	4
1. <u>welcome</u>	1. boarded	1. eleventh	1. doctor
2. <u>aboard</u>	2. clothing	2. remembering	2. guy
3. <u>baggage</u>	3. checkered	3. questioned	3. route
4. <u>toothbrush</u>	4. adults	4. scientists	4. Tokyo
5. <u>underlined</u>	5. provided		5. packed
			6. suit

B

More About Japan

In today's story, you will read about Wendy in Japan.

The map shows the route that her jet plane took to Japan. Name the country the jet left from.

In which direction did the jet fly?

The jet landed in a city in Japan. Name that city.

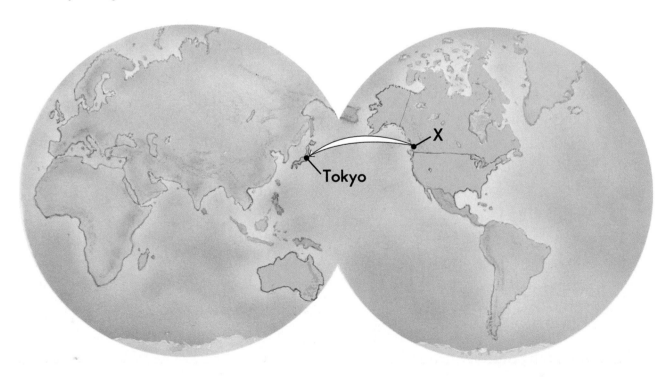

C A Surprise at the Space Station

From the space station, Wendy could see the city of Tokyo, the largest city in Japan. The space station was about twenty miles from Tokyo. Wendy stood in front of the large window and looked down at the beautiful city. She had traveled by jet from Canada to Japan. She had landed at the Tokyo airport. Five other students who were going on the trip to Jupiter were on Wendy's flight. Newspaper reporters met the students at the Tokyo airport. They questioned the students about how they felt about being selected to go on this trip. Wendy said that it was the most important thing that had ever happened to her.

At the airport, Wendy and the other students had boarded a special bus that took them from the airport to the space station. As Wendy looked out of the window, she wondered if she had packed everything she would need on the trip. Part of the letter that told her that she had been selected was a list of things that she should take with her. The list named things like toothbrush and clothing. Part of the letter was underlined: "Your baggage must not weigh more than 100 pounds."

Wendy had her camera, three books, paper and pencils. She didn't have room for her computer and some of the other things she had wanted to take. In fact, before she packed, she had her room filled with things that she wanted to take. But she had to leave most of them behind.

She walked from the window and sat down next to one of the boys who was going on the trip. His name was Bob. She said, "Do you have your list of students?"

"Yeah," he said. He opened a little bag and pulled out the list. She didn't know any of the other students who were going. Sidney's name was not on the list. For a moment Wendy felt sad, remembering how Sidney looked after the test. Wendy imagined how Sidney must have felt today, knowing that the other students were going ⭐ on the trip.

Wendy told herself not to think about Sidney. She asked Bob, "Do you know any of the other kids who are going on this trip?"

"Well, I did," he said. "Tim Mallory was supposed to go, but he's very sick and he can't make it. That poor guy."

"That must be terrible," Wendy said.

"I'm here!" a voice shouted from behind Wendy. "I'm here!"

Wendy turned around and looked. She couldn't believe what she saw.

There was Sidney, standing in a checkered coat with her arms stretched out from her sides. She was laughing. "I'm here!" she repeated.

Wendy jumped up, ran over to Sidney, and threw her arms around her. "Wow," Wendy said. "I can't believe it."

"Me neither," Sidney said. "But I'm here."

"But your name is not on the list," Wendy said.

"That's because I shouldn't be here," Sidney said. "I guess I had the eleventh-highest score." Sidney explained, "They called me last night and told me that somebody got sick and couldn't go. They asked if I could go. Could I go? Could I go?" She laughed. "Could I go? You bet I could."

She grabbed Wendy's shoulders and started to dance and laugh. "What a joke. Could I go? I'm here." The space station was filled with people. Many of them were smiling at Wendy and Sidney.

Suddenly a voice over the loudspeaker said, "Traveler Four will be leaving for Jupiter in fifteen minutes."

Wendy ran over and picked up her bag. She opened it and pulled out her papers. One of the things she had to do before she took the test was to get a report from her doctor. The report told that she was in good health.

She lined up with the other passengers. Most of them were scientists. People did not go to Jupiter for vacations. In fact, very few people went there. Only the most important people had that chance, and only adults had gone in the past. Wendy was in the first group of young people to make the trip.

The voice over the loudspeaker said, "Welcome aboard Traveler Four."

D Number your paper from 1 through 20.

Skill Items

Here are three events that happened in the story.
Write **beginning, middle,** or **end** for each event.

1. Wendy imagined how Sidney must have felt today, knowing that the other students were going on the trip.

2. Newspaper reporters met the students at the airport in Tokyo.

3. The voice over the loudspeaker said, "Welcome aboard Traveler Four."

Write the word from the box that means that same thing as the underlined part of each sentence.

concluded	moaned	ignore	practiced
glance	directed	divided	purchase

4. They will <u>buy</u> a new house next year.
5. We <u>finished</u> our meal with apple pie.
6. She <u>worked on</u> playing the piano.

Use the words in the box to write complete sentences.

worried	gravity	weightless	comfortable
final	equipment	nervous	magnetic	selected

7. She ▨ a ▨ seat.
8. Without ▨, they were ▨.

Review Items

Use these names to answer the questions:
Tyrannosaurus, Triceratops.

9. What is animal **R?**

10. What is animal **T?**

11. What runs an electric eye?

For each picture, tell if the lights in the room are **on** or **off.** The solid arrows show people going into the room. The dotted arrows show people leaving the room.

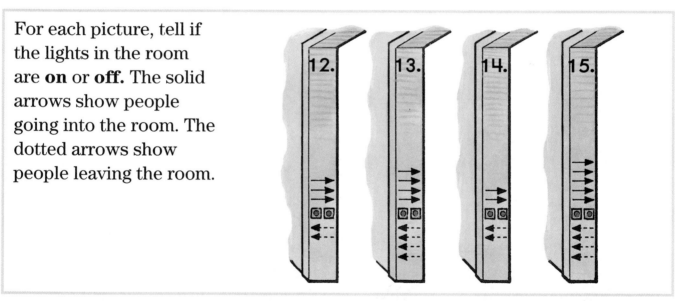

16. The earth is shaped like a ▬▬.

17. The hottest part of the earth is called the ▬▬.

   • pole   • desert   • equator

18. What's the name of the line that goes around the fattest part of the earth?

19. What's the name of the spot that's at the top of the earth?

20. What's the name of the spot that's at the bottom of the earth?

A

1
1. demonstrate
2. computer
3. breakfast
4. aisle
5. gravity

2
1. tremble
2. cabinet
3. darkness
4. oxygen
5. equipment
6. keyboard

3
1. palms
2. gaining
3. guests
4. partly
5. helmets
6. provided

4
1. survive
2. pressure
3. waist
4. suit

5
1. liquid
2. baggage
3. weightless
4. fastened

B

Traveler Four

The inside of Traveler Four was beautiful. It looked even better than the pictures Wendy had seen. The seats were dark red and very comfortable. You could lean them all the way back to form a bed. In front of every pair of seats was a cabinet. Inside the cabinet were two space suits and two space helmets. There was also a little table for writing just below the computer keyboard. And there was even a little TV screen. You could select movies by pressing a button. Or you could just press a button for computer games.

Sidney sat next to Wendy. They kept looking at each other and smiling, but Wendy felt very nervous. She noticed that the palms of her hands were sweaty. And the inside of her mouth felt very dry.

Suddenly, a sharp screeching noise came from below. Then a voice came over the loudspeaker. "You'll hear some strange noises," the voice said. "The one you just heard was the elevator in the cargo section below you."

Wendy noticed that a flight attendant was standing in front of

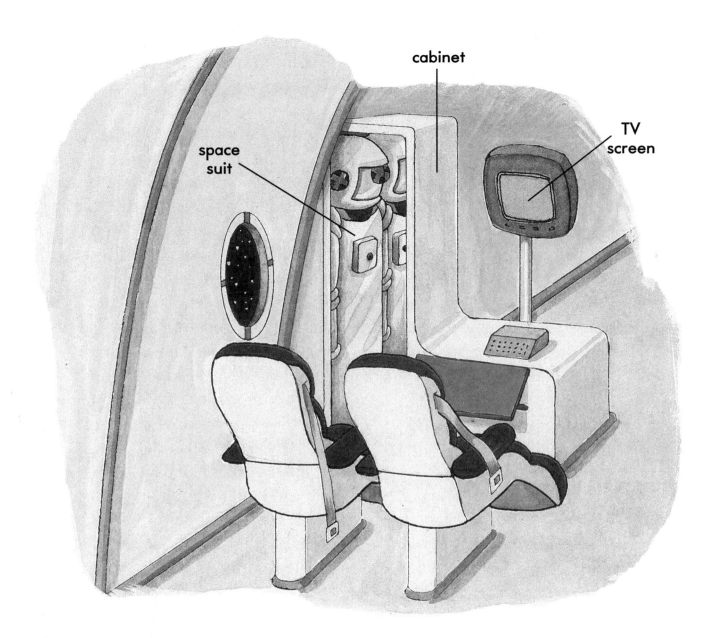

space
suit

cabinet

TV
screen

the passenger section. He said, "I will tell you about the equipment on this spaceship. As you know, there is no oxygen in space. And there is none on Jupiter." The flight attendant continued, "Each passenger has a space suit and all the special equipment needed to survive in space." The attendant said, "When we get close to Jupiter,

I'll show you how to work your space suits and your tanks of oxygen. Until then do not take your suit from the cabinet."

A loud blowing sound seemed to come from behind the passenger section. The flight attendant said, "Those are the engines. We're ready to take off. So lean your seats halfway back. Fasten the seat belts around your waist and across your shoulders."

The flight attendant said, "You will feel a great deal of pressure when the ship takes off because the spaceship is picking up speed very fast. You'll feel as if you're being pressed very hard into your seat. The pressure is no more than you would feel if somebody were sitting on your chest. The pressure lasts for only a few minutes." The flight attendant said, "Remember, when the pressure starts fading, you'll be able to sit up and look out of the window." The flight attendant concluded, "If this is your first trip, you'll be very impressed with what you see when you look out the window."

Wendy leaned her seat halfway back. She fastened the belts around her waist and across her shoulders. Her lips felt very dry. The blowing sound was becoming very loud now, very unpleasant. A voice was saying something over the loudspeaker, but Wendy couldn't hear it over the blowing sound.

The blowing sound was now a roar that seemed to make the spaceship tremble. Then the roar got so loud that Wendy wanted to hold her hands over her ears. Then she felt as if something was pushing her back in her seat. The ship was moving very fast. It had taken off. The roar was even louder. The ship was trembling. For an instant, Wendy was afraid that it might fall apart. But then she told herself that the spaceship was probably going through layers of air so fast that it felt like a car going over a bumpy road. Wendy guessed that the ship was probably already fifteen or twenty miles from Earth and gaining more speed. The pressure was not as great. And the roaring sound suddenly disappeared. Everything was silent. That meant that the ship was now moving faster than the speed of sound. The engines were in the back of the ship. But their sound could not catch up to the front of the ship where Wendy was. So there was no roaring. No noise. And the trembling stopped.

A voice over the loudspeaker said, "Ladies, gentlemen, and special guests, if you want to see the planet Earth as you've never seen it before, look out the window."

Wendy leaned forward and looked out the window. She saw the most beautiful sight she had ever seen. There was a huge green and blue ball, partly covered with white streaks. Part of the ball was in darkness. It was Earth.

C Number your paper from 1 through 20.

Review Items

1. What's the largest city in Japan?

2. How many heat lines are hitting place P on the map?

3. How many heat lines are hitting place R?

4. Write the letter of the place that's the hottest.

5. Write the letter of the place that's the coldest.

6. Write the letter of the place that has the warmest winters.

7. Why is place R hotter than place P?

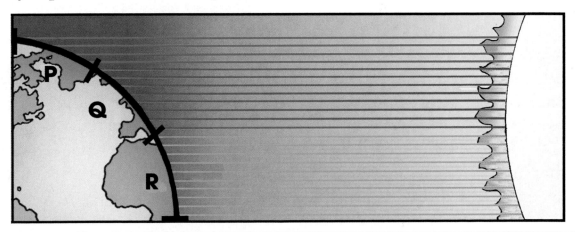

8. Write the letter of the layer that went into the pile **first.**

9. Write the letter of the layer that went into the pile **next.**

10. Which layer went into the pile **earlier,** A or D?

11. Write the letter of the layer where we find the skeletons of dinosaurs.

12. Write the letter of the layer where we find the skeletons of horses.

13. Write the letter of the layer we live on.

14. What's the name of layer C?

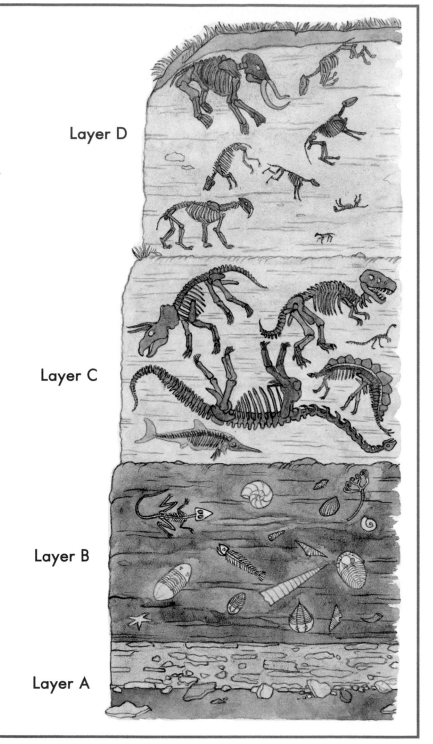

Layer D

Layer C

Layer B

Layer A

15. How many poles are there?

16. The farther you go from the equator, the � it gets.
- colder
- fatter
- hotter

17. At which letter would the winters be very, very cold?

18. At which letter would the winters be very, very hot?

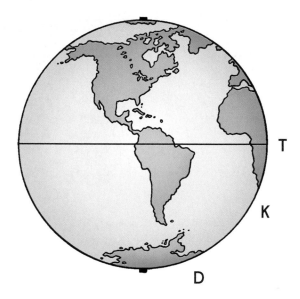

19. The sun shines ▓▓▓.

 • some of the time   • all of the time

20. Can you see the sun all day long and all night long?

A

1	2	3	4
1. upside	1. unfastened	1. demonstrate	1. complained
2. bathroom	2. appeared	2. shower	2. exercise
3. outside	3. rocketing	3. gravity	3. completed
4. workout	4. aimed	4. tank	4. incredible
5. weightless	5. brightly	5. liquid	5. computer
6. sideways			

B

Gravity

In today's story, you will read about gravity.

- Gravity is the force that pulls things back to a planet.
- When you drop something, gravity pulls it down to Earth.
- Not all planets have the same amount of gravity.
- Things weigh more on planets with stronger gravity. If the planet has gravity that is twice as strong as the gravity on Earth, you would weigh two times as much on that planet.

A person who weighs 100 pounds on Earth would weigh 200 pounds on that planet.

Our moon has gravity that is much less than the gravity on Earth. A person who weighs 100 pounds on Earth would weigh only 17 pounds on the moon. Remember, the stronger the gravity of a planet, the more you weigh on that planet.

The planets that have the greatest gravity are the very large planets. On Jupiter, a 100-pound person would weigh more than 200 pounds.

C

The Gravity Device

The people on the spaceship looked out their windows at Earth. They watched it get smaller as the spaceship streaked off into space. The sky in all directions was black now, but the sun was shining brightly. Wendy knew why there was no blue sky. She knew that the sky around Earth looked blue because there was a layer of air around Earth. The spaceship was above the layer of air around Earth.

Now there was nothing outside the spaceship, just empty space.

Because there was no air, the spaceship did not have to use its engines anymore. The pilot just aimed the spaceship in the direction it was supposed to go and then turned off the engines. The spaceship continued to move in that direction. It didn't slow down because there was no air outside to slow it down. There was no strong gravity to pull the spaceship back toward Earth.

A flight attendant appeared in front of the passenger section. She said, "The Traveler Four has a new invention that has not been on any of the earlier Travelers. This invention is a gravity device. It makes you feel just like you do on Earth. If you drop something inside this spaceship, the object falls down. You can stand up and walk on the floor because the gravity device will always pull you down."

The flight attendant continued, "But when the gravity device is not turned on, there is no gravity. And things float without falling. I'll show you how that works."

Wendy heard a high buzzing sound for an instant. Then she felt a little different. She looked at the flight attendant at the front of the passenger section and she could hardly believe what she saw. The flight attendant was not standing on the floor. She was floating in the air about a meter off the floor.

"I'll give you ⭐ a chance to see what it feels like to be weightless. But I would like to warn you about liquids. Let me demonstrate."

The flight attendant held up a paper cup that was covered. She took the cover off and slowly moved the cup downward, leaving a blob of orange juice floating in the air. It was in the same shape it had been when it was in the cup. Now the flight attendant blew on the blob very gently. The blob began to change shape and move away from her. She said, "If I hit this liquid, it will break into a million tiny drops. That's dangerous, because it will make breathing very difficult."

She took a large bag and caught all but a little part of the floating liquid. Then she said, "Watch." And she hit the little blob. It turned into something like a cloud of dust.

"Okay," she said to the passengers. "Take off your seat belts and float around. Don't try to move too fast, or you may hurt yourself."

Wendy had already unfastened her seat belts. She pushed up and floated out of her seat. She looked around. There was Sidney upside down, floating near the ceiling of the spaceship. And there were the other passengers, floating this way and that way, just like a bunch of fish in a fish tank. Wendy laughed. A couple of students were dancing in space. People were bumping into each other.

After a few minutes, the flight attendant said, "Okay, we're going to turn on the gravity device very slowly. You'll find yourself sinking slowly to the floor."

As soon as she finished talking, Wendy felt herself falling slowly to the floor. She stood up. Then she felt herself getting heavier and heavier until she felt like she always did when she stood on Earth. "Wow," she said to Sidney. "That was great."

D Number your paper from 1 through 19.

1. Look at planet A and planet B. Which planet has more gravity?
2. How do you know?

A

B

Skill Items

She demonstrated how animals use oxygen.

3. What word means **showed?**
4. What word names the part of the air you need to survive?

Review Items

5. What are clouds made of?
6. What kind of cloud does the picture show?
7. What happens to a drop of water at **B?**

8. In what part of a spaceship are the engines?
9. The sound of the engines can't reach the passenger section because the spaceship ▢▢▢▢.

Look at the map below.

10. What's the name of the place shown by the letter **E?**

11. Which letter shows the coldest place?

12. Which letter shows the hottest place?

13. Which letter is farthest from the equator?

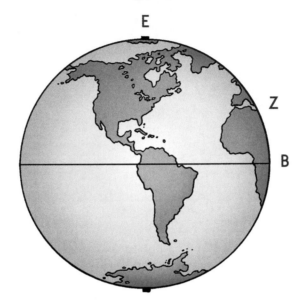

14. Which is bigger, Alaska or Japan?

15. Is Japan a **state** or a **country?**

16. How many people live in Japan?

- 127
- 127 million
- 127 thousand

17. Write the letters of **3** types of products that are used in the United States and manufactured in Japan.

a. rugs
b. CD players
c. Mr. Light Saver
d. TVs
e. books
f. furniture
g. cars

18. The arrow on the map goes from San Francisco to ▢▢▢.
19. Which ocean does the arrow cross?

San Francisco

A

1
1. Io
2. surround
3. instead
4. view
5. area

2
1. circling
2. completed
3. complained
4. bathrooms
5. rocketing

3
1. snored
2. showers
3. serving
4. striped
5. exercises
6. erupting

4
1. incredible
2. aisle
3. breakfast
4. outside
5. sideways
6. workout

5
1. we're
2. were
3. we'll
4. well

B

Jupiter

By dinner time of the first day, Traveler Four had traveled over forty million miles. The spaceship had gone past the planet Mars. That planet looked red. It didn't have many clouds around it, like Earth does. The flight attendant told the passengers about Mars. But Wendy already knew everything the flight attendant said.

Wendy knew that Mars is smaller than Earth. It is also colder because it is much farther from the sun than Earth is.

Sleeping on a spaceship was comfortable enough, but Wendy didn't sleep much that first night. It was very quiet in the spaceship. Nearly all the lights were turned off.

Wendy had moved her seat all the way back so that it became a bed. The only sounds in the spaceship were the buzzing sounds of the gravity device and the sounds of people snoring. Sidney snored very loudly.

From time to time, Wendy went to sleep, but then she would wake

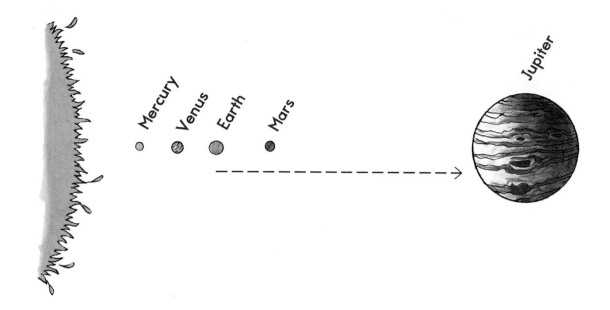

up, feeling strange. For a moment, she wouldn't remember where she was. Then she would look around and remember that she was over fifty million miles from Earth, rocketing through space at one thousand miles per second.

Outside the spaceship, the sun shined brightly, but the sun was getting smaller, because the spaceship was moving away from it.

At 7 the next morning, the lights came on inside the spaceship and people got up. People had to wait in line to use the bathrooms. They took showers, brushed their teeth and changed their clothes. Then they exercised. Not everybody could exercise at the same time because there wasn't enough room. The flight attendants divided the passengers into three groups. The

people in the front of the passenger section were in the first group. Wendy was in the second group. The first group got out in the aisles and did their exercises. They jumped up and down one hundred times. They did as many push-ups as they could. They did sit-ups. They ran in place. They did stretching exercises. Some of the passengers complained.

"You need this exercise," the flight attendant in front of the passenger section said. "We're going to be in this ship for a long time, and you'll get weak if you just sit all that time."

Now the first ★ group sat down and Wendy's group got up. "Now we'll show you how to do it," one of the men in Wendy's group said. "We can do better than the first group."

"Yeah," some of the other people in group two shouted.

So Wendy and the others worked very hard at their exercises. After each exercise, somebody would shout, "We're number one!"

Some of the people in the first group were saying things like, "Boo for group two." But they weren't serious. Everybody was laughing. Some people in the third group said things like, "We can beat both those other groups."

Wendy was tired when the exercises were finished. Her heart was pounding and she was sweating. Sidney said, "That was a good workout."

Now the third group was doing their exercises. "Booooo!" Sidney shouted. "We were twice as good as that group!"

After the exercises were completed, the flight attendants served a big breakfast. As soon as the attendants started serving the people in front of Wendy, she realized that she was very hungry. Wendy ate her breakfast very fast. Sidney didn't eat her roll, so she gave it to Wendy. "I don't know why I'm so hungry," Wendy said, "but I could eat a horse."

Wendy slept well that night. The next day she got up, did her exercises, studied, ate lunch, studied

some more and took a nap in the afternoon. When she woke up, the pilot was talking over the loudspeaker. She said, "We're going to turn the spaceship sideways so that you can ✿ see Jupiter. It is quite a sight."

Slowly, the ship turned. It continued to move in the same direction it had been moving, but it was now moving sideways. Wendy pressed close to the window. And there it was, the largest planet in the solar system—Jupiter. It looked huge. Wendy could clearly see seven moons. She knew that there were 56 others, but she couldn't see them. The planet looked like a great striped ball, with the stripes circling the planet. Some stripes were dark brown, some were orange and some were white. For a moment, Wendy couldn't talk. She heard the other passengers saying things like, "Isn't that beautiful?" and "Incredible!"

C Number your paper from 1 through 21.

Skill Items

Write the word from the box that means the same thing as the underlined part of each sentence.

arithmetic	kneeled	device	tone	mentioned
pace	chuckle	hesitated	energy	suppose

1. He <u>paused for a moment</u> at the corner.
2. I <u>think</u> you know his mother.
3. She <u>quickly told about</u> the movie.
4. The baby's <u>little laugh</u> woke me up.
5. They did their <u>math</u> homework after dinner.

Use the words in the box to write complete sentences.

fancy	demonstrated	appeared	weightless
gravity	headline	oxygen	guessed

6. Without ▮▮▮▮, they were ▮▮▮▮.
7. She ▮▮▮▮ how animals use ▮▮▮▮.

Review Items

8. If something weighted 100 pounds on Earth, how many pounds would it weigh on our moon?

   - 10 pounds   • 17 pounds   • 47 pounds

9. If you drop something on Earth, it falls to the ground. What makes it fall?

10. A person weighs 300 pounds on planet R and 200 pounds on planet T. Which planet has stronger gravity?

11. Planet J has stronger gravity than planet K. On which of those planets would you weigh more?

12. How many suns are in the solar system?

13. How many planets are in the solar system?

14. Write the letter of the best deal for an inventor.

15. Write the letter of the best deal for a manufacturer.

   a. 10 thousand dollars and 3 dollars for every copy sold
   b. 10 thousand dollars and 5 dollars for every copy sold
   c. 10 thousand dollars and 1 dollar for every copy sold

16. Write the letter of the footprint made by the heaviest animal.

17. Write the letter of the footprint made by the lightest animal.

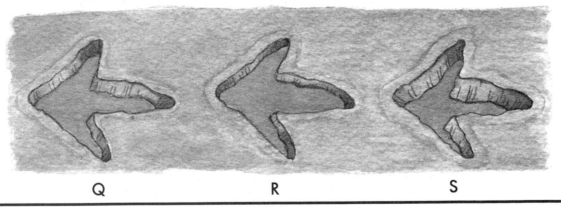

Q   R   S

18. Which is larger, Earth or Saturn?

19. If an object weighed 20 pounds on Earth, would it weigh **more than 20 pounds** or **less than 20 pounds** on Saturn?

20. If an object weighed 20 pounds on Earth, would it weigh more than 20 pounds on our moon?

21. Which planets have stronger gravities, the bigger planets or the smaller planets?

Number your paper from 1 through 36.

1. Name the planet we live on.

2. What's in the middle of the solar system?
3. Name the only part of the solar system that's burning.

4. Is Earth the planet that is closest to the sun?
5. The sun gives ▮▮▮ and ▮▮▮ to all the planets.
6. What's the largest city in Japan?

7. The planets are named below with Mercury first and Venus second. **Write the names of all the planets, including the missing planets.**

   Mercury, Venus, Earth, ▮▮▮, Jupiter, ▮▮▮, Uranus, ▮▮▮, Pluto.

8. Which planet is largest?
9. Which planet is next-largest?

10. How many moons does Saturn have?
11. How many moons does Jupiter have?
12. How far is it from Earth to Jupiter?
    - 40 million miles
    - 400 million miles
    - 800 million miles
13. How many times larger than Earth is the sun?
    - 500
    - 200
    - 100

14. How many suns are in the solar system?
15. How many planets are in the solar system?

16. The arrow on the map goes from San Francisco to ▮▮▮.
17. Which ocean does the arrow cross?

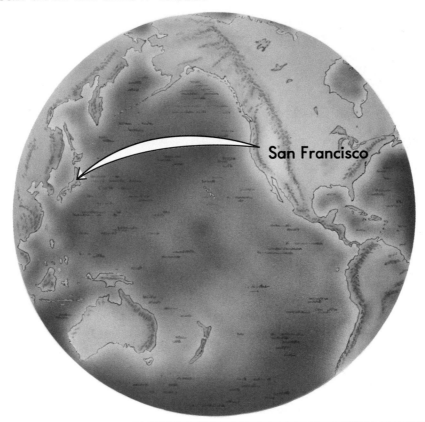

San Francisco

18. Which is smaller, Alaska or Japan?
19. Is Japan a **state** or a **country?**
20. If something weighed 20 pounds on Earth, would it weigh more than 20 pounds on our moon?
21. Which is larger, Earth or Saturn?
22. If an object weighed 20 pounds on Earth, would it weigh **more than 20 pounds** or **less than 20 pounds** on Saturn?
23. A person weighs 100 pounds on planet A and 90 pounds on planet B. Which planet has stronger gravity?
24. Planet P has stronger gravity than planet R. On which of those planets would you weigh more?

25. Which planet has more clouds around it, Earth or Mars?
26. Which planet is bigger?
27. Which planet is warmer?
28. Why is that planet warmer?

29. If something weighed 100 pounds on Earth, how many pounds would it weigh on our moon?

- 57 pounds
- 7 pounds
- 17 pounds

30. If you drop something on Earth, it falls to the ground. What makes it fall?

Skill Items

For each item, write the underlined word or words from the sentences in the box.

> Without <u>gravity</u>, they were <u>weightless</u>.
> She <u>demonstrated</u> how animals use <u>oxygen</u>.
> She <u>selected</u> a <u>comfortable</u> seat.

31. What underlining tells that the seat felt pleasant?
32. What underlining means that something has no weight?
33. What underlining means **chose?**
34. What underlining names the force that pulls things back to Earth?
35. What underlining means **showed?**
36. What underlining names the part of the air you need to survive?

END OF TEST 6

A

1
1. receive
2. assigned
3. telescope
4. lava

2
1. equipped
2. gases
3. erupting
4. surrounded
5. towers
6. impressive

3
1. dome
2. restless
3. instead
4. view
5. soup
6. program

B

Io

The last two days of the trip went slowly. Wendy didn't sleep well on the last night. Wendy was getting very restless. She could hardly wait to get to Jupiter. Actually, the spaceship would not land on Jupiter. It would land on one of Jupiter's larger moons, named Io. Jupiter has a gravity that is much stronger than that of Earth. A large man weighs about 200 pounds on Earth. That same man would weigh 500 pounds on Jupiter. That man would weigh so much on Jupiter that he could hardly stand up. He would feel as if he were carrying two people on his back.

There was another reason that the spaceship would not land on the surface of Jupiter. The planet is surrounded by a thick layer of gas. The surface of the planet is dark. Even with bright lights, it is impossible to see more than a few meters.

So instead of landing on the surface of Jupiter, Traveler Four would land on Io, a moon about as big as our moon. Io is very close to the surface of Jupiter. There are no gases surrounding Io. In fact, there is nothing but empty space surrounding Io. Io floats through space. And it moves around Jupiter very fast. Io goes all the way around Jupiter in about two days.

The last morning on Traveler Four was very busy. The flight attendants showed the passengers how to put on their space suits. "Remember," one of the flight attendants said, "there is no oxygen on Io. There is oxygen inside the space station, but when you go outside, you must wear your space suit or you'll die."

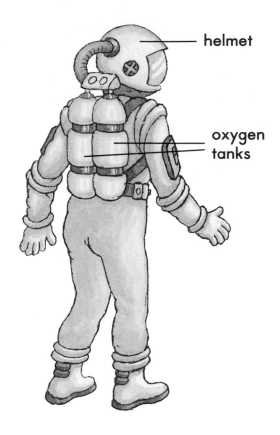

helmet

oxygen tanks

The attendant continued, "When you leave the space station, you must go with another person. Your space suit is equipped with an automatic radio that tells you where you are and how to get back to the space station. The radio also tells you how much more air you have in your oxygen tanks."

The space suit was very heavy. The flight attendants helped Wendy and the other passengers get into their suits. Two large tanks were attached to the back of each space suit. These tanks held oxygen that the person would breathe.

Look at the picture of the space suit.

The passengers could hardly walk in their space suits. "Don't

worry," the flight attendant said. "Io is quite a bit smaller than Earth. So the gravity on Io is less than it is on Earth. That means that you won't feel very heavy ⭐ in your space suit when you walk around on Io. In fact, you should be able to jump 8 feet high on Io. That should make you feel like a super basketball player."

After the passengers walked around in their space suits, they took them off and put them away.

In the middle of the afternoon, the engines of the spaceship started up. "The engines are slowing us down," a flight attendant explained. "It will take us about three hours to slow to the same speed that Io is going."

The view outside the window was incredible. The planet Jupiter was so huge that it seemed to cover half the sky. From time to time, the flight attendant pointed out interesting

facts about the planet. At one time she said, "If you look at the lower half of the planet, you'll see a part that looks something like an eye." Wendy could see it clearly. The attendant said, "That eye is two times as big as Earth."

Wendy shook her head. "Incredible," she said.

As the spaceship got close to Io, the attendant said, "If you look closely, you'll see that there are volcanos on Io. New volcanos erupt all the time. There is a volcano near the top of the moon that is erupting right now."

Wendy looked closely at the moon. Near the top of it, she could see a very thin line of smoke moving up from one of the volcanos. The engines started to slow the ship with greater force. It felt as if something was pulling the ship backward very hard. But the ship was still moving faster than the moon.

Now Wendy could see the space station on the moon. It was a large dome with three towers next to it. Sidney said, "It must have been a hard job to build that station."

Wendy agreed. The spaceship was now getting ready to land on Io.

C Number your paper from 1 through 18.

Story Items

Answer these questions about Jupiter and Io.
1. Which has **more** gravity?
2. Which is **smaller** than Earth?
3. Where can you jump 8 feet high?

4. Which has a stronger gravity, Earth or Jupiter?
5. So where would you feel lighter?

Review Items

6. How many moons does Saturn have?
7. How many moons does Jupiter have?
8. How far is it from Earth to Jupiter?
   - 400 million miles
   - 800 million miles
   - 40 million miles
9. If something weighed 40 pounds on Earth, would it weigh more than 40 pounds on our moon?

10. Which is larger, Earth or Saturn?
11. If an object weighed 40 pounds on Earth, would it weigh **more than 40 pounds** or **less than 40 pounds** on Saturn?

12. When a gravity device is turned on, do things float in the air or fall to the floor?
13. Planet Q has stronger gravity than planet R. On which of those planets would you weigh less?
14. Which planets have stronger gravities, the bigger planets or the smaller planets?

15. Which planet has more clouds around it, Earth or Mars?
16. Which planet is smaller?
17. Which planet is colder?
18. Why is that planet colder?

62

A

1
1. suitcase
2. crunchy
3. program
4. receive
5. Samson
6. close-up

2
1. assigned
2. impressive
3. zipped
4. telescopes
5. unpacked
6. bubbling

3
1. overhang
2. crackle
3. splattered
4. crater
5. warned

4
1. film
2. area
3. lava
4. leak
5. soup

B

Planets and Gravity

You've learned a lot of facts about planets. Here are some of the more important facts.

- Bigger planets have stronger gravity. Smaller planets have weaker gravity.
- The stronger the gravity on a planet, the more somebody would weigh on that planet.
- If a person weighs 100 pounds on Earth, the person will weigh more than 100 pounds on planets that have stronger gravity than Earth. The person will weigh less than 100 pounds on planets that have weaker gravity than Earth.

- A person who weighs 100 pounds on Earth weighs over twice as much on Jupiter but weighs only 17 pounds on our moon.
- Saturn has 47 moons. Jupiter has 63 moons. Earth has one moon.
- Io is the moon that is closest to Jupiter.
- It takes about 2 days for Io to go all the way around Jupiter.
- There is no oxygen around Io and no oxygen around our moon.
- A person can jump 8 feet high on Io.

The Space Station on Io

As Traveler Four approached Io, the engines came on with great force. The engines didn't sound the way they sounded near Earth because there was no air around Io. So Wendy didn't hear the great roaring sounds of the engines. But she felt the engines buzzing and making everything inside the spaceship tremble.

Traveler Four floated slowly down to the surface of the moon, right between two towers. When it landed, the passengers clapped and cheered. Wendy could hardly wait to leave the ship. The flight attendants helped the passengers get into their space suits. The attendants checked everybody to make sure that they had zipped up the suit so that no air would leak out.

One flight attendant announced that the suits would not feel heavy because the pilot had turned off the gravity device. With the gravity device turned off, Wendy felt much lighter than she did on Earth.

The flight attendant talked to the passengers over the radio that was in their helmets. "Go directly into the space station. Inside you will receive information about Io. You will also receive a map of the places you may visit on Io. You can pick up your baggage inside the space station."

The attendant continued, "We're going to let the air out of the spaceship now. You may feel a little dizzy for a few seconds. Take your time and walk slowly to the space station."

Wendy waited with the other passengers as the air was let out of Traveler Four. Then the doors opened and the passengers walked outside. Wendy felt very light as she left the spaceship. The ground was crunchy. She took a couple of steps on it. Then she decided to take a little jump. She jumped about five feet high. She started to laugh and was ready to jump again when she heard a voice over her radio. "Take it easy," the voice said. "Just walk to the space station."

Before walking inside the space station, Wendy turned around and looked at Io. She could see three volcanos, but they were not erupting. One was very close to the space station. The sky was almost completely covered by Jupiter. It was the biggest thing that Wendy had ever seen. And it was beautiful. The sight of Jupiter was so impressive that she just stood there, looking.

"Keep moving," a voice said over the radio. "There will ⭐ be lots of time to look at Jupiter later on."

The inside of the space station looked very strange. There was a large meeting area in the middle of the dome. Around one side were tiny rooms. Each passenger was assigned one of these rooms. Wendy's room was right next to Sidney's room. The rooms were so small that there was just enough space inside for a bed and a chair. Wendy hung her space suit in the closet and unpacked her suitcase. She took out her camera and made sure that there was film in it. Then she went out into the meeting area.

A very tall man told the passengers to sit down. "Welcome to Io," he said. "My name is Rod Samson. I know that most of you will be busy during most of the day, but everybody will have time to look around. Everybody will get a map that shows the places you might visit."

Rod Samson continued, "The favorite spot that people visit is a volcano about half a mile away. We call it Soup Pot because it has a large lake of lava just inside the cone. And the lava boils and bubbles like a great pot of boiling soup. It's safe to walk around the rim of Soup Pot because it has given no signs that it will erupt. But be careful when you walk around the rim. If you fall inside, there won't be much left of you."

"Let's go there," Sidney said. "I've never seen the inside of a volcano."

"Me, neither," Wendy said.

Rod Samson told about other things that people might look at on Io. Then he pointed to a row of telescopes near the windows of the space station. "Of course, you may want to look at Jupiter. Through those telescopes you can get a close-up view of the clouds that surround the great planet. Also, we have thousands of pictures of Jupiter. And we have hundreds of books and CD-ROMs that show and tell everything we know about the planet. If you look on the back of your map, you'll find a list of the more important facts about Jupiter. The planet is bigger than all the other planets in the solar system put together. It spins around one time every ten hours. The gases that surround it are poisonous."

When the meeting was over, Sidney said, "Let's go see the volcano."

 **Number your paper from 1 through 22.**

Skill Items

> **Lava erupted from the volcano's crater.**

1. What word means **coughed out** or **spit out?**

2. What word means **melted rock?**

3. What do we call the enormous dent at the top of a volcano?

Review Items

4. The gravity device is off. What would happen if you hit a big blob of floating liquid?

5. Do things fall to the floor when the gravity device is off?

6. A person weighs 100 pounds on planet A and 300 pounds on planet B. Which planet has stronger gravity?

7. Which planets have stronger gravities, the bigger planets or the smaller planets?

8. Which has a stronger gravity, Earth or Jupiter?

9. So where would you feel **lighter?**

10. Could you see very far on Jupiter with bright lights?

11. Does Io move around Jupiter **fast** or **slowly?**

12. It takes Io about ▩ to go all the way around Jupiter.

13. When a person makes an object for the first time, the person _____ the object.

14. Write the letter of the clouds that have frozen drops of water.
15. Write the letter of the clouds that may stay in the sky for days at a time.
16. Write the letter of the storm clouds.

A

B

C

17. Female animals fight in the spring to protect _____.
18. Name **2** kinds of Alaskan animals that are dangerous in the spring.
19. Which came **earlier** on Earth, dinosaurs or horses?
20. Which came **earlier** on Earth, strange sea animals or dinosaurs?

- On planet A you can jump 10 feet high.
- On planet B you can jump 30 feet high.
- On planet C you can jump 5 feet high.
- On planet D you can jump 20 feet high.
- On planet E you can jump 3 feet high.

21. Write the letter of the planet that has the most gravity.
22. Write the letter of the planet that has the least gravity.

1	2	3
1. manage	1. <u>over</u>hang	1. crater
2. numb	2. <u>close</u>-up	2. splattered
3. swallow	3. <u>rest</u>less	3. strings
4. vehicle	4. <u>suit</u>case	4. bubbling
	5. <u>red</u>-hot	5. crackle
	6. <u>butter</u>flies	6. warned
		7. tingles

A Trip to the Volcano

The temperature outside the space station was almost 200 degrees below zero. But Wendy was warm inside her space suit. She could look out through the helmet. She walked with Sidney toward the volcano. Little red flags were lined up along the path to mark the way to the volcano rim. The ground was crunchy and Wendy could feel it crackle under her feet as she walked along. Then she suddenly thought about running. She wondered how it would feel to run where you weigh much less than you weigh on Earth.

So she began running. Her first step must have covered nine feet. In a moment, she must have been running faster than a deer could run on Earth. And she wasn't even trying to go as fast as she could. She leaped high above the surface of Io

and landed as softly as a feather. "Wow," she said into her helmet, "this is great."

Sidney's voice answered, "Yeah. Watch this."

Wendy turned her head and saw Sidney running next to her. Sidney was leaping very high. Then suddenly she did a somersault above the surface of the ground and landed on her feet. "That's great," Wendy said.

"You are using up your oxygen too fast," a voice said over Wendy's radio. "If you keep using it this fast, your oxygen will last only 35 minutes."

"I'd better take it easy," Wendy said. The voice that warned her about the oxygen was part of the space suit. It was the automatic

radio that told how much oxygen was left.

Sidney said, "When we exercise very hard like that, we're using up much more oxygen than we do when we take it easy."

The girls slowed to a walk and continued toward the volcano. The red flags marked a path that circled around the right side of the volcano. The rim of the volcano was over half a mile above the surface of Io, but the climb was not difficult. Within half an hour the girls were standing on the huge rim that circled the volcano. They looked down inside the cone-shaped crater of the volcano. Sidney said, "Now I see why they call it Soup Pot."

About one hundred meters below the rim was lava. Most of it looked gray. There were cracks running through it. The cracks went this way and that way.

There were a few huge bubbling places. The bubbling lava was not gray. It was bright orange. And it boiled up slowly, making huge bubbles that burst slowly and splattered great strings of lava on the gray surface. These strings would slowly turn color as they cooled. They would first turn  a brown color. Then they would become more and more gray until you couldn't see them anymore.

Wendy knew that the lava was melted rock. When it cooled, it hardened into gray rock again. When it was boiling hot, it was like red-hot mud.

The crater of the volcano was very large. A city block could easily fit inside the volcano crater.

The girls stood on the rim for a few minutes, watching the lava boil and splatter. Then they started to walk around the rim. The path was marked with red flags. As they started to walk, the voice came over Wendy's radio. "Your oxygen supply will last 45 minutes if you keep using it as fast as you are using it."

Wendy thought, "If we have 45 minutes of oxygen, we should have plenty of time to walk around the rim and get back to the space station."

The girls walked around the rim until they came to a place where there was an overhang. The overhang was like a little shelf that stuck out about three meters over the rim. Sidney pointed to the overhang. "Let's stand out on the end of that overhang," she said.

The overhang looked scary. Wendy thought for a moment, then said, "Okay. Let's go out there."

So the girls walked onto the overhang. They walked to the end of it and looked down. They were almost above the lava. When Wendy looked down, she got a little dizzy looking at the boiling hot rock. Then suddenly, she felt the ground move. She quickly turned around and saw that the overhang was cracking off and starting to fall into the crater.

She started to run back to the rim, but it was too late. The overhang broke off with Wendy and Sidney standing on it. Wendy reached out and grabbed a rock on the edge of the rim. She felt Sidney behind her, trying to grab on to her. But Sidney could not hold on. She fell. Wendy could hear her yelling something over the radio, but Wendy couldn't turn around. She was hanging on to the rock with all her might.

 Number your paper from 1 through 18.

Skill Items

Use the words in the box to write complete sentences.

oxygen	crater	assigned	area	erupted
impressive	demonstrated		crackle	lava

1. She ▢▢ how animals use ▢▢.

2. ▢▢ ▢▢ from the volcano's ▢▢.

Here are 3 events that happened in the story. Write **beginning, middle** or **end** for each event.

3. Wendy and Sidney started walking toward the volcano.

4. She quickly turned around and saw that the overhang was cracking off and starting to fall into the crater.

5. Within half an hour, the girls were standing on the huge rim that circled the volcano.

Review Items

6. Name the largest city in Japan.

7. After Traveler Four took off, the pilot turned off the engines. Did the spaceship slow down?

8. Was there any air outside the spaceship?

9. Do gases surround Io?

10. How much oxygen surrounds Io?

11. Name the largest planet in the solar system.

12. How long does it take Jupiter to spin around one time?

13. Which has **more** gravity, Jupiter or Io?

14. Which is **smaller** than Earth?

15. Where can you jump 8 feet high?

16. In what season are animals most dangerous in Alaska?

17. During what season do female animals in Alaska have babies?

18. Write the letters of the 5 things that tell about Jupiter.

      a. It has stripes.

      b. It has 15 moons.

      c. It has more gravity than Earth.

      d. It's brown, orange and white.

      e. It's small.

      f. It's huge.

      g. It's green and blue.

      h. It's beautiful.

A

1	2	3
1. <u>tingles</u>	1. numb	1. slumped
2. <u>purple</u>	2. swallow	2. scariest
3. <u>managed</u>	3. vehicle	3. attaching
4. <u>butterflies</u>	4. shapes	4. smoked

B

Help

The overhang fell into the crater. Wendy had managed to grab the rim and hang on. She easily pulled herself up and stood up on the rim. She turned around and looked down into the crater. She could see the overhang sticking out of the lava. It was slowly sinking down. But where was Sidney?

Wendy looked at the surface of the lava. No Sidney. Then she looked near the edge of the lava. There was Sidney. She wasn't in the lava. She was hanging on to a rock and her feet were only a couple of meters above the lava.

"Help," Sidney shouted over the radio. "I think I'm slipping. Help me."

Wendy didn't know what to do. She couldn't climb down to where Sidney was, because the inside wall of the crater was almost straight up and down. Wendy didn't have a rope or any way to reach Sidney and pull her out.

"You just hang on," Wendy said. "I'll be right back."

Wendy started to run back to the space station. And this time, she ran as fast as she could go. Down the side of the volcano she went. She took steps that were four and five meters long. She leaped down the side of the mountain like a deer. The automatic voice came over her radio. "You are using your oxygen too fast. You will be out of oxygen in two minutes."

"I don't care," Wendy said and ran faster.

She reached the bottom of the volcano and ran toward the space station. When she was about 200 meters from the space station, another voice came over her radio. "Wendy, what's wrong?" the voice said. "You shouldn't be running that fast."

It was Rod Samson's voice.

"Sidney!" Wendy shouted. "She fell off the rim. She's almost in the lava. She . . . she . . . she can't hang on much longer."

"Stop right there," Rod shouted. "Just sit down and rest. We'll be there in less than a minute."

The automatic voice came over her radio. "You have fifteen seconds of oxygen left."

Wendy stopped running. She was breathing so hard that she couldn't catch her breath. "Sidney's in trouble," she yelled over her radio. "Help her . . . Help . . ."

"Don't say anything," Rod said over the radio. "Just sit down and take it easy."

"You are out of oxygen," the automatic voice said. Wendy sat down and realized that it was very hard to breathe. The harder she tried, the less she could breathe. She started to see spots in front of her eyes. Things were becoming purple and spotted. Her hands felt numb. She couldn't tell if she was sitting down or standing up. She wanted to cry. "Sidney," she said. "She's caught in the volcano. Help . . . her . . ." She shook her head and tried to clear the spots away. Her hands and arms were covered with tingles. Her mouth was dry. She tried to swallow but she couldn't. She tried to talk but nothing happened. Her voice wasn't working. She started to see butterflies—purple ones. She . . .

•   •   •

Wendy suddenly saw the shapes of people. "Help . . ." she said.

"Be quiet," a woman's voice said. Wendy realized that she was inside a vehicle that was bouncing over the surface of Io. Wendy's helmet was off. There was air inside the vehicle. Rod Samson was driving the vehicle. Another man was sitting next to him. A woman was in back with Wendy. The woman was attaching fresh oxygen tanks to Wendy's space suit.

Wendy tried to sit up, but the woman gently pushed her back down. The woman said, "Take it easy. We'll be up at the top of Soup Pot in just a minute."

"You've got to get there fast," Wendy said. "Sidney is just hanging on. She's . . ."

"We're going as fast as we can," the woman said. "Everything is going to be all right."

Wendy looked at the woman's face. The woman looked worried.

The woman said, "I'll put your helmet back on. You have fresh tanks of oxygen now."

Rod said to the woman, "Fasten her helmet. We're almost there."

The woman helped Wendy put on the helmet. The vehicle stopped. Wendy looked outside. The vehicle had stopped on the rim of Soup Pot, right near the place where the overhang had been.

C Number your paper from 1 through 19.

Review Items

1. Which planet is largest?

2. Which planet is next-largest?

3. How many times larger than Earth is the sun?

4. Write the names of the 9 planets, starting with Mercury.

5. If something weighed 100 pounds on Earth, how many pounds would it weigh on our moon?
   - 25 pounds
   - 100 pounds
   - 17 pounds

6. If something weighed 50 pounds on Earth, would it weigh more than 50 pounds on our moon?

7. Which is larger, Earth or Jupiter?

8. If an object weighed 50 pounds on Earth, would it weigh **more than 50 pounds** or **less than 50 pounds** on Jupiter?

9. If you drop something on Earth, it falls to the ground. What makes it fall?

10. What color is lava when it's very hot?
- gray   • orange   • brown

11. What color is lava after it cools a little bit?
- gray   • orange   • brown

12. What color is lava after it's completely cooled?
- gray   • orange   • brown

Use these names to answer the questions:
Tyrannosaurus, Triceratops.

13. What is animal **A?**

14. What is animal **B?**

15. The men who invented the first airplane saw a need. What need?

16. Captain Parker's ship passed through a place where hundreds of ships have sunk or been lost. Name that place.

17. Name 2 things that can make an ice chunk drift.

18. Which globe shows how the earth looks on the first day of winter?

19. Which globe shows how the earth looks on the first day of summer?

L

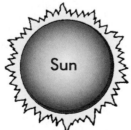

Sun

K

A

> 1
> 1. slumped
> 2. pale
> 3. sipped
> 4. scariest
> 5. smoked
> 6. tea
> 7. Terry

Sidney

"Where is she?" the woman asked as Wendy and the others got out of the vehicle.

Wendy led the way to the edge of the rim. She pointed down. "She's right there," Wendy said and pointed. But Sidney was not where she had been. Wendy could see the rock that Sidney had been hanging on to. But Sidney was no longer hanging on to that rock.

"Sidney," Wendy yelled over the radio. "Where are you? Sidney!"

The others started to call. Then Rod said, "Be quiet and listen." Nobody said anything. The only sounds that came over the radio were the sounds of people breathing.

Then suddenly a small voice came over the radio. "Help," it said.

It was Sidney's voice.

"There," Rod shouted and pointed straight down. Just above the rock that Sidney had been hanging on to was a little cave. A foot and leg of a space suit were sticking out of that cave. Sidney must have climbed up the rock and into that cave.

"Fasten the rope to the front of the vehicle," Rod told the other man. "I'm going down."

The other man took one end of the rope and tied it to the vehicle. Then Rod tossed the rest of the rope over the rim. Down and down it fell. The end of the rope reached the surface of the lava. It touched a part that was bright orange. The end of the rope smoked for a second. Wendy could see that the end had burned off.

Rod slid down the rope very fast. For a moment, it seemed as if he would slide right into the lava. He was swinging back and forth just a few meters above it. Some of the huge bubbles that were breaking sent strings of lava very close to him. He kept swinging until he was able to swing right into the little cave. Wendy could not see him now. She saw Sidney's leg disappear and she could hear Rod talking to Sidney.

"Are you hurt?" he asked.

"Just a little bit," she said. "But I'm very scared."

"I don't blame you," Rod said. "Climb onto my back and put your arms around my neck . . . There. That's good. Now just hang on tight and I'll get you out of here."

Rod then called, "Terry, back the vehicle up slowly. Back  away from the rim."

Terry ran to the vehicle and got in. A moment later, the vehicle began to move backward. The rope that was attached to it started to move up. Now Wendy could see Rod and Sidney. They swung out of the little cave and they were slowly swinging over the lava. Slowly, Rod

and Sidney moved up as the vehicle continued to back up. Up, up, up. Now they were almost at the rim.

"Okay, stop it there," Rod called. "We'll climb up the rest of the way."

Rod reached over the rim and began pulling himself up. Sidney was hanging tightly on to his neck. The woman helped pull Rod and Sidney onto the rim. Then she grabbed Sidney and helped her stand up. Sidney's face looked very pale. Wendy hugged her. "I'm so glad that you're okay," Wendy said.

"Me, too," Sidney said. "That was the scariest thing that ever happened to me. But I'm so glad that Rod . . . "

Everybody got into the vehicle. The vehicle moved slowly down the side of the volcano and along the row of flags back to the space station. A door opened in the space station and the vehicle went inside. The door closed behind the vehicle.

The woman helped Sidney from the vehicle. Then the others got out. They walked through a door to the meeting place in the space station. When they were inside, they took off their helmets. The woman helped Sidney to one of the chairs. Sidney slumped into the chair.

"I don't feel scared anymore," Sidney said. Then she added, "But am I ever tired. I feel as if I've been working for a hundred years."

Wendy said, "When we came back to the volcano and didn't see you, I thought I was going to die. I thought you had fallen into that lava."

"I was close," Sidney said. "I was hanging on to that rock. Then after a while I got one foot into a little crack in the rocks and I pushed up. I climbed into that cave."

"I'm glad," Wendy said.

Rod handed Sidney a cup of tea. "Sip this," he said. "Watch out. It's hot."

Sidney sipped the tea, looked up, and smiled. Then she said, "Oh, am I glad to be back here."

C Number your paper from 1 through 19.

Review Items

1. What planet is shown in the picture?
2. Which is bigger, the "eye" of the planet or Earth?

3. Which uses up more oxygen, jumping or sitting?

4. What's another name for hot, melted rock?

5. Write the names of the 9 planets, starting with the planet that's closest to the sun.

Write the name of each numbered object in the picture. Choose from these names:

- kayak
- fishing pole
- spear
- sled
- Eskimo
- sled dogs

12. Write the letter of the layer that went into the pile **first.**

13. Write the letter of the layer that went into the pile **next.**

14. Write the letter of the layer that went into the pile **last.**

15. Which layer went into the pile **earlier,** A or B?

16. Which layer went into the pile **earlier,** C or B?

17. Write the letter of the layer we live on.

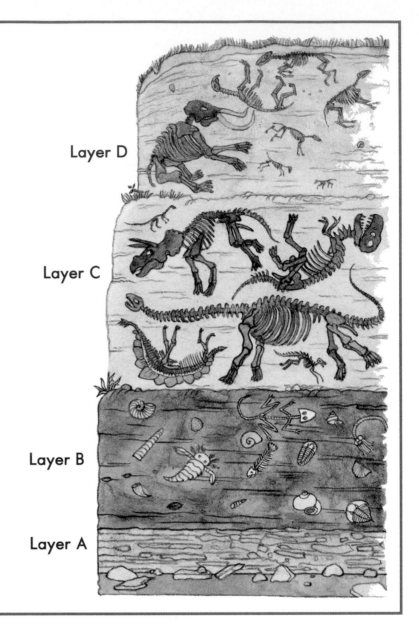

Layer D

Layer C

Layer B

Layer A

Study Items

Today's story told about a vehicle that goes on the surface of Io. No people have gone to Io yet. But people have gone from Earth to the moon. They have taken a vehicle with them. See if you can find out some facts about that vehicle.

18. Find out what makes it run.

19. Find out the name of the vehicle.

A

1
1. pigeon
2. giraffe
3. squirrel
4. spaghetti
5. ridiculous
6. Michael
7. serious

2
1. great
2. meals
3. ready
4. least
5. earn
6. clean

3
1. gather
2. enjoying
3. meow
4. hamburger
5. parrot
6. hometown

4
1. prepare
2. kitchen
3. zebra
4. yeah

B

Back to Earth

Wendy and Sidney and the other students stayed on Io for five days. They went with the scientists who were studying the rocks on Io. They went on a land vehicle that took them two hundred miles from the space station to a place where there were big volcanos—much bigger than Soup Pot. One of these big volcanos was erupting. The girls and the other students took pictures of the things they saw. Wendy took over two hundred pictures. She even took some pictures through a telescope. She attached her camera to one end of the telescope and took pictures of the eye of Jupiter. She also took pictures of some of the other parts of the huge planet. She took one picture of a small moon that looked as if it was almost touching the surface of Jupiter.

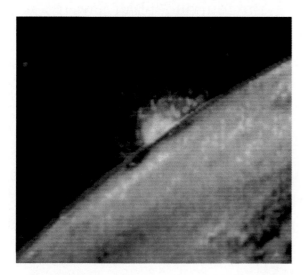

The five days seemed to pass very quickly. Then it was time to go back to Earth. Wendy felt both happy and sad. She was looking forward to getting back and telling her friends and her family about the things she had seen. She could hardly wait to show her pictures to her friends. She could almost hear what they would say when they saw some of the pictures. She imagined that their eyes would get big and they would say things like, "Wow," and "That's incredible."

On the day that Traveler Four was to leave for Earth, Wendy and Sidney went back to Soup Pot. They felt very strange walking up the path to the rim of the volcano. But they wanted to take one more look at the place where they had their most frightening adventure. They didn't plan to stay long this time, just long enough to take some pictures. They wanted pictures of the place where the overhang had been and pictures of the inside of the crater. Wendy wanted these pictures more than any of the others.

She took six pictures. For the last one that she took, she got down on her belly and leaned over the rim to take a picture of the crater. Sidney said, "Be careful. We don't want to have to save you." Wendy was careful.

•   •   •

As the girls entered the space station again, the automatic voice inside Wendy's helmet said, "You have forty minutes of oxygen left."

Later that day, the students and most of the passengers who had come to Jupiter with them boarded Traveler Four. Some of the scientists stayed on Io. And some of the scientists that had been on Io for months left with Wendy ⭐ and the other students. Two of these scientists had been on Io for over a year.

Wendy and Sidney hugged Rod. They knew him very well by now. He was a scientist, a very smart one. He was also a very nice person.

During the time the girls were on Io, he had explained things to them, had eaten with them, and had been a good friend. For Wendy, it was sad to say goodbye to him. After she hugged him, she had to turn away, because she didn't want him to see that she had tears in her eyes.

The trip back to Earth on Traveler Four didn't seem to take as long as the trip out to Jupiter. In fact, the four-and-a-half days seemed to go by quickly. Wendy read a lot and made plans about things that she would do when she got back to her hometown.

When Traveler Four landed at the space station in Japan, the sun was just starting to come up. Everybody cheered when the huge spaceship landed. Then the students said goodbye to each other. Sidney

and Wendy made a lot of plans. They planned to see each other the following year. They planned to write to each other. They planned to phone each other and to send each other good pictures.

As Wendy and Sidney got out of the bus at the airport in Japan, Wendy realized that she had a lot to tell Sidney and not much time to tell those things. So she talked very fast. Sidney did too. The girls seemed to say the same things over and over. "I'll never forget that day on Io," Sidney said for about the tenth time.

"Me, neither," Wendy said.

Then the girls said goodbye to each other. They hugged each other. They cried more. Then Sidney went to her plane and Wendy went to hers.

Wendy felt sad for the first hour of the plane trip back to her hometown. Slowly, she started to feel better as she looked forward to getting home. Suddenly, she noticed that the woman next to her was reading a book about the solar system. The woman was reading a page that had pictures of Jupiter and Io. When the woman noticed that Wendy was looking at the book, the woman said, "Our solar system is incredible."

Wendy agreed.

Then the woman said, "I was just reading the most amazing facts about Jupiter. Did you know that one of the moons near Jupiter has volcanos on it?"

Wendy laughed and said, "Yes, I do." Then she told the woman about her frightening adventure.

C Number your paper from 1 through 23.

Skill Items

The incredible whales made them anxious.

1. What word names warm-blooded animals that look like fish?
2. What word means **nervous** or **scared?**
3. What word means **amazing?**

Review Items

4. If you drop something on Earth, it falls to the ground. What makes it fall?
5. A person weighs 200 pounds on planet X and 100 pounds on planet Y. Which planet has stronger gravity?
6. Planet P has stronger gravity than planet R. On which of those planets would you weigh more?

7. Which planet has fewer clouds around it, Earth or Mars?
8. Which planet is bigger?
9. Which planet is colder?
10. Why is that planet colder?

11. Which has **more** gravity, Jupiter or Io?
12. Which is **smaller** than Earth?
13. Where can you jump 8 feet high?

14. Write the names of the 9 planets, starting with the planet that's closest to the sun.

15. What is a person doing when the person makes an object for the first time?
16. The person who makes an object for the first time is called an ▮▮▮.
17. The object the person makes is called an ▮▮▮.

18. How old are geese when they mate for the first time?

19. After male and female geese mate, how long do they stay together?

20. Most geese live for about ▓▓▓ years.

21. Geese live in large groups called ▓▓▓ .

22. Where are most wild geese born?

23. The ▓▓▓s are the coldest places on the earth and the ▓▓▓ is the hottest place on the earth.

END OF LESSON 66 INDEPENDENT WORK

SPECIAL PROJECT

Make a wall chart that shows these planets:
Mercury, Venus, Earth, Mars, Jupiter.

For each planet, find the answers to these questions:

- How big is the planet?

- How many hours does it take to turn around? (How long is a day on that planet?)

- How long does it take to circle the sun?

- How many moons does it have?

- How far from the sun is it?

A

1	2	3	4
1. Waldo Greem	1. zebras	1. Fran	1. elephants
2. solve	2. trainer	2. world's	2. yeah
3. serious	3. parrots	3. prepare	3. pigeons
4. kitchen	4. fainted	4. zoo	4. trucks
5. hamster	5. screeching	5. disturb	5. audience

B

Kinds of Animals

The pictures below show some of the animals that you'll be reading about. Read the name for each animal.

The story that you'll read will also talk about an elephant's trunk. Touch that part of the elephant.

A. elephant

B. zebra

C. squirrel

D. parrot

E. rabbit

F. tiger

K. giraffe

G. sheep

H. pigeon

I. hamster

J. goat

Waldo's Cooking

Waldo Greem became the world's greatest animal trainer because of his cooking. Waldo cooked from the time he was ten years old. He loved to cook eggs and big meals like spaghetti. There was one serious problem with the things he cooked—nobody could stand them.

His mother and father didn't want to make him feel bad about his cooking, so they tried to eat the things that he cooked. They tried to pretend that they were enjoying his hamburgers or his spaghetti, but they didn't enjoy anything that Waldo cooked.

Waldo's brother Michael and his sister Fran wouldn't eat anything that Waldo cooked. When they found out that he had cooked something, they would just say, "Ugh, I'm not hungry." Instead of eating one of his meals, they would eat a peanut butter sandwich.

Waldo didn't give up. He kept trying to be a better cook, but no matter how hard he tried to make better meals, people couldn't stand his cooking. Sometimes his school would have a party and Waldo would bring something that he fixed. When the party was over, everything that the other students brought for the party would be gone. Everything that Waldo brought would still be on the table.

For years Waldo cooked and for years nobody could stand his cooking—at least, no human could stand his cooking. Animals were different. Every time Waldo cooked, many animals would gather around his house—usually more than twenty animals. They didn't just like Waldo's cooking. They <u>loved</u> it. Cats, dogs, birds, squirrels, rabbits, sheep, goats and even cows and horses would come into the yard and stand near the kitchen window. When Waldo fixed big meals that took a long time to prepare, over a hundred animals would gather in the yard. The dogs would howl; the cats would meow; the other animals would make other noises. "This has got to stop," Waldo's father said after Waldo had fixed a huge meal. "Our yard is like a zoo every time Waldo cooks."

On that day, the yard really did look like a zoo. It was a warm day and the windows in the kitchen were open. The smell of his cooking must have drifted to the other side of the town where a circus was being held. As soon as the smell reached the circus animals, they went crazy and ran from the circus. They followed their noses to Waldo's yard. Just as Waldo was getting ⭐ ready to put his meal on the table, he noticed that there was a large elephant trunk coming through the window. He looked outside and almost fainted. Elephants, zebras, monkeys, parrots and all the other animals from the circus were in the yard. The animal trainers from the circus were also in the yard. They were tugging and pulling at the animals, trying to lead them into trucks and take them from the yard. But the animals would not move. They were crowding around the windows, howling and screeching and making all kinds of noises.

That day was a very bad one for Waldo, but it was also a very good one, because that was the day that Waldo found out how to train any animal. When the people in Waldo's family saw the animals in the yard, they became very angry. His sister Fran said, "Make Waldo stop cooking. This is ridiculous." His brother Michael said, "Yeah, make Waldo stop cooking." His mother said, "Waldo, I think you had better not cook anymore."

One of the trainers from the circus was leaning in the window. She said, "What do you have in there that's making the animals go crazy?"

Another trainer appeared at the window. "How are we going to get them into the trucks?" he said. "They just won't move."

Waldo looked at the meal he had made. He felt very sad. Then he said, "I'll help you get them back into the truck."

Waldo dumped some of the meal into a large bowl. Then he walked outside with the bowl. The animals crowded around him. Then he walked to the truck. All the animals followed. The circus animals followed and so did all the cats and dogs and squirrels and goats that usually came around the house when Waldo cooked.

Waldo climbed into the truck and all the animals followed. Then he gave all the circus animals a little bit of food. That seemed to make them very happy. One of the trainers said, "That's amazing. He just gives them a little bite of food and they're happy."

Waldo jumped out of the truck and all the animals that had not been fed followed him—the dogs and cats and squirrels and birds. He gave each of these animals a little bite of food and they were happy. A trainer said to Waldo, "I don't know what you put in that food, but I've never seen anything like this before."

D Number your paper from 1 through 16.

Skill Items

Use the words in the box to write complete sentences.

numb	whales	vehicle	lava	pale
managed	anxious	crater	incredible	erupted

1. ▨▨ from the volcano's ▨ .
2. The ▨▨ made them ▨ .

Review Items

3. Write the letters of **3** types of products that are used in the United States and manufactured in Japan.

      a. rugs   e. TVs
      b. Mr. Light Saver   f. books
      c. CD players   g. cars
      d. furniture

4. Which planet has more clouds around it, Earth or Mars?

5. Which planet is bigger?

6. Which planet is hotter?

7. Why is that planet hotter?

8. Which has more gravity, Jupiter or Io?

9. Which is smaller than Earth?

10. Where can you jump 8 feet high?

11. Which has a stronger gravity, Earth or Jupiter?

12. So where would you feel lighter?

13. Does Io move around Jupiter **fast** or **slowly?**

14. It takes Io about ▨ to go all the way around Jupiter.

15. How long does it take Jupiter to spin around one time?

16. Which uses up more oxygen, sitting or jumping?

1

1. deliver
2. folks
3. cute
4. applaud

2

1. funniest
2. answering
3. solve
4. fried

B A Problem

Many people had gathered in the yard when the circus animals had crowded around the kitchen windows. Most of those people remained in the yard after the circus truck left with the circus animals.

The people stayed because more animals were gathering in the yard. People laughed and pointed at all the dogs and cats and birds and squirrels that were trying to stay close to Waldo. There were so many animals around him that you couldn't see any part of Waldo from his waist down to his feet. When he moved, all the animals moved. When he stopped, all the animals stopped.

Waldo's father tried to get close to Waldo, but he couldn't. "Waldo," he shouted, "You're just going to have to stop cooking things."

The people who were watching laughed.

His brother and sister said, "Yeah, stop cooking."

Waldo was going to say, "But I love to cook." Just as he started to talk, a large dog jumped up and licked him on the face. Waldo turned his head away. A bird landed on his head. As he brushed the bird away, a squirrel climbed up his leg. "But," Waldo said, "I love . . ."

The people who were watching Waldo laughed harder and harder. One person said, "This is the funniest show I've ever seen. Look at those animals."

Waldo's mother said, "Waldo, you better go inside so these animals will go away."

Waldo walked up the back steps of his house and the crowd of animals followed him. He reached into the bowl and grabbed a little handful of food. He threw the food as far as he could. The whole crowd of animals went after the food. Birds were flying. Rabbits were leaping. Dogs and cats and horses were running. The people who were watching laughed and laughed. Then they began to applaud. Waldo smiled and waved. He felt embarrassed but he didn't know what to say.

Waldo went inside. His father followed him. "Waldo," he said. "This has to stop."

Waldo felt very sad as he slowly slumped into a kitchen chair. "Yes, Waldo," his mother said. "We are not running a zoo here. Every time you cook a large meal, more than a hundred animals appear in the yard."

"Yeah," his brother Michael said. "Every time you cook, the phone rings all evening long. Everybody wants to know if we've seen ⭐ their dog or their cat."

"Yeah," his sister Fran said. "I'm getting tired of answering the phone. Some of those calls are ridiculous. I hate it when somebody asks if I've seen a striped cat. I tell them I've seen a whole yard full of striped cats."

Waldo's brother said, "We see more than striped cats. We see black cats and brown cats and yellow cats and cats with one eye and cats with . . ."

"All right," Waldo's mother said. "That's enough."

"And cats with long hair and cats with no hair and cats with . . ."

"I said, that's enough!"

Waldo covered his face with his hands and started to cry. "I don't want to make any trouble," he said. "I just love to cook and I love animals. . . ."

Waldo's father patted him on the back. "I know how you feel, son. But you can see that we've got a big problem here."

"Yes, Dad," Waldo said.

"Make him stop cooking," his sister said. "Make him stop."

His brother said, "Yeah, make him stop. Or make him answer all the phone calls."

"That's enough from you two," Waldo's mother said. She continued, "Waldo is a good boy. We just have to figure out some way to solve this problem."

His sister said, "I know how to solve the problem. We could make Waldo . . ."

"Go into the other room," Waldo's mother said. Then his mother added, "We'll work out a solution to this problem."

So Waldo, his mother, and his father sat in the kitchen and talked about the problem. There were still many animals outside. Two big dogs were standing on their hind legs, looking through the kitchen window. One of them kept howling. The phone was ringing in the other room. Every now and then, one of the neighbors would yell something like, "Get out of here. Go home."

After Waldo and his parents talked for a while, Waldo's father said, "I don't see any solution except one. You're going to have to stop cooking."

Waldo's mother said, "I'm afraid that's right. It costs a lot of money to cook all that food. Then nobody can eat it except those animals."

Waldo said, "But I'll pay for the food. I'll get a job and make enough to pay for my own food. And I'll . . ."

"I'm sorry, son," his father said. "I think you'll just have to stop cooking."

C Number your paper from 1 through 22.

Skill Items

Here are three events that happened in the story. Write **beginning, middle** or **end** for each event.

1. After Waldo and his parents talked for a while, Waldo's father said, "I don't see any solution except one."

2. Most of those people remained in the yard after the circus truck left with the circus animals.

3. Waldo walked up the back steps of his house and the crowd of animals followed him.

Review Items

4. Which is bigger, Alaska or Japan?

5. Is Japan a **state** or a **country?**

6. How many people live in Japan?

- 127   • 127 million   • 127 thousand

7. Do gases surround Io?

8. How much oxygen is on Io?

9. What color is lava when it's very hot?

- orange   • brown   • gray

10. What color is lava after it cools a little bit?

11. What color is lava after it's completely cooled?

- On planet P you can jump 4 feet high.
- On planet L you can jump 15 feet high.
- On planet J you can jump 7 feet high.
- On planet M you can jump 10 feet high.
- On planet Z you can jump 20 feet high.

12. Write the letter of the planet that has the most gravity.

13. Write the letter of the planet that has the least gravity.

14. How many moons does Jupiter have?

15. How many moons does Saturn have?

16. Which planet has more moons, Saturn or Jupiter?

17. How far is it from Earth to Jupiter?

18. Write the names of the 9 planets, starting with Mercury.

19. Is Earth the planet that is closest to the sun?

20. The sun gives ____ and ____ to all the planets.

21. Which planet in the picture has more gravity?

22. How do you know?

T   S

A

1	2	3
1. fried	1. backyard	1. dust
2. masks	2. wagging	2. whew
3. mobbed	3. attracting	3. cage
4. folks	4. owner	4. wore
5. delivering	5. cleaning	5. screech
		6. cute

B

Training Animals

You're going to read about how animals are trained to do tricks. Here's how to train animals:

First, you tell the animal what to do. If the animal does what you tell it to do, you reward the animal. You reward the animal by giving it something it likes.

If the animal does not do what you tell it to do, you do not reward the animal.

You may have to wait a long time before the animal does the trick you want it to do. But if you reward the animal the right way, the animal will learn that the only way to get the reward is to do the trick. The animal wants the reward, so the animal does the trick.

Remember: Reward the animal each time the animal does the trick. Do not reward the animal if the animal does not do the trick.

C

Waldo Gets a Job

After all those circus animals came to Waldo's house, his parents told him that he had to stop cooking. After they told him what they had decided, he tried to think of ways that he could cook without attracting animals. He thought about closing all the windows in the house when he cooked, but he knew that his brother and sister would not like this plan. They were always complaining about the smell of Waldo's cooking, even when the windows were open. He thought of giving them masks they could wear, but he didn't think they would like that plan.

After Waldo hadn't cooked for two months, he came up with a plan that he thought would work. He decided to get a job and earn money so that he could pay for the food that he cooked. That was part of his plan, but not all of it. He also planned to fix up the garage so that he could cook there and sleep there. Then he could have animals around to eat his cooking, but they wouldn't disturb the neighbors or disturb his parents.

Waldo didn't tell anybody about his plan. He just put his plan into action. First, he got a job. Actually, he tried three jobs before he found one that he liked.

Waldo's first job was delivering newspapers. He didn't like that job because he had to get up very early in the morning. The second job that he got was cleaning up in a shoe store. He hated that job. All he did was take boxes of shoes from the shelves and dust the boxes. Then he would sweep the floor in the back room. It was the most boring job in the world, but Waldo would have kept that job if he hadn't found the third job. He would have kept working in the shoe store because he liked earning money more than he hated dusting boxes. So he dusted boxes and dusted boxes and dusted boxes. The box dusting went on for two weeks.

Then, one day after work, he was walking home thinking about what a terrible job he had. Suddenly, he heard a dog barking. He turned toward the barking and noticed that he was in front of a pet shop. Waldo looked at the dog that was barking. He said to himself, "I have seen that dog in my yard before." The dog continued to bark. At last the owner of the pet store went over to the dog's cage. "Stop that barking," the owner shouted. But the dog didn't stop.

Waldo walked inside the pet shop. The dog began wagging his tail. Waldo looked at the owner, and before he knew what he was saying, he said, "I can help you keep those animals happy."

The owner looked at Waldo. She was a tall woman who wore glasses. "What did you say?" she asked.

"I said that I can help you make these animals happy," Waldo said. Then he kept on talking. He hadn't planned to make a big speech, but the speech came out. He told the owner that people like to buy happy pets, not pets that bark or cry. He told her that more people would stop and look in the window if the animals looked friendly and did funny tricks. Then he told her that he knew how to make the animals happy.

"How can you do that?" she asked.

He said, "If I show you how, could you give me a job working with these animals?"

"Maybe," she said. "But first you'll have to show me what you can do."

Waldo asked, "Do you have a kitchen in the back of this pet shop?"

"Yes, I do," she said. "But I don't understand what…"

Waldo asked, "Do you have some food that I can cook?"

"Yes, I do," she said. "But I don't understand what . . ."

"Let me cook up some stuff and I'll show you what I can do."

So the owner led Waldo into the kitchen and showed him where the food was. Waldo went to work. He fried things. He boiled things. He cooked things in the oven. Then he mixed things together. When he was done, the owner said, "Whew, that stuff stinks."

Waldo didn't say anything. He dumped all the things he had cooked into a large bowl. The owner opened the windows in the kitchen and stood near one of the windows, holding her nose.

Outside, the animals were beginning to gather. "This is strange," she said to Waldo, as she held her nose. "There are three goats in the backyard. I wonder where they came from. And look at the squirrels."

"Close the window," Waldo said, "or they'll come inside."

"I've never seen anything like this," the owner said.

The animals inside the pet shop were starting to howl and screech and run around in circles and jump up and down. The owner of the pet shop said, "My, my. I've never seen anything like this in my whole life."

Waldo smiled and said, "Just wait and see what they do when I bring the food out to them."

D Number your paper from 1 through 19.

Skill Items

The boring speaker disturbed the audience.

1. What's another word for **bothered?**

2. What word is the opposite of **interesting?**

3. What do we call all the people who watch an event?

Review Items

4. The map shows a route. What state is at the north end of the route?

5. What country is at the south end of the route?

6. About how many miles is the route?

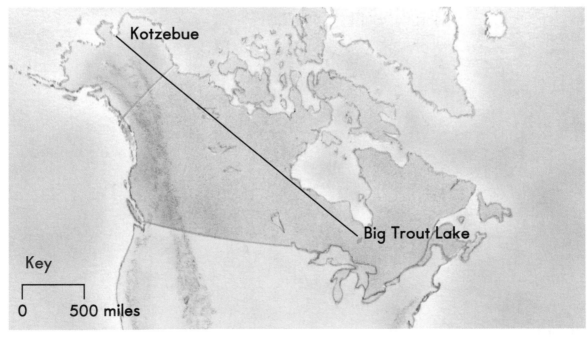

Kotzebue

Big Trout Lake

Key

0   500 miles

7. What are clouds made of?

8. What kind of cloud does the picture show?

9. What happens to a drop of water at **B?**

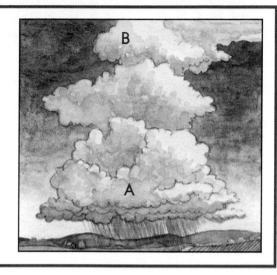

Write the name of each animal in the picture.

10.

11.

12.

13.

14.

15.

16. What's another name for hot, melted rock?

17. When days get longer, is the North Pole tilting **toward** the sun or **away from** the sun?

18. When days get shorter, is the North Pole tilting **toward** the sun or **away from** the sun?

19. In April, the sun shines for more than ▮ hours each day in Alaska.

Number your paper from 1 through 36.

1. Which has more gravity, Jupiter or Io?
2. Which is smaller than Earth?
3. Where can you jump 8 feet high?

4. Which has stronger gravity, Earth or Jupiter?
5. So where would you feel heavier?

6. Do gases surround Io?
7. How much oxygen is on Io?
8. Does Io move around Jupiter **fast** or **slowly?**
9. It takes Io about ▬▬▬ to go all the way around Jupiter.

10. What planet is shown in the picture?
11. Which is bigger, the "eye" of the planet or Earth?

12. Write the letter of the **5** things that tell about Jupiter.
   a. It's small.
   b. It's brown, orange and white.
   c. It has 7 moons.
   d. It has more gravity than Earth.
   e. It has stripes.
   f. It's huge.
   g. It's green and blue.
   h. It's beautiful.

- On planet F you can jump 5 feet high.
- On planet T you can jump 30 feet high.
- On planet K you can jump 8 feet high.
- On planet B you can jump 15 feet high.
- On planet R you can jump 6 feet high.

13. Write the letter of the planet that has the most gravity.

14. Write the letter of the planet that has the least gravity.

15. How long does it take Jupiter to spin around one time?

16. Which uses up more oxygen, reading or hopping?

17. What's another name for hot, melted rock?

18. What color is lava when it's very hot?

- brown   • orange   • gray

19. What color is lava after it cools a little bit?

20. What color is lava after it's completely cooled?

Write the name of each animal in the picture.

21.

22.

23.

24.

25.

26.

27. When you're training an animal, what do you do each time the animal does the trick?

28. What do you do if the animal does not do the trick?

29. Name **2** things you could give a dog to reward it.

Skill Items

For each item, write the underlined word from the sentences in the box.

Lava erupted from the volcano's crater.

The incredible whales made them anxious.

The boring speaker disturbed the audience.

30. What underlining means **melted rock?**

31. What underlining means **amazing?**

32. What underlining names warm-blooded animals that look like fish?

33. What word is the opposite of **interesting?**

34. What underlining means **coughed out** or **spit out?**

35. What underlining means **nervous** or **scared?**

36. What's another word for **bothered?**

Fact Game Answer Key

Lesson 10

2. a. Z
   b. north

3. a. R
   b. T

4. a. M
   b. B

5. a. Q
   b. R

6. a. F
   b. M
   c. Q

7. A — Summer
   B — Fall
   C — Winter
   D — Spring

8. a. 24 hours
   b. 365 days
   c. 5

9. a. three years old
   b. until one goose dies; for life
   c. about 30 years

10. a. south
    b. north

11. a. Y
    b. Y
    c. X

12. a. J
    b. P

Lesson 20

2. a. spring
   b. spring

3. a. north
   b. west
   c. south

4. a. J
   b. F

5. a. away from the sun
   b. toward the sun

6. a. winter
   b. summer

7. a. B
   b. G

8. a. T
   b. P

9. a. X
   b. P and T

10. a. Ideas: (any three) fish, ants, snakes, frogs, and so on
    b. Ideas: (any three) bears, humans, dogs, cows, horses, cats, whales, and so on

11. a. no
    b. warm-blooded

12. a. not warm; cold
    b. 12

Lesson 30

2. a. A
   b. B

3. a. water
   b. funnel

4. a. dinosaurs
   b. horses

5. a. C
   b. D

6. a. A
   b. B
   c. D

7. a. D
   b. Mesozoic

8. a. D
   b. D
   c. C

9. A. Triceratops
   B. Tyrannosaurus

10. a. dinosaurs
    b. earlier

11. a. (tiny) drops of water
    b. storm clouds

12. A, D, E

Lesson 40

2. a. shoe
   b. rock

3. a. rock
   b. cup

4. R
5. 1800

6. pens, paper, shoes, houses, stoves

7. a. inventor
   b. invention

8. a. need
   b. figure out how to meet that need

9. to get places faster; to use shorter routes

10. millions of years ago

11. earthquake

12. It cools and gets hard.

Lesson 50

2. a. 2
   b. 2

3. a. into the room
   b. out of the room

4. A — on
   B — off
   C — off
   D — on

5. a. need
   b. model
   c. patent

6. manufacturers

7. a. yes
   b. 2

8. a. patent
   b. patent attorneys

9. a. counts forward; plusses one
   b. counts backward; minuses one

10. a. outside beam
    b. inside beam
    c. on

11. a. off
    b. on

12. a. zero
    b. They turn off.

Lesson 60

2. a. Mars
   b. Earth
   c. Earth

3. a. yes
   b. no
   c. 17 pounds

4. a. 40 million miles
   b. Earth

5. planet Y

6. a. no
   b. heat and light

7. a. sun
   b. Earth
   c. sun

8. a. 47
   b. 63

9. Mercury, Venus, Earth, Mars, Jupiter, Saturn, Uranus, Neptune, Pluto

10. a. Jupiter
    b. Saturn
    c. 100

11. a. 9
    b. 1

12. a. Alaska
    b. country
    c. Tokyo

Lesson 70

2. lava

3. A — giraffe
   B — goat
   C — parrot

4. D — sheep
   E — tiger
   F — zebra

5. a. 10 hours
   b. running

6. a. Jupiter
   b. Io
   c. Io

7. a. fast
   b. 2 days

8. a. Reward the animal.
   b. Do not reward the animal.

9. a. Jupiter
   b. Earth

10. a. red
    b. gray

11. a. no
    b. none

12. a. Jupiter
    b. eye of the planet

VOCABULARY SENTENCES

Lessons 1—70

1. The horses became restless on the dangerous route.

2. Scientists do not ignore ordinary things.

3. She actually repeated that careless mistake.

4. The smell attracted flies immediately.

5. The rim of the volcano exploded.

6. The new exhibit displayed mysterious fish.

7. She automatically arranged the flowers.

8. They were impressed by her large vocabulary.

9. He responded to her clever solution.

10. The patent attorney wrote an agreement.

11. The applause interrupted his speech.

12. She selected a comfortable seat.

13. Without gravity, they were weightless.

14. She demonstrated how animals use oxygen.

15. Lava erupted from the volcano's crater.

16. The incredible whales made them anxious.

17. The boring speaker disturbed the audience.

Glossary

actually   *Actually* means *really*.

adventure   An *adventure* is a new, exciting experience.

Africa   *Africa* is a large area of land that is bigger than North America.

agreement   An *agreement* is a paper that tells what two people promise to do.

Andros Island   *Andros Island* is an island that is close to Florida.

anxious   *Anxious* is another word for *nervous* or *scared*.

appear   Something *appears* when it first comes into sight.

applause   *Applause* is another word for *clapping*.

approach   When you *approach* something, you move toward it.

arithmetic   *Arithmetic* is another word for *math*.

armor   *Armor* is a hard covering that is made to protect anything inside the armor.

arrange   When you *arrange* things, you put them where you want them.

assigned   A person who is *assigned* a book is the only person who can use the book.

assignment   A job that somebody gives you to do is called an *assignment*.

Atlantic Ocean   The *Atlantic Ocean* is the ocean that touches the eastern shore of the United States.

attorney   An *attorney* is a lawyer.

attracted   If you are *attracted* to something, you are really interested in that thing.

audience   All the people who watch an event are the people in the *audience*.

automatically   Things that happen *automatically* don't require any thought.

Bermuda Triangle   The *Bermuda Triangle* is an area in the Atlantic Ocean where very strange things happened to ships.

blisters   *Blisters* are sore bubbles that form from rubbing or burning.

boring   *Boring* is the opposite of *interesting*.

bow   The *bow* of the ship is the front of the ship.

breath   Your *breath* is the air you take in or let out.

business   If you sell flowers, you are in the *business* of selling flowers.

careless   *Careless* is the opposite of *careful*.

character   When you say that somebody is a *character,* you mean the person is unusual.

checker   A person or a machine that checks things is called a *checker.*

chuckle   A *chuckle* is a little laugh.

clearing   A *clearing* is a place in a forest or a jungle where there are no trees.

clever   *Clever* is another word for *very smart.*

cliff   A *cliff* is like a side of a hill that goes almost straight up and down.

comfortable   Things that are *comfortable* feel very pleasant.

conclude   *Conclude* is another word for *finish.*

constant   Something that is *constant* doesn't change.

crater   A volcano's *crater* is the enormous dent in the top of the volcano.

crooked   *Crooked* is the opposite of *straight.*

current   A water *current* is a stream of water that moves in the same direction.

danger   Something that's a *danger* is something that is not safe.

dart   When something *darts* around, it moves like a dart, very fast and straight.

daydream   When you *daydream* you think about things that you would like to be doing.

deliver   When you bring something to a place, you *deliver* it to that place.

demonstrate   When you *demonstrate* something, you show it.

device   A *device* is a machine or fixture that is made by people.

diagram   A *diagram* is a picture that is something like a map.

direct   When you *direct* people to do something, you order them to do it.

disappointed   When something you want does not happen, you feel *disappointed.*

display   Another word for *show* is *display.*

disturb   When you bother something, you *disturb* it.

divided   Things that are *divided* are separated into parts.

dome   Another word for a *rounded ceiling* is a *dome.*

electricity   *Electricity* is the power that runs appliances like washing machines and televisions.

embarrassed   When you are *embarrassed,* you feel foolish or silly.

energy   The amount of work something can do depends on how much *energy* it has.

engineer   The *engineer* on a ship is the crew member who makes sure that the engine is running well.

equator   The *equator* is a make-believe line around the middle of the earth.

equipment   The supplies or tools needed to do something is the *equipment* needed to do it.

equipped   When you're well *equipped* for doing something, you have all the supplies you need to do the job.

erupted   When lava *erupts* from a volcano, the lava is spit or coughed out.

Eskimo   *Eskimos* are native people that live in Alaska and Canada.

example   A dog is an *example* of an animal.

excellent   Something that is very, very good is *excellent.*

exhibit   An *exhibit* has things arranged for people to see.

expect   When you *think* something will happen, you *expect* it to happen.

explanation   When you give an *explanation,* you tell how something works.

explode   When things *explode,* they make a loud bang and fly apart.

expression   The *expression* on your face shows what you're feeling.

faint   If something is *faint,* it is very hard to hear or see.

female   Girls and women are called *females.*

first mate   The *first mate* is a crew member who is the captain's main helper.

flock   A *flock* of birds is a group of birds that lives together and flies together.

Florida   *Florida* is one of the states in the United States.

foolish   Something that is *foolish* is the opposite of *wise.*

funnel-shaped   Things that are *funnel-shaped* are shaped like a round tube that is wide on one end and narrow on the other end.

galley   The *galley* is the kitchen on an airplane or ship.

gallon   A *gallon* is a unit of measurement that is the same as four quarts.

gases   *Gases* float in the air.

gather   When you pick up things from different places and put them in one place, you *gather* those things.

gentle   Things that are *gentle* are the opposite of things that are rough.

glance   When you *glance* at something, you give that thing a quick look.

glide   When a bird *glides,* it goes through the air without flapping or moving its wings.

gravity   *Gravity* is the force that pulls things back to Earth.

grinding   When two hard things rub together, they *grind,* and they make a *grinding* sound.

guest   A *guest* is a visitor.

gulp   When you *gulp* something, you swallow it quickly.

hardened   Something that becomes hard is called *hardened.*

hesitate   When you *hesitate,* you pause for a moment.

hind   Another word for the *back* part of animals is the *hind* part.

hitch   When you *hitch* two things together, you attach them to each other.

however   Another word for *but* is *however.*

ice flow   An *ice floe* is a flat sheet of ice that floats in the ocean.

ignore   When you don't pay attention to something, you *ignore* that thing.

immediately   *Immediately* means *right now.*

impressed   When you're *impressed* by something, you think it is very good.

incredible   *Incredible* is another work for *amazing.*

interest   If you have an *interest* in something, you pay attention to that thing.

interrupt   *Interrupt* means *break into.*

invent   When a person makes an object for the very first time, the person *invents* the object.

invisible   If something is *invisible,* you can't see it.

Io   *Io* is a large moon that circles Jupiter.

Jupiter   *Jupiter* is one of the planets in the solar system.

kayak   A *kayak* is a small boat with an opening in the center for a person.

Kentucky   *Kentucky* is a state that you might go through if you went from Michigan to Florida.

kneel   When you *kneel,* you get down on your knees.

lava   *Lava* is hot melted rock.

lawyer   People who need help with the law go to a *lawyer.*

leathery   If something is *leathery,* it looks or feels like leather.

male   Men and boys are called *males.*

manage   If you *manage* to do something, you work hard until you do it.

manufacturer   Somebody who makes a product is a *manufacturer* of the product.

mast   A *mast* on a ship is a tall pole.

mention   When you *mention* something, you quickly tell about it.

Michigan   *Michigan* is one of the states that touches Canada.

migration   A *migration* is a long journey that animals make every year.

moan   A *moan* is a sound that people make when they are in pain.

mukluks   *Mukluks* are very warm boots that Eskimos wear.

museum   A *museum* is a place with many different kinds of exhibits.

mysterious   Things that you do not understand are *mysterious.*

no-see-ums   *No-see-ums* are tiny biting insects that live in Alaska and Canada.

nudge   When you *nudge* something, you give it a little push.

numb   When part of your body gets *numb,* you don't have any feeling in that part.

ordinary   Things that you see all the time in different places are *ordinary* things.

owe   Something that you *owe* is something that you must pay.

oxygen   *Oxygen* is the part of the air your body needs to survive.

pace   The *pace* of something is the speed of that thing.

pale   If something is *pale,* it is whiter than it normally is.

palms   The insides of your hands are called *palms.*

patent   A *patent* is a license that says that only one person can make a particular product.

patent attorney   A *patent attorney* is a lawyer whose special job is getting patents for a new invention.

pebbled   Things that are *pebbled* are covered with small stones.

permission   Someone who has approval to do something has *permission* to do it.

planet   The Earth that we live on is a *planet.*

possible   Things that are *possible* are things that could happen.

practice   When you *practice* something, you work on it.

prepare   When you get ready for something, you *prepare* for that thing.

pressure   *Pressure* is a push.

products   Things that are made by people are *products.*

protection   *Protection* is something that protects.

purchase   *Purchase* is another word for *buy.*

quake   When something *quakes,* it shakes very hard.

receive   *Receive* means *get.*

remains   The *remains* of something are the parts that are left.

repeat   When you *repeat* something, you do it again and again and again.

respond   *Respond* is another word for *react*.

restless   When you feel *restless*, you don't want to keep doing what you're doing.

ridge   A *ridge* is a long strip of land that is raised above the land around it.

ridiculous   When you think something is really silly, you think it is *ridiculous*.

rim   Things with a thin top edge have a *rim*.

rose   Something that moved up yesterday *rose* yesterday.

route   The different ways you can go to get to a place are the different *routes* that you can take to get there.

scientists   *Scientists* are highly-trained people who study different things about the world.

scrambled   Things that are *scrambled* are all mixed up.

seagulls   *Seagulls* are birds that are seen around the ocean.

section   *Section* is another word for *part*.

select   When you *select* something, you choose it.

sense   If you have a good *sense* of sight, you can see well.

serious   The opposite of something funny is something *serious*.

shaft   The *shaft* of a pencil is the part with long straight sides.

shallow   *Shallow* is the opposite of *deep*.

sharp-minded   A person who is *sharp-minded* has a quick mind or a smart mind.

shrank   Things that get smaller now shrink; things that got smaller yesterday *shrank*.

shriek   A *shriek* is a very sharp scream.

sight   A *sight* is something you see.

sir   An important man is sometimes called *sir*.

slosh   If you swing a bucket of water back and forth, the water *sloshes* around.

slump   When people *slump,* they slouch and do not sit up straight or stand up straight.

solar system   The *solar system* is the group of planets and moons that move around the sun.

solution   The *solution* to a problem is how to solve the problem.

solve   When you *solve* a problem, you figure out the answer to that problem.

son   If parents have a male child, that child is the parents' *son*.

speckled   Things that have small spots are *speckled*.

splatter   When wet things hit something, they *splatter* and spread out.

sprang   If an animal jumped at something yesterday, it *sprang* yesterday.

stern   The *stern* of a ship is the back of the ship.

stern   A *stern* expression is a frowning expression.

stumble   When you *stumble*, you trip.

suggest   When you *suggest* a plan, you tell about a possible plan.

supplies   The *supplies* you need for a job are the things you'll use up when you do that job.

suppose   Another word for *believe* or *think* is *suppose*.

surface   The *surface* of the water is the top of the water.

surround   If something *surrounds* you, it is all the way around you.

survive   If you *survive*, you live.

swarm   When insects *swarm*, hundreds of them fly very close to each other.

swift   Something that is *swift* is very fast.

tangle   A *tangle* is a mixed-up mass.

telescope   A *telescope* is a device that makes distant things look large.

throat   The front of your neck is sometimes called your *throat.*

Tokyo   *Tokyo* is the largest city in Japan.

tone   Your *tone* of voice tells what you are feeling.

tremble   Something that *trembles* shakes a little.

trout   A *trout* is a fish.

tumble   When things *tumble,* they turn over and over and over.

unfasten   When you *unfasten* something, you undo it.

Uranus   *Uranus* is one of the planets in the solar system.

vocabulary   A person's *vocabulary* is all the words the person knows.

volcano   A *volcano* is a mountain that is made from hot, flowing rock that comes from inside the earth.

weightless   Things that are *weightless* float in space.

whales   *Whales* are warm-blooded animals that live in the ocean.

whether   In some sentences, *whether* means *if.*

wrist   Your *wrist* is the joint between your hand and your arm.

Index

Mychela
2011